Vygotsky and Research

Despite the changes that have taken place in social science since Vygotsky's death in 1934, his work remains a vital source for the creative processes of research. *Vygotsky and Research* provides a number of glimpses of the Vygotskian imagination at play, whilst updating key elements of the theoretical arguments developed in *An Introduction to Vygotsky* and *Vygotsky and Pedagogy*, also written by Harry Daniels.

Starting with a concise introduction to Vygotsky's original thesis and a discussion of his own approach to research methods, the book explores the research practices which have developed in a number of fields on the basis of his writings. These include:

- Sociocultural studies with a focus on mediated action
- Distributed cognition
- Situated cognition
- Activity theory.

A chapter devoted to each area provides examples of specific studies in order to illustrate the underlying methodological principles and specific methods at work. In each case, both the assumptions and limitations of practices will be comprehensively discussed. The conclusion outlines proposals for future developments at both methodological and conceptual levels, in order to develop approaches to research that acknowledge and integrate a broad understanding of social, cultural and historical features into research designs.

The book will be of particular interest to academics and students in the social sciences and education, and some sections relate to the interests of those whose research involves studies of management in and across institutions and human–computer interaction.

Harry Daniels is Professor of Education at the University of Bath, UK.

Vygotsky and Research

Harry Daniels

LONDON AND NEW YORK

First published 2008
by Routledge
2 Park Square, Milton Park, Abingdon, Oxon OX14 4RN

Simultaneously published in the USA and Canada
by Routledge
270 Madison Ave, New York, NY 10016

Routledge is an imprint of the Taylor & Francis Group, an informa business

© 2008 Harry Daniels

Typeset in Bembo by Wearset Ltd, Boldon, Tyne and Wear
Printed and bound in Great Britain by TJ International, Padstow, Cornwall

All rights reserved. No part of this book may be reprinted or
reproduced or utilised in any form or by any electronic,
mechanical, or other means, now known or hereafter invented,
including photocopying and recording, or in any information
storage or retrieval system, without permission in writing from
the publishers.

British Library Cataloguing in Publication Data
A catalogue record for this book is available from the British
Library

Library of Congress Cataloging in Publication Data
Daniels, Harry.
Vygotsky and research / Harry Daniels.
p.cm.
1. Vygotskii, L. S. (Lev Semenovich), 1896–1934. 2.
Psychology–Research. 3. Social sciences–Research. I. Title.
BF109.V95D362008
150.92–dc22
2008004924

ISBN10: 0-415-39592-5 (hbk)
ISBN10: 0-415-39593-3 (pbk)
ISBN10: 0-203-89179-1 (ebk)

ISBN13: 978-0-415-39592-2 (hbk)
ISBN13: 978-0-415-39593-9 (pbk)
ISBN13: 978-0-203-89179-7 (ebk)

Contents

List of figures and tables		vi
Acknowledgements		viii
1	An introduction to Vygotskian theory	1
2	An overview of research undertaken by Vygotsky and some of his colleagues	29
3	The sociocultural tradition	51
4	Researching distributed cognition	76
5	Situated action and communities of practice	91
6	Activity theory and interventionist research	115
7	Institutions and beyond	148
References		179
Index		203

Figures and tables

Figures

1.1	The basic triangular representation of mediation	5
1.2	Discourse and knowledge structures	19
4.1	Integrated research activity map	83
6.1	The hierarchical structure of activity	119
6.2	The structure of a human activity system	122
6.3	Two interacting activity systems	123
6.4	Typical DWR workshop layout	133
6.5	Stages of data gathering for series of workshops	136
6.6	Representation of activity with a focus on objects and outcomes (stage 2)	138
6.7	Representation of activity with a focus on objects and outcomes (stage 3)	139
6.8	Representation of activity with a focus on objects and outcomes (stage 4)	140
6.9	Representation of activity with a focus on objects and outcomes (stage 5)	141
6.10	Representation of activity with a focus on objects and subsequent tool development	142
6.11	Overall sequence of transformations of the activity	144
7.1	Overall model of description	157
7.2	Percentage of correct discriminations agreed by both teachers for each school	159
7.3	Dominance in networks of activity systems through time	167
7.4	Example of coding grids applied to model of description	171
7.5	Representation of the structure of pedagogic practices at each study site	173

Tables

2.1	Findings from Shif's experiments on *because* and *although*	40
3.1	The inseparability/separability difference between sociocultural theorists	55
5.1	Characteristics of a community	99
5.2	Focus of psychological and anthropological views of situativity theory	100
5.3	Comparison between the knowledge community and the knowledge collectivity	101
5.4	Rogoff's inseparable, mutually constituting planes	102
6.1	Bateson's levels of learning	126
7.1	Extract from the coding frame for describing the classification and framing at the classroom level	158
7.2	Coding of classroom practice in the four schools	158
7.3	The codings for each site	172
7.4	Features of the local authority	172
7.5	Sequences of communicative action	174
7.6	Tentative typology of hybridities	176

Acknowledgements

My thanks are due to the Department of Education at the University of Bath which provides me with an appropriately challenging and yet congenial setting in which to work. I am grateful to my colleagues in the Centre for Sociocultural and Activity Theory Research reading group for lively and thought provoking discussion. It is a privilege to work with people who bring a richness of ideas and generosity of spirit to conversation.

The Economic and Social Research Council, Teaching and Learning Research Programme provided funding for the Learning in and for Interagency Working (ESRC TLRP RES 139-25-0100) project which provided me with the much valued opportunity for research and reflection with close research colleagues.

I owe a great debt of gratitude to Sarah Cox who, with tenacity and gentle humour, helped to bring the manuscript to order.

Chapter 1

An introduction to Vygotskian theory

In 1959 Wright Mills argued the case for sociology as an imaginative pursuit which necessarily retained a certain playfulness (Mills, 1959). In this book I intend to scope some of the possibilities for a Vygotskian research imagination. In so doing I will try to avoid the sense of singularity that Mills imposed with his title *The Sociological Imagination* (Morgan, 1998). My argument is that Vygotsky and his followers provide a rich and vivid palette of theoretical and methodological ideas which can be utilised as we struggle to understand the processes through which the human mind is formed. He argued that creativity is a social process which requires appropriate tools, artefacts and cultures in which to thrive (Vygotsky, 2004). A central argument of this book is that Vygotsky and those who have been influenced by him provide us with tools and artefacts which can be deployed in creative social science. These are the tools and artefacts for imagining ways of researching and ways of thinking about the objects of our research.

The original texts are themselves rich and complex. They afford a multiplicity of stimulating avenues for exploration and development. The nature and extent of this source of inspiration is captured in the following intriguing statement made by a modern-day Russian writer whose own imagination is inspired by his early twentieth-century countryman.

> Vygotsky's cultural-historical theory (like any great theory) resembles a city. A city with broad new avenues and ancient, narrow backstreets known only to longtime residents, with noisy, crowded plazas and quiet, deserted squares, with large, modern edifices and decrepit little buildings. The individual areas of that city may not be situated on a single level: while some rise above the ground, others are submerged below it and cannot be seen at all. In essence, it is as though there were a second city that has intimate and complex associations with the ground-level city but completely invisible to many. And the sun rises above it all and the stars come out over it at night. Sometimes dust storms and hurricanes rage, or the rain beats down long and hard and 'the sky is overcast.' Life is a constant feeling of effervescence. Holidays and the humdrum follow one another. The city changes, grows, and is rebuilt.

Whole neighborhoods are demolished. The center is sometimes over here, sometimes over there. And so it goes.

(Puzyrei, 2007, pp. 85–6)

This image of a city, with its popular as well as relatively unknown spaces, visible and invisible structures that change in time with a variety of tempos and rhythms, captures the complexity and excitement of Vygotsky's legacy. It points to the political nature of the development of ideas ('sometimes dust storms and hurricanes rage, or the rain beats down long and hard and "the sky is overcast"') as well as the subtlety and complexity that underpins ostensible simplicity and the processes of its renewal.

His work has influenced the development of many research imaginations which share core assumptions and celebrate their own distinctiveness. In this first chapter I will draw on, extend and update the arguments laid down in Daniels (2001) in order to discuss the core elements of Vygotsky's theoretical framework. I must emphasise that this will inevitably be a partial account. I am not attempting to give a full history of his theoretical work. That is not the purpose of this chapter. Such a history can be found in Yaroshevsky (1989), Van der Veer and Valsiner (1991) or Veresov (1999). My intention is to provide an introduction to the key theoretical moves that Vygotsky made in his somewhat frenetic period of research in the social sciences. This was a relatively brief period of furious creative activity in which he drew on the ideas of other European thinkers such as Marx, Hegel, Durkheim, Spinoza, Janet and the Gestalt psychologists, amongst many others. It gave rise to a body of writing that continues to inspire and excite a large number of social scientists today.

The Russian cultural-historical school of social theory that developed in the wake of Vygotsky's contribution placed great emphasis on the need to develop robust theories and methodologies which would enable social scientists to study the ways in which humans both shape and are shaped by the artefacts which mediate their engagement with the world. Theories themselves are, of course, cultural-historical products. This book brings together several culturally and historically shaped interpretations and developments of the work of that Russian school. At the outset, I must draw attention to the culturally situated interpretations of Vygotsky's work which have been developed:

> The Vygotsky described in the books of J. Wertsch (1985a) does not resemble the Vygotsky in the works of A.V. Brushlinskii (1994) or V.P. Zinchenko (1996). M.G. Iaroshevskii (1991) and Kozulin (1990) do not agree in their evaluations of Vygotskian theory with Van der Veer and Valsiner (1991), Veresov (1992), or Leontiev (1998).
>
> (Koshmanova, 2007, p. 62)

This is an important moment in the development of social theory. The material and communicative circumstances which obtain at this point at the beginning of the twenty-first century present new challenges for conceptions of learning. These challenges are themselves mediated and shaped by the culturally and historically specific understandings of learning that have been developed and are available at specific moments in time and space.

Vygotsky's ideas were originally forged at another time of rapid and intense social upheaval: the Russian Revolution. It is arguably the case that his involvement with the development of state system for the education of 'pedagogically neglected' children (Yaroshevsky, 1989, p. 96) also had a formative effect. This group included the homeless, of which there were a very large number. In many respects, this was a group of young people whose engagement with the social world was mediated by the cultures of the street rather than those of Russian homes and schools. They were disconnected from the historical legacy of Russian culture as sedimented in the practices of family-based upbringing and schooling. They were deprived of access to these legacy understandings and ways of thinking by dint of their social circumstances of isolation, marginalisation and deprivation. It is hardly surprising that Vygotsky's gaze should been directed to the development of the cultural-historical theory of the formation of mind. He was also working in a political world which was developing new priorities for the development of Russian or, more specifically, Soviet society and its citizens. This political world was directly informed by the writings of Marx and there is no doubt that this tradition energised Vygotsky's efforts to create an approach to social science that was commensurate with the aspirations of this new political order. In July 1924, the 28-year-old Lev Vygotsky was appointed to work in the People's Commissariat for Public Education. He argued that the culture of education as it had existed was itself in need of profound transformation and that this was possible in the new social circumstances that obtained in Russia. He embarked on the creation of psychological theories that he and others used as tools for the development of new pedagogies for all learners.

The development of Psychology as a discipline has passed through several stages. Each part of this history provides an important legacy for the next. One of the reasons that so many Western psychologists are reading the writings of a long-dead Russian may be that they are seeking to extend the insights of the so-called 'cognitive revolution' and yet are painfully aware of the shortcomings of so many of its products (e.g. Hirst and Manier, 1995). The research practice of experimentation in artificial situations has provided valuable insights but incurred significant costs. Questions of the extent to which cognition is situated in particular contexts and distributed across individuals acting in those settings remain a challenge to theories and methodologies that are deployed in the study of human functioning. Vygotsky provided some key concepts and proposals that are now regarded as important contributions to the development of a contemporary social theory that acknowledges these features of cognitive and affective processes. The rest of this chapter consists of a discussion of some of these key ideas and in so doing surfaces some of the theoretical and methodological challenges that confront researchers who wish to adopt and adapt this tradition in their own studies. Chapter 2 will move on to an examination of some of the methodologies and methods developed by Vygotsky and his co-workers, before moving on in the rest of the book to consider how this legacy has been developed and applied in the emergent dialects of post-Vygotskian and related social theory.

Mediation

Wertsch (1985a) proposed that Vygotsky's theoretical approach can be understood in terms of three major themes. These are: (1) the claim that an adequate account of human mental functioning must be grounded in an analysis of the tools and signs that mediate it; (2) a reliance on a genetic or developmental method; and (3) the claim that higher mental functioning in the individual has its origins in social life. I will now explore each of these themes.

Vygotsky (1978, p. 87) viewed the concept of mediation as being central to his account of social formation. It opens the way for the development of a non-deterministic account in which mediators serve as the means by which the individual acts upon and is acted upon by social, cultural and historical factors in the course of ongoing human activity. Engeström (2001a) has summarised the significance of this start:

> The insertion of cultural artifacts into human actions was revolutionary in that the basic unit of analysis now overcame the split between the Cartesian individual and the untouchable societal structure. The individual could no longer be understood without his or her cultural means; and the society could no longer be understood without the agency of individuals who use and produce artifacts. This meant that objects ceased to be just raw material for the formation of logical operations in the subject as they were for Piaget. Objects became cultural entities and the object-orientedness of action became the key to understanding human psyche.
>
> (Engeström, 2001a, p. 134)

Figure 1.1 represents the possibilities for subject–object relations in such an activity. Such relations are either unmediated, direct and in some sense natural or they are mediated by culturally available artefacts. It is important to note that Vygotsky's thoughts on the nature of mediation changed during the course of his writing. Wertsch (2007) distinguishes between the accounts of mediation that appear to be rooted in the psychology of stimuli and stimulus means and those that seem to owe more to Vygotsky's roots in semiotics, literary theory, art and drama. He invokes the terms 'explicit' and 'implicit mediation' in order to distinguish between the two conceptions. The following quotation provides an illustration of his attempts to develop an idea in the prevailing language of early Soviet psychology. Here explicit mediation refers to the incorporation of signs into human action as a means of reorganising that action:

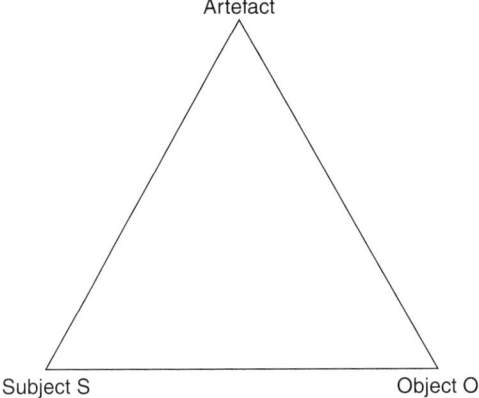

Figure 1.1 The basic triangular representation of mediation.

> In natural memory, the direct (conditioned reflex) associative connection A-B is established between two stimuli A and B. In artificial, mnemotechnical memory of the same impression, instead of this direct connection A-B, two new connections, A-X and B-X, are established with the help of the psychological tool X (e.g., a knot in a handkerchief, a string on one's finger, a mnemonic scheme).
>
> (Vygotsky, 1981c, p. 138)

Wertsch contrasts explicit mediation with implicit mediation. In so doing he discusses the dialectical relation between thinking and speech in the development of one of Vygotsky's preferred units of analysis: word meaning.

> In his critique of the kind of false and misleading isolation of thought and word that he saw in the research of his day, Vygotsky (1987) proposed taking 'word meaning' as a unit of analysis, something that allows us to recognize that it is 'a phenomenon of both speech and intellect' (p. 244). Throughout this chapter Vygotsky emphasized the need to focus on the dialectic between thought and word. He viewed this dialectic as a sort of developmental struggle and asserted that this was 'the primary result of this work [and] ... the conceptual center of our investigation' (p. 245). In his view 'The discovery that word meaning changes and develops is our new and fundamental contribution to the theory of thinking and speech.'
>
> (Wertsch, 2007, p. 183)

Hasan (2005) argues it is in this way that Vygotsky links the development of consciousness to semiosis, and specifically to linguistic semiosis, and thus links the specifically human aspects of our practical and mental life to sociohistorical contexts (Hasan, 2005, p. 135–6). Bakhtin's (1981, 1986) suggestion that language is 'over populated with the intentions of others', reminds us that the processes of mediation are processes in which individuals operate with artefacts (e.g. words/texts) which are themselves shaped by, and have been shaped in, activities within which values are contested and meaning negotiated. In this sense, cultural residues reside in and constrain the possibilities for communication. Thus the mediational process is one which denies neither individual or collective agency nor social, cultural or historical constraint. For Wertsch (2007), implicit mediation involves signs, especially natural language, whose primary function is communication, that are part of a pre-existing, independent stream of communicative action that becomes integrated with other forms of goal-directed behaviour. The emphasis here is on the negotiation of meaning in implicit semiotic mediation. This is also the case for Hasan (2005), who agrees with Vygotsky's identification of speech as a most powerful means of mediation:

> of all the semiotic modalities only language at once defies time, is capable of being reflexive, classifies reality, construes communicable human experience, and articulates the many voices of a culture with equal facility, which is not to say that it ensures their social privilege, or that other modalities make no contribution.
>
> (Hasan, 2005, p. 134)

Importantly, however, in an earlier paper, Hasan (2002) also echoes Wertsch's (2007) distinction between implicit and explicit mediation with the introduction and discussion of visible and invisible semiotic mediation. For her, visible semiotic mediation is aimed at mediating a specific category of reasoning, a certain range of technical concepts and a particular relation to the physical phenomena of the world whereby the world is classified and categorised in a certain way (Hasan, 2002, p. 152); whereas invisible semiotic mediation occurs in discourse embedded in everyday, ordinary activities of a social subject's life. However, she draws on Bernstein (1990) to argue that, whilst the context for mediation is always the social practices of discourse, an important qualification is that in such practices individuals take up specific social positions and are positioned. The same context offers different possibilities for socially positioned actors.

> Participation in social practices, including participation in discourse, is the biggest boot-strapping enterprise that human beings engage in: speaking is necessary for learning to speak; engaging with contexts is necessary for recognising and dealing with contexts. This means, of course, that the contexts that one learns about are the contexts that one lives, which in turn means that the contexts one lives are those which are specialised to one's social position.
>
> (Hasan, 2005, p. 153)

This argument advances the case for an account of the structuring of discourse in relation to that of implicit and/or invisible semiotic mediation. Bernstein (1990, p. 13) used the concept of social positioning to refer to the establishing of a specific relation to other subjects and to the creating of specific relationships within subjects. He relates social positioning to the formation of mental dispositions in terms of the identity's relation to the distribution of labour in society. I will return to the methodological implications of this assertion in Chapter 7.

In this section I have identified two approaches to the notion of mediation as announced by Vygotsky. These have been nuanced and developed in the writings of Wertsch (2007) and Hasan (2005). This central concept in the Vygotskian thesis is, as with so much of his work, a rich and inspirational starting point in the development of social theory. At this point I wish to flag the point that the notions of invisible or implicit mediation may well be developed through the incorporation of sociological understandings of the ways in which practices of semiotic mediation are structured and in which individuals take up, contest, resist and reformulate social positions.

Tools, signs and artefacts as mediators

When writing in the language of what Wertsch (2007) terms 'explicit mediation', Vygotsky (1978) announces the importance of psychological tools as cultural artefacts which could be used to 'control behaviour from the outside': 'Because this auxiliary stimulus possesses the specific function of reverse action, it transfers the psychological operation to higher and qualitatively new forms and permits the humans, by the aid of extrinsic stimuli, to control their behaviour from the outside' (Vygotsky, 1978, p. 40). Vygotsky described psychological tools as devices for mastering mental processes. They were seen as artificial and of social rather than organic or individual origin. He gave the following examples of psychological tools: 'language; various systems for counting; mnemonic techniques; algebraic symbol systems; works of art; writing; schemes, diagrams, maps and mechanical drawings; all sorts of conventional signs' (Vygotsky, 1981c, pp. 136–7). From Vygotsky's perspective, the use of psychological tools:

1   introduces several new functions connected with the use of the given tool and with its control;
2   abolishes and makes unnecessary several natural processes, whose work is accomplished by the tool, and alters the course and individual features (the intensity, duration, sequence, etc.) of all the mental processes that enter into the composition of the instrumental act, replacing some functions with others (i.e. it recreates and reorganises the whole structure of behaviour just as a technical tool recreates the whole structure of labour operations) (Vygotsky, 1981c, pp. 139–40).

In line with Wertsch's (2007) distinction between Vygotsky's writing which seems to be located within the psychology of stimuli and stimulus means and that which seems to owe more to his roots in semiotics, literary theory, art and drama, the notion of psychological tool moved from its initial somewhat instrumental form to an emphasis on the development of meaning. As Knox and Stevens note:

> Vygotsky was stating that humans master themselves from the 'outside' through symbolic, cultural systems. What needs to be stressed here is his position that it is not the tools or signs, in and of themselves, which are important for thought development but the *meaning* encoded in them. Theoretically, then, the *type* of symbolic system should not matter, as long as meaning is retained. All systems (Braille for the blind and for the deaf, dactylology or finger spelling, mimicry or a natural gesticulated sign language) are tools embedded in action and give rise to meaning as such. They allow a child to internalise language and develop those higher mental functions for which language serves as a basis. In actuality, qualitatively different mediational means may result in qualitatively different forms of higher mental functioning.
> (Knox and Stevens, 1993, p. 15)

Prawat (1999) argues that Vygotsky's later work offers a mediational account of meaning-making which is also social, embodied and transactional. This position is elaborated by Kozulin (1998), who discusses three possible generators of consciousness:

- the historical nature of human experience: 'human beings make a wide use of non-biological heredity transmitting knowledge, experiences and symbolic tools from generation to generation';
- the social environment and experiences of others: through drawing out the similarities between Mead and Vygotsky he emphasises that 'an individual becomes aware of him- or herself only in and through interactions with others';
- the existence of mental images and schemas prior to actual action: 'human experience is always present in two different planes – the plane of actual occurrences and the plane of their internal cognitive schematizations' (Kozulin, 1998, p. 10).

Where Prawat speaks of social, embodied and transactional, Kozulin speaks of history, interaction and internal cognitive schematisations. There are tensions between the two positions: Kozulin's emphasis on history which is not made explicit in Prawat's use of the term 'social'; Prawat's use of transaction has a more dialectical turn than 'interaction' within Kozulin's work; and schematisations is much more specific than embodied. Whilst differences of emphasis are clear, there remains an agreement about the existence of multiple levels of representational activity which occurs between and within persons.

Vygotsky was arguing that humans master themselves through external symbolic, cultural systems rather than being subjugated by and in them. This emphasis on the self-construction through and with those tools that are available brings two crucial issues to the foreground. First, it speaks of the individual as an active agent in development. Second, it affirms the importance of sociocultural context in that development takes place through the use of those tools which are available at a particular time in a particular place. He distinguished between psychological and other tools and suggested that psychological tools can be used to direct the mind and behaviour. In contrast, technical tools are used to bring about changes in other objects. Rather than changing objects in the environment, psychological tools are devices for influencing the mind and behaviour of oneself or of another. Vygotsky saw tools and symbols as two aspects of the same phenomena: a tool being technical and altering 'the process of a natural adaptation by determining the form of labour operations'; a sign being psychological and altering 'the entire flow and structure of mental functions' (Vygotsky, 1981c, p. 137).

In the discussion of memory and thinking that constitutes Chapter 3 of one of the more widely available collections of his writing, *Mind in Society*, Vygotsky stipulates that radical transformations take place in the relationships between psychological functions as a result of such mediated psychological activity. He suggests that 'for the young child, to think means to recall; but for the adolescent, to recall means to think' (Vygotsky, 1978, p. 51). Human memory is seen as a function that is actively supported and transformed through the use of signs.

> Just as a mould gives shape to a substance, words can shape an activity into a structure. However, that structure may be changed or reshaped when children learn to use language in ways that allow them to go beyond previous experiences when planning future action ... [O]nce children learn how to use the planning function of their language effectively, their psychological field changes radically. A view of the future is now an integral part of their approaches to their surroundings.
>
> (Vygotsky, 1978, p. 28)

The notion of artefact, which subsumes that of psychological tool, raises questions about the relation between the ideal and the material. Bakhurst (e.g. 1995) has done much to clarify the contribution of the Russian philosopher, Ilyenkov, to our understanding of the framework within which so much of the Russian perspective on mediation may be read. The idea of meaning embodied or sedimented in objects as they are put into use in social worlds is central to the conceptual apparatus of theories of culturally mediated, historically developing, practical activity. He provides an account of the way in which humans inscribe significance and value into the very physical objects of their environment (Bakhurst, 1995, p. 173). A theory of mediation through artefacts implies that in the course of human activity meaning is sedimented, accumulated or deposited in things. These meanings are remembered both collectively and individually. Thus as Cole (1996) reminds us, cultural artefacts are always material and ideal and Leander provides an illustration of their embedded nature:

> A broad definition of artifact as any mediational means ... would not draw sharp distinctions between semiotic and material artifacts for various reasons. It is difficult not to find at least some material dimension in all mediational means; even sound waves are material.... Secondly, the materiality of artifacts is always deeply embedded in their ideational (cultural and historical) meanings.... Third, transformations between semiotic and material realizations of any artifact are in constant flux, as are the realizations of any artifact as *internal* (e.g., mental models, scenarios) or *external* (charts, diagrams, materials tools).
>
> (Leander, 2002, p. 202)

Cole (1996) employs Wartofsky's definition of artefacts (including tools and language) as objectifications of human needs and intentions already invested with cognitive and affective content (Wartofsky, 1973, p. 204). He distinguishes between three hierarchical levels of the notion of artefacts. Primary artefacts are those such as needles, clubs, bowls, which are used directly in the making of things. Secondary artefacts are representations of primary artefacts and of modes of action using primary artefacts. They are therefore traditions or beliefs. Tertiary artefacts were referred to by Wartofsky as imagined worlds. He sees works of art as examples of these tertiary artefacts or imagined worlds. He proceeds to outline how these three levels of artefact function in processes of cultural mediation.

Holland and Cole (1995) use discourse and schema theory to elaborate the concept of cultural artefact. Discourse theory is used to initiate a discussion of how representations/artefacts that operate in the social world may be regarded as cultural products and exhibit historical legacies. Speech genres and stories both reveal these qualities. Schema theory is used to explore the possibilities for mental representations which are socially formed and are modifiable.

Wertsch (1998) and Bruner (1990) both analyse narrative and historical texts as cultural tools. Wertsch (1998) emphasises that tools or artefacts such as 'conventional' stories or popular histories may not always 'fit' well with a particular personal narrative. As ever with a Vygotskian account, there is no necessary recourse to determinism. Wertsch suggests that individuals may resist the way in which such texts 'shape their actions, but they are often highly constrained in the forms that such resistance can take' (Wertsch, 1998, p. 108). This emphasis on the individual who is active in shaping a response to being shaped by engagement with cultural artefacts is central to the Vygotskian argument. The relative emphasis on agency (whether individual or collective – Wertsch, 1998) and the affordances (Gibson, 1986) that social, cultural and historical factors offer form the stage on which the development of new and improved forms of thought is enacted.

As is now well known, Vygotsky was involved in a variety of intellectual pursuits. These ranged from medicine and law to literary theory. Kozulin reminds his readers that Vygotsky was a member of the Russian intelligentsia for whom literature assumed a particular significance.

> A particular feature of the Russian intelligensia was the importance they attached to literature, which they saw not only as the ultimate embodiment of culture but as the most concentrated form of life itself. Literary characters were routinely judged by the Russian intelligensia as real social and psychological types, while political and historical debates were commonly conducted in the form of literature and about literature.
> (Kozulin, 1990, pp. 22–3)

He has subsequently expanded on this position in an essay on literature as a psychological tool in which he discusses the notion of human psychological life as 'authoring' alongside a consideration of the role of internalised literary modalities as mediators of human experience (Kozulin, 1998, p. 130).

The relationship between Wartofsky's tertiary artefacts or imagined worlds and the schemas and scripts of cognitive psychology has been made possible through the understanding of artefact as simultaneously material and ideal that is available in Ilyenkov's work.

Engeström (1999b) has also suggested that the distinction between external or practical artefacts and internal or cognitive artefacts is not helpful. He argues that there is a constant movement between the forms and they are inextricably linked. His insistence is that a more profitable move is to distinguish between different ways of using artefacts and he discusses the ways in which artefacts may be used to serve different functions, providing the following typology of functions:

'WHAT' artefacts	Used to identify and describe objects
'HOW' artefacts	Used to guide and direct processes and procedures on, within or between objects
'WHY' artefacts	Used to diagnose and explain the properties and behaviour of objects
'WHERE TO' artefacts	Used to envision the future state or potential development of objects, including institutions and social systems

(after Engeström, 1999b, pp. 381–2)

The understanding of artefacts carrying out different functions, being both material and ideal and circulating between inner and outer worlds in which meaning is developing, presents a complex, layered, dialectical view of human engagement with the world which carries with it a significant methodological challenge for research which aims to study processes of artefact-mediated formation of mind.

Social origins of higher mental functioning in the individual

Vygotsky's (1978) 'general genetic law of cultural development' asserts the primacy of the social in development:

> every function in the child's cultural development appears twice: first, on the social level, and later, on the individual level; first between people (interpsychological), and then inside the child (intrapsychological). This applies equally to voluntary attention, to logical memory, and to the formation of concepts. All the higher functions originate as actual relations between human individuals.
>
> (Vygotsky, 1978, p. 57)

The general genetic law of cultural development introduces the notion of some form of relationship between something which is defined as 'social' and something which is defined as 'individual'. There is an important methodological question with respect to which the individual is seen as separable from the context or general environment (Sawyer, 2002). Cole (1996) provides an example of the inseparability thesis:

> The dual process of shaping and being shaped through culture implies that humans inhabit 'intentional' (constituted) worlds within which the traditional dichotomies of subject and object, person and environment, and so on cannot be analytically separated and temporally ordered into independent and dependent variables.
>
> (Cole, 1996, p. 103)

As Van der Veer and Valsiner (1991) remind us, Vygotsky most definitely adopted a dialectical world view. This was the case for his theories as well as his approach to method and criticism.

> A present day psychologist is most likely to adopt a non-dialectical 'either – or' perspective when determining the 'class membership' of one or other approach in psychology. Hence the frequent non dialectical contrasts between 'Piagetian' and 'Vygotskian' approaches, or the wide spread separation of psychologists into 'social' versus 'cognitive' categories which seem to occupy our minds in their meta-psychological activities ... in direct contrast, for Vygotsky any two opposing directions of thought serve as opposites united with one another in the continuous whole – the discourse on ideas. This discourse is expected to lead us to a more adequate understanding of the human psyche, that is, to transcend the present state of theoretical knowledge, rather than force the existing variety of ideas into a strict classification of tendencies in the socially constructed scientific discipline of psychology.
>
> (Van der Veer and Valsiner, 1991, pp. 392–3)

This dialectical stance pervaded all aspects of his thinking, as is clear from the way in which he theorises the genetic influence on development:

> Development is not a simple function which can be wholly determined by adding X units of heredity to Y units of environment. It is a historical complex which, at every stage, reveals the past which is a part of it.... Development, according to a well-known definition, is precisely the struggle of opposites. This view alone can support truly dialectical research on the process of children's development.
>
> (Vygotsky, 1993, pp. 282–3)

Genetic or developmental method

Vygotsky's (1978) accounts of mediation by tools or artefacts and of the social origins of higher mental functioning may be read solely in terms of a movement from exchange between people to the development of individual competence. This reading ignores the origins of artefacts themselves. They are the products of individual and collective endeavour. 'Like Ilyenkov after him, Vygotsky recognises that as much as culture creates individuals, culture itself remains a human creation' (Bakhurst and Sypnowich, 1995, p. 11). As Bakhurst and Sypnowich imply, ways of thinking and feeling may be influenced and shaped by the availability of cultural artefacts which are themselves the products of mediated activity. Whilst I will return to the debates about the validity of propositions concerning processes of internalisation and appropriation in Chapters 3 and 4, it is clear that his was a theory which took account of the mediational function of artefacts which were human products. He was also concerned with the development of methodologies which would facilitate the study of such processes. In line with his account of artefact-mediated sociocultural formation, he proposed that the focus of observation and experiment should be on the mediated processes through which higher forms of functioning are established.

> To study something historically means to study it in the process of change; that is the dialectical method's basic demand. To encompass in research the process of a given thing's development in all its phases and changes – from birth to death – fundamentally means to discover its nature, its essence, for 'it is only in movement that a body shows what it is.' Thus, the historical study of behavior is not an auxiliary aspect of theoretical study, but rather forms its very base.
>
> (Vygotsky, 1978, pp. 64–5)

His account of mediation formed the basis of his formulation of the method of dual stimulation which is discussed in what is, perhaps, his best known publication, *Thinking and Speech*:

> In using this method, we study the development and activity of the higher mental functions with the aid of two sets of stimuli. These two sets of stimuli fulfill different roles *vis-à-vis* the subject's behavior. One set of stimuli fulfills the function of the object on which the subject's activity is directed. The second functions as signs that facilitate the organization of this activity.
>
> (Vygotsky, 1987c, p. 127)

Chapter 2 will include a full discussion of this important contribution which continues to influence research. The insight that in order to study and understand the psychological functioning we must do more than consider whether a problem can be solved, we must study how a problem is solved, was a crucial step in the development of a distinctive approach to methodology.

Wertsch (1985b) reminds us that a full account of the development of human mental functioning involved several intertwined genetic domains. Vygotsky was concerned with the relations between ontogenesis, phylogenesis, sociocultural history and microgenesis.

> The use and 'invention' of tools in humanlike apes crowns the organic development of behavior in evolution and paves the way for the transition of all development to take place along new paths. It creates *the basic psychological prerequisites for the historical development of behavior.* Labor and the associated development of human speech and other psychological signs with which primitives attempt to master their behavior, signify the beginning of the genuine cultural or historical development of behavior. Finally, in child development, along with processes of organic growth and maturation, a second line of development is clearly distinguished – the cultural growth of behavior. It is based on the mastery of devices and means of cultural behavior and thinking.
>
> (Luria and Vygotsky, 1930, p. xi)

Again, the methodological challenges are clear and these will be explored in Chapters 2, 6 and 7.

I will now consider aspects of Vygotsky's theory which follow from the themes identified by Wertsch (1985a): namely reliance on a genetic, or developmental method; the claim that higher mental functioning in the individual has its origins in social life; and the claim that an adequate account of human mental functioning must be grounded in an analysis of the tools and signs that mediate it. I will make specific reference to his work on scientific and everyday concepts, lower and higher elementary functioning, the zone of proximal development and the relation between sense and meaning

Scientific and everyday concepts

Vygotsky (1987a) and his co-worker Shif were particularly interested in two types of concepts: the scientific and the everyday or spontaneous. Using the term 'scientific concepts', Vygotsky referred to concepts introduced by a teacher in school; while spontaneous concepts were those that were acquired by the child outside contexts in which explicit instruction was in place. Scientific concepts were described as those which form a coherent, logical hierarchical system. For Vygotsky, scientific concepts were characterised by a high degree of generality and their relationship to objects is mediated through other concepts:

> the dependence of scientific concepts on spontaneous concepts and their influence on them stems from the unique relationship that exists between the scientific concept and its object ... [T]his relationship is characterised by the fact that it is mediated through other concepts. Consequently, in its relationship to the object, the scientific concept includes a relationship to another concept, that is it includes the most basic element of a concept system.
> (Vygotsky, 1987a, p. 192)

According to Vygotsky (1987a), children can make deliberate use of scientific concepts, they are consciously aware of them and can reflect upon them. The editors of the most recent translation of *Thinking and Speech* suggest that when Vygotsky (1987a) uses the terms 'spontaneous thinking' or 'spontaneous concepts', he is referring to a context of formation which is that of immediate, social, practical activity as against a context of instruction in a formal system of knowledge. Scientific concepts are, through their very systematic nature, open to the voluntary control of the child.

For Vygotsky, co-operation and collaboration are crucial features of effective teaching:

> The development of the scientific concept, a phenomenon that occurs as part of the educational process, constitutes a unique form of systematic co-operation between the teacher and the child. The maturation of the child's higher mental functions occurs in this co-operative process, that is, it occurs through the adult's assistance and participation.... In a problem involving scientific concepts, he must be able to do in collaboration with the teacher something that he has never done spontaneously ... we know that the child can do more in collaboration that he can independently.
> (Vygotsky, 1987a, pp. 168, 169 and 216)

Vygotsky argued that the systematic, organised and hierarchical thinking that he associated with scientific concepts becomes gradually embedded in everyday referents and thus achieves a general sense in the contextual richness of everyday thought. Vygotsky thus presented a model of an interdependent relationship between scientific and everyday or spontaneous concepts in the process of true concept formation. He argued that everyday thought is given structure and order in the context of systematic scientific thought. Vygotsky was keen to point out the relative strengths of both as they both contributed to each other:

> the formation of concepts develops simultaneously from two directions: from the direction of the general and the particular ... [T]he development of a scientific concept begins with the verbal definition. As part of an organised system, this verbal definition descends to concrete; it descends to phenomena which the concept represents. In contrast, the everyday concept tends to develop outside any definite system; it tends to move upwards toward abstraction and generalisation ... [T]he weakness of the everyday concept lies in its incapacity for abstraction, in the child's incapacity to operate on it in a voluntary manner ... [T]he weakness of the scientific concept lies in its verbalism, in its insufficient saturation with the concrete.
>
> (Vygotsky, 1987a, pp. 163, 168 and 169)

In arguing that conceptual thinking positively influences not only the cognitive domain but also aesthetic reactions and emotions, Van der Veer (1994) suggests that Vygotsky's view of conceptual development is overly rationalistic. For Wardekker (1998), the development of scientific concepts also includes a moral dimension. He argues that 'scientific (or 'scholarly') concepts are the products of reflection in a practice that includes choices about the future development of that praxis and are, in that sense, of a moral nature' (Wardekker, 1998, p. 143). This issue is recognised if not developed in the original writing.

> [Thought] is not born of other thoughts. Thought has its origins in the motivating sphere of consciousness, a sphere that includes our inclinations and needs, our interests and impulses, and our affect and emotions. The affective and volitional tendency stands behind thought. Only here do we find the answer to the final 'why' in the analysis of thinking.
>
> (Vygotsky, 1987a, p. 282)

In the emergent, radically transformed society of early twentieth-century Russia, the school was to be the state's agency for ensuring the development of advanced conceptual tools. Instruction was the educational driving force of development for Vygotsky. Co-operation and collaboration were seen as crucial within effective teaching.

Vygotsky argued that scientific concepts are not assimilated in ready-made or pre-packaged form. He insisted that the two forms of concept are brought into forms of relationship within which they both develop. An important corollary of this model of is the denial of the possibility of direct pedagogic transmission of concepts.

> [P]edagogical experience demonstrates that direct instruction in concepts is impossible. It is pedagogically fruitless. The teacher who attempts to use this approach achieves nothing but a mindless learning of words, an empty verbalism that stimulates or imitates the presence of concepts in the child. Under these conditions, the child learns not the concept but the word, and

this word is taken over by the child through memory rather than thought. Such knowledge turns out to be inadequate in any meaningful application. This mode of instruction is the basic defect of the purely scholastic verbal modes of teaching which have been universally condemned. It substitutes the learning of dead and empty verbal schemes for the mastery of living knowledge.

(Vygotsky, 1987a, p. 170)

In *Educational Psychology* he uses the analogy of a gardener trying to affect the growth of a plant by directly tugging at its roots with his hands from underneath when criticising teachers who directly influence concept development in the student (Vygotsky, 1997b, p. 49). If it is to be effective in the formation of scientific concepts, instruction should be designed to foster conscious awareness of conceptual form and structure and thereby allow for individual access and control over acquired scientific concepts. It must also foster the interaction and development of everyday concepts with scientific concepts. One of his better-known examples is that of learning a foreign language, which for Vygotsky raises the level of development of mother-tongue speech through enhanced conscious awareness of linguistic forms. Similarly, he suggests that by learning algebra, the child comes to understand arithmetic operations as particular instantiations of algebraic operations. The scientific concepts of grammar and algebra are seen as means by which thought is freed from concrete instances of speech or numerical relations and raised to a more abstract level (Vygotsky, 1987a, p. 180). Scientific concepts are developed through different levels of dialogue: in the social space between teacher and taught; and in the conceptual space between the everyday and scientific. The result is the production of webs or patterns of conceptual connection.

[T]he concept of 'flower' is not actually more general than the concept of 'rose'. When the child has mastered only a single concept, its relationship to the object is different than it is after he masters a second. However, after he masters a second concept, there is a long period during which the concept of 'flower' continues to stand alongside, rather than above, the concept of 'rose'. The former does not include the latter. The narrower concept is not subordinated. Rather, the broader concept acts as a substitute for the narrower one. It stands alongside it in a single series. When the concept 'flower' is generalized, the relationship between it and the concept of 'rose' changes as well. Indeed, there is a change in its relationship with all subordinate concepts. This marks the emergence of a concept system.

(Vygotsky, 1987a, p. 193)

Vygotsky's writing on scientific and everyday concepts continues to cause controversy. Ageyev (2003) speaks of the need for contextual and cultural interpretations of Vygotsky. The notion that Vygotsky's writing appears as though drawn through some kind of cultural mediator is an interesting way of applying the theory to its own development. In a discussion of the interpretations that have arisen from the writing on scientific and everyday concepts, Karpov (2003) notes the discrepancies that exist between those influenced by a constructivist theory of learning and those who have drawn on Davydov's (1988) distinction between theoretical learning (which results in scientific concepts) and empirical learning (which results in spontaneous concepts). He is critical of both traditional and guided discovery forms of classroom practice; arguing that they may often give rise to misconceptions, he advocates instruction in a combination of conceptual and procedural knowledge in a particular curriculum/knowledge context. The tension between constructivist and instructional interpretations persists.

What I am calling the 'instructional approach' has also developed its own factions: e.g. Davydov (1993, pp. 88, 90), Hedegaard (2002, 1998, p. 90) and Karpov (2003). The analysis of knowledge within such approaches requires further work. Some headway has been made by Bernstein (1999), who distinguishes between vertical and horizontal discourse. Horizontal discourse arises out of everyday activity and is usually oral, local and context dependent as well as specific, tacit, multilayered and contradictory across, but not within, contexts. Its structure reflects the way a particular culture is segmented and its activities are specialised. Horizontal discourse is thus segmentally organised. In contrast, vertical discourse has a coherent, explicit and systematically principled structure which is hierarchically organised or takes the form of a series of specialised languages with specialised criteria for the production and circulation of texts.

Bernstein's paper serves as important reminder that the theoretical derivation of 'scientific and everyday' in the original writing was somewhat provisional. For example, the association of the scientific with the school does not help to distinguish those aspects of schooling that merely act to add to everyday understanding without fostering the development of scientific concepts. Bernstein's analysis is suggestive of a more powerful means of conceptualising the forms which Vygotsky announced. Bernstein's (1999b) endeavour was to develop a language of description which could produce greater differentiation within and between these forms and explore the social basis of this differentiation. For him, horizontal discourse is segmentally organised and its realisation varies with the way the culture segments and specialises activities and practices. It entails a set of strategies which are local, segmentally organised, context specific and dependent, for maximising encounters with persons and habitats. Within a horizontal discourse an individual's *repertoire* is drawn from a community *reservoir* and it is practices of social stratification that produce distributive rules that control the flow of procedures from reservoir to repertoire. This argument alone serves to locate the Vygotskian notion of the 'everyday' or 'spontaneous' back into the social and cultural structures of everyday practices.

Bernstein (1999b) further argued that hierarchical knowledge structures create very general propositions and theories which integrate knowledge at lower levels, whereas horizontal knowledge structures create a series of specialised languages.

Within hierarchical knowledge structure, a theoretical development takes place through the formulation of a theory which is more general/integrating than any that preceded it. Within horizontal knowledge structures, the specialised languages are not 'translatable'. Advancement does not take place through the production of theories capable of greater generality; rather it takes place through the introduction of a new language which may displace old languages and speakers. He further suggested that horizontal knowledge structures may embody strong or weak grammars. He cited economics, linguistics and mathematics as examples of strong grammars, each with an explicit syntax capable of relatively precise empirical descriptions and rigorous restrictions on the empirical phenomena they address. He offered sociology and cultural studies as examples of weak grammars in which work is referenced through persons and associated with a notional gaze. In a horizontal knowledge structure with a weak grammar, power relations establish 'truth' within a gaze as against the case of hierarchical knowledge structures where reference is to a theory, albeit with choices between options. Within horizontal knowledge structures, Bernstein argues the case of linguistic hegemony (being able to speak with a particular voice) and the acquisition of a gaze (a way of seeing) that constitutes competence with weak powers of empirical description.

Figure 1.2 provides an illustration of Bernstein's (1999b) proposal. Such a schema is one way of developing the scientific/everyday distinction and hints at the kind of analysis that might be required in order to identify the conceptual and procedural knowledge which Karpov (2003) states is necessary for the kind of instructional practice that will lead to the development of 'scientific concepts'.

The zone of proximal development

A casual reading of late twentieth-century texts concerning Vygotsky might well leave a reader with the impression that the 'Zone of Proximal Development'

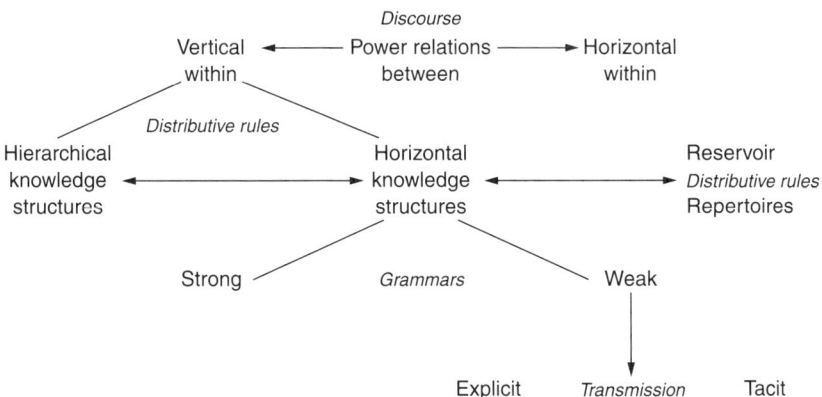

Figure 1.2 Discourse and knowledge structures.

(ZPD) was his central contribution. However, he did not introduce the concept until 1933 and it does not feature widely in his writing. As Valsiner and Van der Veer (2000) note, it has given rise to many 'interesting interpretations', many of which have been subjected to strident criticism (e.g. Chaiklin, 2003).

Vygotsky discussed the ZPD in terms of assessment and instruction. Within both frames of reference, he discussed the relationship between an individual learner and a supportive other or others, even if that other was not physically present in the context in which learning was taking place, as revealed in the following:

> when the school child solves a problem at home on the basis of a model that he has been shown in class, he continues to act in collaboration, though at the moment the teacher is not standing near him. From a psychological perspective, the solution of the second problem is similar to this solution of a problem at home. It is a solution accomplished with the teacher's help. This help – this aspect of collaboration – is invisibly present. It is contained in what looks from the outside like the child's independent solution of the problem.
> (Vygotsky, 1987a, p. 216)

According to Valsiner and Van der Veer (2000), Vygotsky was an active participant in the Russian testing movement which was particularly active during the 1920s. He was, however, an opponent of the use of IQ tests and the suggestion that they gave direct access to genetic endowment. His work with disadvantaged children makes it clear why Vygotsky would be extremely anxious to find 'the optimal student-education fit and why he would be looking for methods to optimise this fit' (Valsiner and Van der Veer, 2000, p. 378). Within the first, assessment-oriented account, Vygotsky defines the ZPD as 'actual developmental level as determined by independent problem solving' and the higher level of 'potential development as determined through problem solving under adult guidance or in collaboration with more capable peers' (Vygotsky, 1978, p. 86). He elaborates on this definition in order to emphasise the difference between aided and unsupported performance:

> Suppose I investigate two children upon entrance into school, both of whom are twelve years old chronologically and eight years old in terms of mental development. Can I say that they are the same age mentally? Of course. What does this mean? It means that they can independently deal with tasks up to the degree of difficulty that has been standardized for the eight-year-old level. If I stop at this point, people would imagine that the subsequent course of development and of school learning of these children will be the same, because it depends on their intellect.... Now imagine that I do not terminate my study at this point, but only begin it.... Suppose I show ... [these children] have various ways of dealing with a task ... that the children solve the problem with my assistance. Under these circumstances it

> turns out that the first child can deal with problems up to a twelve-year-old's level. The second up to a nine-year-old's. Now are these children mentally the same? When it was first shown that the capability of children with equal levels of mental development to learn under a teacher's guidance varied to a high degree, it became apparent that those children were not mentally the same and that the subsequent course of their learning would obviously be different. This difference between twelve and eight, or between nine and eight, is what we call the zone of proximal development.
>
> (Vygotsky, 1978, pp. 85–6)

His interest was in assessing the ways in which learners make progress. The focus on process as well as product in assessment has become embedded in the range of techniques now called 'dynamic assessment' (e.g. Lidz and Elliot, 2000). The general practice of dynamic assessment is either explicitly or tacitly inspired by the work of Vygotsky. This contrasts sharply with practices which theorise a lag of learning behind development as in the case of Piaget or which theorise learning as development as in the case of Skinner. There are stark differences in the ways in which this idea, which has, at least, some root in Vygotskian theory, becomes embedded in other psychological traditions.

The second account of the ZPD is to be found in *Thinking and Speech* (1987c), and is embedded in Chapter 6 in which he discussed 'The development of scientific concepts in childhood':

> We have seen that instruction and development do not coincide. They are two different processes with very complex interrelationships. Instruction is only useful when it moves ahead of development. When it does, it impels or awakens a whole series of functions that are in a stage of maturation lying in the zone of proximal development. This is the major role of instruction in development. This is what distinguishes the instruction of the child from the training of animals. This is also what distinguishes instruction of the child which is directed toward his full development from instruction in specialised, technical skills such as typing or riding a bicycle. The formal aspect of each school subject is that in which the influence of instruction on development is realized. Instruction would be completely unnecessary if it merely utilized what had already matured in the developmental process, if it were not itself a source of development.
>
> (Vygotsky, 1987c, p. 212)

As Valsiner and Van der Veer (1993) note, it was in this way that he brought the notion of the ZPD together with his account of the relationship between scientific and everyday concepts. He also integrated the ZPD notion into his theory of play. It was argued that in play the child could temporarily become 'higher than his average age, higher than his usual everyday behaviour; he is in play as if a head above himself' (Valsiner and Van der Veer, 1993, p. 44).

Chaiklin (2003) reminds us that the reference made by Vygotsky was to instruction that is designed to support the development of psychological functions as they are transformed and reconfigured through particular age periods. Chaiklin suggests that much of what has been discussed under the rubric of the ZPD misses the central insistence on instruction leading *development*. The distinction between microgenesis and ontogenesis is missed in what, for Chaiklin, are misinterpretations of the original formulation of the ZPD in its instructional frame of reference. Valsiner provides another important cautionary note that must enter into this debate. He reminds us that much of the empirical work that has been undertaken runs the risk of confusing microgenetic and ontogenetic processes: 'There exists an unwarranted (and implicit) assumption in received empirical practices in developmental psychology to consider the microgenetic and ontogenetic levels of development similar in their organisation' (Valsiner, 1997, p. 241). Chaiklin (2003) suggests that terms such as 'scaffolding' should be reserved for practices which are designed to teach specific skills and subject matter concepts as against instruction designed to serve explicitly developmental purposes (Chaiklin, 2003, p. 59).

The term scaffolding could be taken to infer a 'one-way' process within which the 'scaffolder' constructs the scaffold alone and presents it for use to the novice. Newman *et al.* (1989) argued that the ZPD is created through negotiation between the more advanced partner and the learner, rather than through the donation of a scaffold as some kind of prefabricated climbing frame. There is a similar emphasis on negotiation in Tharp and Gallimore (1988), who discussed 'teaching as assisted performance' in those stages of the ZPD where assistance is required. The key question here seems to be with respect to where the 'hints', 'supports', or 'scaffold' come from. Are they produced by 'the more capable partner' or are they negotiated? Vygotsky is unclear on this matter.

Cole and Griffin (1984) mount a strong criticism of the scaffolding metaphor based on the extent to which the child's creativity is underplayed. They draw on the work of the Russian physiologist Nicholas Bernstein and A.N. Leontiev. From Bernstein they borrow an emphasis on essential creativity in all forms of living movement and from Leontiev they pursue the notion of 'leading activity'. The argument that different settings and activities give rise to 'spaces' within the ZPD for creative exploration rather than pedagogic domination is at the heart of their position: 'Adult wisdom does not provide a teleology for child development. Social organization and leading activities provide a gap within which the child can develop novel creative analyses' (Griffin and Cole, 1984, p. 62). In a seminal article, Vygotsky (2004) recognised the importance of the development of creativity through schooling and also rejected the notion of creativity as the product of sudden inspiration. He argued that the active promotion of creativity was a central function of schooling.

> [W]e should emphasize the particular importance of cultivating creativity in school-age children. The entire future of humanity will be attained through

the creative imagination; orientation to the future, behavior based on the future and derived from this future, is the most important function of the imagination. To the extent that the main educational objective of teaching is guidance of school children's behavior so as to prepare them for the future, development and exercise of the imagination should be one of the main forces enlisted for the attainment of this goal.

(Vygotsky, 2004, pp. 87–8)

His analysis of the development of creativity is marked by an emphasis on interfunctional relations which resonates throughout his work. He argued that children are not necessarily more creative than adults; rather that they have less control and critical judgement over the products of their imagination. He suggests that as rational thought develops so does critical judgement and that the tendency is for adolescents to become increasingly dissatisfied with the products of their imagination, if they do not acquire appropriate 'cultural and technical factors' or tools with which to engage in creative activity. Adults dismiss their creative output if they are not given the tools to do this sort of work.

He argues that creativity is a social process which requires appropriate tools, artefacts and cultures in which to thrive. He extends this analysis to social class with a comment on creativity which will doubtless cause a little discomfort when read by twenty-first-century Western eyes.

Every inventor, even a genius, is also a product of his time and his environment. His creations arise from needs that were created before him and rest on capacities that also exist outside of him. This is why we emphasize that there is a strict sequence in the historical development of science and technology. No invention or scientific discovery can occur before the material and psychological conditions necessary for it to occur have appeared. Creation is a historical, cumulative process where every succeeding manifestation was determined by the preceding one. This explains the disproportionate distribution of innovators and creators among different classes. The privileged classes supply an incomparably greater percentage of scientific, technical, and artistic creators, because it is in these classes that all the conditions needed for creation are present.

(Vygotsky, 2004, pp. 30–1)

This position has been adapted by Wertsch and Tulviste, who talk of creativity as 'transformation of an existing pattern of action, a new use for an old tool' (Wertsch and Tulviste, 1996), and Wertsch (1991, 98) reminds us that individuals' histories with regard to cultural tools are an important element in the development of mediated action. He argues that when Vygotsky uses the term 'mental function' he does so with reference to social interaction and to individual processes. In this sense mental functions may be seen to be carried by groups as well as by individuals. Like Pea, he sees ability as the capacity to function with the tool and citing Middleton, Bartlett, Resnick and Salomon, he also talks of mind being socially distributed, belonging to dyads and larger groups who can think, attend and remember together (Wertsch, 1991, 1998).

If we follow Vygotsky's own insistence on the use of genetic (historical/developmental) analysis it is possible to discern a trajectory in his own writing towards a more socially connected account:

> Vygotsky seemed to be coming to recognise this issue near the end of his life. It is reflected in the difference between Chapters five and six of Thinking and Speech (1987). Both chapters deal with the ontogenetic transition from 'complexes' to 'genuine', or 'scientific' concepts. However, the two chapters differ markedly in what they see as relevant developmental forces. In Chapter five (based on research with Shif and written during the early 1930s), concept development is treated primarily in terms of intramental processes, that is, children's conceptual development as they move from 'unorganised heaps' to 'complexes' to 'concepts'. In Chapter six (written in 1934), there is an essential shift in the way Vygotsky approaches these issues. He clearly continued to be interested in intramental functioning, but he shifted to approaching concept development from the perspective of how it emerges in institutionally situated activity. Specifically, he was concerned with how the forms of discourse encountered in the social institution of formal schooling provide a framework for the development of conceptual thinking. He did it by the teacher-child intermental functioning found in this setting.
>
> (Wertsch *et al.*, 1993, p. 344)

The notion of 'forms of discourse encountered in the social institution of formal schooling [that] provide a framework for the development of conceptual thinking' expands the formulation of the ZPD beyond the confines of a dyadic setting and sets this approach apart from much of the work that is presented under the rubric of 'scaffolding'. On the basis of his interpretation of Activity Theory, Engeström (1999a) has developed an approach to the study of what he terms 'expansive learning', which deploys an account of the collective formation of the ZPD. In Chapter 6 I will discuss the assumptions and methodologies of this body of work.

In another variant of the understanding of the ZPD, Holzman (1999) seeks to promote an account of the ways in which both the learner and that which is being learned are mutually transformed. The emphasis here is on creation and transformation rather than transmission:

> For Vygotsky human development was revolutionary activity – development (more properly developing) is inseparable from creating environments for development. The social-cultural-historical process of creating what he called zpds is the revolutionary activity of people jointly (collectively,

socially) transforming totalities. Zpds are not instrumental means-ends tools for results, but simultaneously prerequisite and product, tool and result.

(Holzman, 1999, p. 100)

It is possible that the sheer popularity of the notion of the ZPD is attributable to its perceived malleability: it can adapted to meet the meet the demands/expectations/aspirations of researchers with a wide range of methodological and theoretical orientations. There would appear to be a need for greater clarity in the explication of the background assumptions that are in play when the concept ZPD is deployed. Chaiklin (2003) provides a good example of this move to transparency. His differentiation between microgenesis and ontogenesis is clearly of great importance. There is also a need to clarify the scope of the social, cultural-historical formation that is envisaged within the ZPD. Most empirical work appears to assume that an account of the dynamics of a working dyad is all that is necessary. Engeström (1999b) makes a strong case for an extended analysis of the activity settings. The methodological implications of these arguments will be explored in Chapters 6 and 7.

Lower and higher elementary functioning

Ratner (1998) insists that a central principle within the framework of Vygotsky's developmental psychology is the transition from 'lower' processes to 'higher' functions. The 'lower' psychobiological processes include reflexes and spontaneous, rudimentary conscious processes. The 'higher' conscious psychological functions include developed, voluntary mental functions, categorical perception, voluntary attention and voluntary movements. He understood the development of higher functions in terms of mediated social, collaborative activity.

> [C]onsidering the history of the development of higher mental functions that comprise the basic nucleus in the structure of personality, we find that the relation between higher mental functions was at one time a concrete relation between people; collective social forms of behaviour in the process of development become a method of individual adaptations and forms of behaviour and thinking of the personality.... Put more simply, higher mental functions arise from collective forms of behaviour.
>
> (Vygotsky, 1998b, p. 168)

He argued that with its onset in childhood thought becomes linguistic and speech rational. He argued that speech acts develop the interrelation of all the higher mental functions and and in so doing developed a dialectical concept of the relation between speech and thinking which incorporated biological and cultural influences, as shown in the two extracts below:

> [A]ll higher mental functions are mediated processes. A central and basic aspect of their structure is the use of the sign as a means of directing and mastering mental processes ... [higher mental functions] are an aspect of the child's cultural development and have their source in collaboration and instruction ... initially these [higher mental] functions arise as forms of cooperative activity. Only later are they transformed by the child into the sphere of his own mental activity.
>
> (Vygotsky, 1987a, pp. 126, 213 and 259)

> If we include this history of higher psychological functions as a factor in psychological development, we must arrive at a new concept of development itself. Within a general process of development, two qualitatively different lines of development, differing in origin, can be distinguished: the elementary processes, which are of biological origin, on the one hand, and the higher psychological functions, of sociocultural origin, on the other. The history of child behavior is born from the interweaving of these two lines. The history of the development of the higher psychological functions is impossible without a study of their prehistory, their biological roots, and their organic disposition. The developmental roots of two fundamental, cultural forms of behavior arise during infancy: the use of tools and human speech. This alone places infancy at the center of the prehistory of cultural development.
>
> (Vygotsky, 1978, p. 46)

Wertsch (1985a) summarises the four major differences between higher and lower mental functions as: the shift of control from the environment to the individual, that is, the emergence of voluntary regulation; the emergence of conscious realisation of mental process; the social origins and social nature of higher mental functions; and the use of signs to mediate higher mental functions.

Vygotsky's (1981b) suggestion was that mastery of a psychological tool and, through it, mastery of a natural mental function are involved in the development of a lower function to a higher stage. In its higher form it is restructured and its field of application widened. Davydov (1988) disagreed with Vygotsky's division of functions into higher and lower or elementary forms. He argued that all mental processes arise and are maintained through complex mediational processes, albeit that the onset of speech marks a particularly important phase. Van der Veer and Van Ijzendoorn (1985) also criticise the distinction between lower and higher psychological processes in Vygotsky's cultural-historical theory. They also argued that what is often considered to be the problem of the sharp distinction drawn by Vygotsky between higher and lower psychological processes may be resolved through recent studies in activity theory which consider the possibility of demonstrating that 'natural' processes may be influenced by direction and instruction/training.

Veresov's (1999) detailed analysis of Vygotsky's work makes claims for transitions in the way in which the notions of higher and lower are handled. He discusses the writing in which higher functions were presented as inhibited reflexes to 1925 when he defined 'higher psychical functions' and 'higher forms of behaviour' as synonyms. This was the phase in which Minick (1985) notes that Vygotsky was concerned with interfunctional relationships. By around 1927, Veresov argues that Vygotsky began to represent higher functions as higher psychical processes which gradually replace the natural (not elementary) processes in the development of consciousness. Whether one agrees with the details of Veresov's assertions is, perhaps, not as important as the recognition that Vygotsky's ideas were changing rapidly.

One of the great dangers with the early interpretations of this work was the suggestion that children whose elementary functions were damaged or deficient were beyond the reach of education. Children would be assessed to see if they could benefit from education. This assessment would consist of a means of scrutinising those functions deemed elementary. Those who 'failed' the assessment were removed from the educational community. Davydov's work gives ground for rejecting the sharp delineation between functions deemed higher and lower and the practices that were associated with the demarcation. The development of Vygotsky's own thinking on this matter was incomplete. He certainly changed his views on several occasions. He was also working at a time when the cultural artefacts of the late twentieth century were not even imagined. He had no access to tape recorders, freeze-frame video recorders, etc. and was not in a position to 'see' the data on development that those who followed him have examined. Nelson (1995) depicts three levels of conceptual development: the first is constructed by individuals on the basis of direct experience with the world without the mediational effects of language; the second is that level of knowledge is a product of the 'language using community'; and the third level is that of a formally organised cultural system – theoretical knowledge. Thus she proposes the transitions from the natural to the sociohistorical and from spontaneous to scientific. The spontaneous and the scientific are located in the sociohistorical.

Sense/meaning

Within the analysis of the semiotic mode of mediation, speech, the most powerful and pervasive of semiotic devices, functions as a psychological tool in the construction of individual consciousness. The social becomes individual not through a process of simple transmission. Individuals construct their own sense from socially available meanings. Inner speech is the result of a constructive process whereby speech from and with others has become speech for the self. Egocentric speech, rather than being a form of thinking aloud as in the Piagetian thesis, is a transitionary phase between ordinary communicative speech and inner speech. The social voice becomes the inner voice. Changes in social circumstances (particularly patterns of communication) give rise to changes in the patterns of construction.

Lave and Wenger's (1991) representation is of the scientific as 'understood' or 'cultural' and the everyday as 'active' and 'individual'; the 'mature' concept being achieved when they have merged. The complexity of mastering scientific concepts is brought home by the distinction between the 'sense' (*smyl*) and the 'meaning' (*znachenie*) of a word.

> A word's sense is the aggregate of all the psychological facts that arise in our consciousness as a result of the word. Sense is a dynamic, fluid and complex formation which has several zones that vary in their stability. Meaning is only one of these zones of sense that the word acquires in the context of speech. It is the most stable, unified and precise of these zones. In different contexts, a word's sense changes. In contrast, meaning is a comparatively fixed and stable point, one that remains constant with all the changes of the word's sense that are associated with its use in various contexts.
> (Vygotsky, 1987a, pp. 275–6)

In Chapter 7 of *Thinking and Speech* Vygotsky discusses the complexities of the relationships between sense and meaning on the one hand and oral and inner speech on the other. In this rather beautiful and poetic chapter, Vygotsky provided what could be taken as the background for the preceding chapters on concept development. The ongoing dynamic between the use of social speech and relatively stable social meanings in the creation of particular forms and patterns of personal sense is construed as the motor of development. The notion of the scientific concept can be seen as a particular historical-cultural form of relatively stable meaning which is brought into productive interchange with the sense of the world that is acquired in specific everyday circumstances.

In this chapter I have briefly sketched an outline of some of the key concepts in Vygotsky's overall thesis. I have attempted to show how his ideas developed over time and hinted at some of the ways in which interpretations of his work have been contested. This body of work fulfils the specification of a system of interconnected concepts which derive their full meaning in relation to each other. Just as Halliday (1975) proposed the notion of 'talking one's way in' to social and cultural understanding and meaning-making, so I would argue that there is no direct route to an understanding of the Vygotskian thesis. Following the quotation I gave from Puzyrei (2007) at the outset of this chapter, this body of work is like a complex city that must be walked through in multiple transects both above and below ground to gain an appropriately multidimensional view of its subtlety and complexity.

Chapter 2

An overview of research undertaken by Vygotsky and some of his colleagues

In this chapter I will provide a selective overview of the approach to research adopted and developed by Vygotsky and his colleagues in post-revolutionary Russia. I have written elsewhere about the difficulties which confront non-Russian speakers when they attempt to read and understand Vygotsky's writing (Daniels, 2001). In addition to difficulties with translation and cultural differences in orientation to certain key psychological constructs, Van der Veer and Valsiner (1991) comment on the unfinished or half-developed nature of some of Vygotsky's ideas which in no small part have their origins in the thoughts of others. His attempts at synthesis and development of a wide range of ideas have their own developmental trajectory and present their own challenges of interpretation. As Meshcheryakov notes:

> There are many reasons for the difficulties readers encounter in analyzing and understanding Vygotsky's terminology. He developed his psychology in constant direct and indirect dialogue with many other authors. In doing so, he absorbed and processed all the ideas and terms that he believed could be useful. These ranged from the philosophy of Spinoza and Marx to the American behaviorism of Watson and the linguistics of Sapir. However, when one meets a seemingly familiar term borrowed from some predecessor in Vygotsky's writings, one should keep in mind that he was likely to have modified the term's meaning.
>
> (Meshcheryakov, 2007, p. 155)

In an editorial footnote to a chapter written by two Russian colleagues, Wertsch drew attention to differences in the use of the terms 'methodology' and 'methodologist' in Soviet psychology. Rather than being restricted to problems of designing and conducting empirical research, he suggests that the terms refer to the study of 'general theoretical and metatheoretical issues that underlie any investigation of psychological phenomena' (Wertsch, in Davydov and Radzikhovskii, 1985, p. 61). In the same chapter, Davydov and Radzikhovskii themselves argue that fundamental to Vygotsky's methodology or metatheory is the insistence that psychological theory must involve the elucidation of the 'explanatory principle', the object of study (or analytic unit) and the dynamics of the relations between these two.

Bakhurst (1991) adds a further dimension to this position in that he describes Vygotsky as 'concerned with the question of how psychologists' methodology (including general theoretical suppositions) can *infect* the object of their analysis' (p. 61; italics added). In his search for methods, Vygotsky drew on a wide range of ideas which themselves brought changes in the way in which research objects were construed. Kozulin (1986) cites the work of the Soviet philosopher of psychology Georgy Schedrovitsky, who suggests that Vygotsky's methodological activity transformed the understanding of the object of study in psychological work:

> The range of ideas introduced by Vygotsky, alien to traditional psychology, called for special means of discussion and analysis. And he drew many of these means from philology and linguistics ... [I]t turned out, however that in the process Vygotsky broke down the traditional object of psychology.
> (Schedrovitsky, 1982, p. 62)

It remains the case that the research tools and artefacts developed by Vygotsky do not easily submit to classification and categorisation. Van der Veer (1997) suggests it is quite possible that we still do not possess a complete collection of the original texts. There is even some debate as to when his work in the social sciences actually commenced (Veresov, 1999). Descriptions of the historical stages or phases through which his thinking progressed have been proposed by Das (1995) and Minick (1987), and contested by Veresov (1999). Van der Veer (1997) further regards any attempt at dividing Vygotsky's work into categories such as theoretical, developmental or pedological as arbitrary.

However, they all agree that Vygotsky should be thought of as a researcher and thinker who was primarily concerned with the development of methodology.

> The search for method becomes one of the most important problems of the entire enterprise of understanding the uniquely human forms of psychological activity. In this case, the method is simultaneously prerequisite and product, the tool and the result of the study.
> (Vygotsky, 1978, p. 65)

Bakhurst (1988, p. 82) restates this in terms of his search for a method that is necessary and sufficient for studying a specific object which involves scrutiny of the nature of the object itself. This effect has been noted at both the micro-level of specific research intervention (cf. Newman and Holzman, 1993) and at the macro-level of his entire activity within the social sciences. It is well known that a wide range of sources fired Vygotsky's methodological imagination. For example, at one point he argued that psychology must be developed in the concepts of drama, not in the concepts of processes (Vygotsky, 1989, p. 71).

Despite the reservations noted above, Minick's (1985) analysis of three phases of Vygotsky's work enables the reader to gain an overview and perspective on the development of Vygotsky's methodological writings. In his account of the trajectory of Vygotsky's work, Minick suggests that the first transition was from a focus on an analytic unit called the instrumental act in 1925–30, to an analytic unit of the psychological system in 1930. This was followed in 1933–4 by a refinement of the explanatory principle which became the differentiation and development of systems of interaction and action in which the individual participates (Minick, 1987). This final phase is evidenced in papers and lectures written in the last two years of his life. These sources are often difficult to obtain and remain elusive, as his work was often left in the form of sketches rather than fully fledged arguments (e.g. Vygotsky, 1983). This final phase of Vygotsky's work suggests the need to move towards a broad analysis of behaviour and consciousness which articulates and clarifies the social, cultural and historical basis of development.

Across these three stages, particular themes emerge and develop and are transformed. These themes have been identified by Van der Veer and Valsiner (1991, p. 398), who characterise Vygotsky's fundamental contributions to psychology in terms of:

- his emphasis on the process of dialectical synthesis;
- his consistent developmental perspective;
- his overall anti-reductionist stance;
- his development of the method known as double or dual stimulation.

I will explore all four of these matters in the rest of this chapter. In so doing, I will draw attention to the studies and methodological breakthroughs that Vygotsky made in the latter part of his career. I will not be discussing the early work which Minick (1987) suggests was dominated by the assumption that the stimulus–response unit was 'the basic building block of behaviour' (Minick, 1987, p. 23). As mentioned above, there is some disagreement between writers as to the exact point at which Vygotsky's work took the cultural-historical turn which has proved to be so influential. Minick suggests that this change is to be seen in 'The genetic roots of thinking and speech', which was written in 1929 and became Chapter 4 of *Thinking and Speech* (Vygotsky, 1987a). Van der Veer and Valsiner (1991) point to 'The problem of the cultural development of the child II', originally published in 1928 (in English as Vygotsky, 1929). They further suggest that the theory reached its most complete account in the 300 pages of the much-revised text which was eventually published under the title *The History of the Development of the Higher Mental Functions* (Vygotsky, 1997c). Whatever the date of its inception, it is this cultural-historical aspect of his work which continues to attract the attention of researchers today.

The process of dialectical synthesis

Van der Veer and Valsiner (1991) remind us that Vygotsky adopted a dialectical world view. This was the case for his theories as well as his approach to method and criticism.

> A present day psychologist is most likely to adopt a non-dialectical 'either – or' perspective when determining the 'class membership' of one or other approach in psychology. Hence the frequent non dialectical contrasts between 'Piagetian' and 'Vygotskian' approaches, or the wide spread separation of psychologists into 'social' versus 'cognitive' categories which seem to occupy our minds in their meta-psychological activities ... [I]n direct contrast, for Vygotsky any two opposing directions of thought serve as opposites united with one another in the continuous whole – the discourse on ideas. This discourse is expected to lead us to a more adequate understanding of the human psyche, that is, to transcend the present state of theoretical knowledge, rather than force the existing variety of ideas into a strict classification of tendencies in the socially constructed scientific discipline of psychology.
> (Van der Veer and Valsiner, 1991, pp. 392–3)

Vygotsky's intention was to consider the synthesis and qualitative transformation of oppositional or in some way contradictory elements into new coherent wholes (Moran and John-Steiner, 2003). I will illustrate Vygotsky's argument through quotations from the essay 'Problems of method', which constitutes Chapter 5 of *Mind in Society* (Vygotsky, 1978), in the next section. This account rests on his dialectical orientation which posits reciprocal transformation of the individual and the social-cultural setting. This is witnessed in the phrase 'shape and shaped by', which is deployed by writers such as Michael Cole (1996) in his account of object-oriented, artefact-mediated activity. This is exemplified in the following extract from *Mind in Society*:

> ...between natural and dialectical approaches to the understanding of human history. Naturalism in historical analysis, according to Engels, manifests itself in the assumption that only nature affects human beings and only natural conditions affect historical development. The dialectical approach, while admitting the influence of nature on man, asserts that man, in turn, affects nature and creates through his changes in nature new natural conditions for his existence. This position is the keystone of our approach to the study and interpretation of man's higher psychological functions and serves as the basis for the new methods of experimentation and analysis that we advocate.
> (Vygotsky, 1978, pp. 60–1)

Developmental perspective

In the essay 'Problem of method', Vygotsky identifies three analytical principles that form the basis of his approach to the analysis of higher psychological functions. First, he insisted on a developmental or genetic approach in which processes rather than objects are analysed: 'Psychology should be developmental; we should reconstruct stages of development rather than focusing on milestones. We should 'trace' development' (Vygotsky, 1978, pp. 61–2). Second, he criticised the associationist and introspective psychology of his day for its emphasis on description rather than explanation. Vygotsky deploys the example that a description of a whale would suggest that it was more like a fish than a cow or a deer, rather than an analysis which reveals that a whale is, of course, a mammal. He refers to the work of Lewin and argues that genotypic (explanatory) rather than phenotypic (descriptive) explanations should be invoked: 'By a developmental study of the problem, I mean the disclosure of its genesis, its causal dynamic basis. By phenotypic I mean the analysis that begins directly with an object's features and manifestations' (Vygotsky, 1978, p. 62). He also provides an example from early speech development in which he again refers to Lewin in his argument that two apparently identical descriptions may in fact be underpinned by radically different processes. He goes on to enlist support from Marx in this fundamental aspect of his work which was further evidenced in his discussions of assessment and his critique of static tests of performance that mask the developmental pathways through which progress has been achieved.

Vygotsky's interest in the study of processes and their explanations gives rise to a third problem which he terms 'fossilized behavior'. He explains that 'processes that have already died away, that is, processes that have gone through a very long stage of historical development and have become fossilized' (Vygotsky, 1978, p. 63) or mechanised or automated inhibit development. He continues that '[t]hey have lost their outer appearance', and so 'their automatic character creates great difficulty for psychological analysis' (Vygotsky, 1978, p. 64). In order to understand such automatic, mechanised or fossilised behaviour, Vygotsky argues that its development must be reconstructed to 'turn it back to its source through the experiment' (Vygotsky, 1978, p. 64).

He summarises his position on a dialectical approach to the study of development of psychological functions as follows:

> To study something historically means to study it in the process of change; that is the dialectical method's basic demand. To encompass in research the process of a given thing's development in all its phases and changes – from birth to death – fundamentally means to discover its nature, its essence, for 'it is only in movement that a body shows what it is.' Thus, the historical study of behavior is not an auxiliary aspect of theoretical study, but rather forms its very base.
>
> (Vygotsky, 1978, pp. 64–5)

Towards the end of this essay on 'Problems of method', he reasserts his insistence on the need for the developmental/historical/genetic study of qualitative transformation and change:

> Our concept of development implies a rejection of the frequently held view that cognitive development results from the gradual accumulation of separate changes. We believe that child development is a complex dialectical process characterized by periodicity, unevenness in the development of different functions, metamorphosis or qualitative transformation of one form into another, intertwining of external and internal factors, and adaptive processes which overcome impediments that the child encounters.
> (Vygotsky, 1978, p. 73)

There remains a question as to whether Vygotsky fulfilled his own methodological aspirations. Davydov and Radzikhovskii (1985) argue that there is a major gulf between 'Vygotsky the psychologist' and 'Vygotsky the methodologist'. For example, Minick suggests that Vygotsky's theoretical concerns with the interplay between biology and sociocultural influences were not realised in his research practice during the period in which he was concerned with interfunctional relations and the development of word meaning (1930–2):

> he criticized paradigms that failed to differentiate the biological and the social in psychological development. Because he was unable to adapt his explanatory principle to his new conception of psychological development, however, Vygotsky's writings were open to precisely these criticisms during this period.
> (Minick, 1987, pp. 24–5)

Anti-reductionism

Another of his primary methodological assertions was cast in terms of *analysis in units*. Vygotsky (1987c) discussed the difference between analysis into elements and analysis into units which preserved the characteristics of the whole. He explained, 'A unit designates a product of analysis that possesses all the basic characteristics of the whole. The unit is a vital and irreducible part of the whole' (p. 46). The example given was of the difference between the analysis of the component parts (elements) of water (oxygen and hydrogen) and the analysis of the water itself. He suggested that the analysis of mental processes into reflexes or stimulus–response bonds as in behaviourism was an analysis of elements which lost the psychological meaning of the whole. This can also be read in relation to the way in which Vygotsky wrote about Marx's method and its implications for psychological method:

> I want to find out how science has to be built, to approach the study of the mind having learned the whole of Marx's method.... In order to create such

an enabling theory-method in the generally accepted scientific manner, it is necessary to discover the essence of the given area of phenomena, the laws according to which they change, their qualitative and quantitative characteristics, their causes. It is necessary to formulate the categories and concepts that are specifically relevant to them – in other words; to create one's own Capital. The whole of Capital is written according to the following method: Marx analyzes a single living 'cell' of capitalist society – for example, the nature of value. Within this cell he discovers the structure of the entire system and all of its economic institutions. He says that to a layman this analysis may seem a murky tangle of tiny details. Indeed, there may be tiny details, but they are exactly those, which are essential to 'microanatomy.' Anyone who could discover what a 'psychological' cell is – the mechanism producing even a single response – would thereby find the key to psychology as a whole.

(Vygotsky, 1978, p. 8)

This emphasis on unity and preserving the essence of the whole is also often related to the influence of Gestalt theory, which he saw as a form of monistic materialism (Van der Veer, 1997, p. 4). Whilst he proffered an extended critique of Gestalt psychology, his emphasis on retaining the whole is witnessed in many aspects of his writing:

Indeed, mental life is characterized by breaks, by the absence of a continuous and uninterrupted connection between its elements, by the disappearance and reappearance of these elements. Therefore, it is impossible to establish causal relationships between the various elements and as a result it is necessary to refrain from psychology as a natural scientific discipline ... We must not study separate mental and physiological processes outside their unity, because then they become completely unintelligible. We must study the integral process which is characterized by both a subjective and an objective side at the same time.

(Vygotsky, 1997a, pp. 111–13)

If, then, Vygotsky was suggesting analysis in units rather than elements, what did he offer by way of inspiration in the search for such units? Van der Veer (2001) suggests that Vygotsky provides us with three important requirements for the analysis of higher mental processes. The seminal text to which Van der Veer refers is Vygotsky's (1997c) *The History of the Development of the Higher Mental Functions*. The three requirements that Van der Veer (2001) identified are that we should:

1   focus on the genesis of actions;
2   distinguish between the analysis of things from the analysis of process; and
3   distinguish between explanatory and descriptive analysis.

As Leontiev (1997) notes, Vygotsky brought an emphasis on historicism to bear on the holistic, integrative approach which he acknowledges was influenced by the Gestalt theorists. In Vygotsky's hands these two approaches became inseparable: 'they are two dimensions of one idea – the idea of the mediated nature of mental processes conceived from dialectical positions' (Leontiev, 1997, p. 20). The analysis of process led Vygotsky to work on ways in which the developmental process itself can be constructed and reconstructed. This theme of unpicking the processes of formation was also in play in his discussion of behaviours that have become automatic or fossilised and static. The method of dual or double stimulation was a key moment in this work and will be discussed later in this chapter.

As Van der Veer (2001) notes, Vygotsky's emphasis on the need for explanatory analysis was revealed in his comparison of what may appear as phenomenological similarities in particular moments of development in thinking with the momentary similarity in two trains that arrive and depart from one place by different routes.

I will now explore the creation of Vygotsky's own approach to the explanatory analysis of the mental processes as they develop and as understood in terms of their origins.

> Word meaning is a unity of both processes (i.e. both thinking and speech) which cannot be further decomposed ... the word without meaning is not a word but an empty sound. Meaning is a necessary, constituting feature of the word itself.... It is the word viewed from the inside. In psychological terms, however, word meaning is nothing other than a generalization, that is a concept ... Thus, word meaning is also a phenomenon of thinking ... it is a unity of word and thought.
>
> (Vygotsky, 1987a, p. 244)

By 1929 he had rejected the notion of signs including speech as simple stimuli along with the idea that the stimulus–response unit derived from Soviet reflexology constituted the basic unit of analysis for studies of human development. This came about after his empirical work during the period 1925–30 when, along with others, he studied the ways in which simple sign systems mediate behaviour (e.g the tying of knots in material to mediate remembering) and thus examined the ways in which humans use signs to manipulate their own behaviour. His next move was to posit the development of interfunctional relationships between mental functions and thus the study of the progressive formation of psychological systems. This is clearly shown in the following extract from Chapter 2 of *Thinking and Speech*:

> In one of our experiments, a child of five and a half was drawing a picture of a tram. While drawing a line that would represent a wheel, the child put too much pressure on the pencil and the lead broke. The child attempted,

> nonetheless, to complete the circle by pressing the pencil to the paper. But nothing appeared on the paper other than the imprint of the broken pencil. As if to himself, the child quietly said, 'Broken'. Laying the pencil aside, he took a paintbrush and began to draw a broken tram car that was in the process of being repaired after an accident, continuing to talk to himself from time to time about the new subject of his drawing. This egocentric utterance is clearly linked to the whole course of the child's activity. It constitutes a turning point in his drawing and clearly indicates his conscious reflection on the situation and its attendant difficulties. It is so clearly fused with the normal process of thinking that it is impossible to view it as a simple accompaniment of that thinking.
>
> (Vygotsky, 1987c, p. 70)

Such systems were not thought of in purely cognitive terms and he moved to include motivation and the effect in the analysis. As Minick (1987) notes, the emergent weakness was in the absence of an account as to *why* new interfunctional relationships emerge and develop. He levels this criticism at the work conducted with Leonid Sakharov on the development of word meaning.

> Vygotsky insisted that the analysis of concept development cannot be divorced from the analysis of the development of word meaning and he insisted that the development of concepts is not the development of thought as such, but the development of the word, the development of the functional relationship between thought and speech in verbal thinking. Conspicuously absent in this work, however, is any explanation of how and why this development occurs.
>
> (Minick, 1987, p. 25)

I will return to these experiments and the interpretation of the data below. However, at this point, the crucial absence was the linkage between transformations and developments in patterns of social interaction and psychological systems. It was to this linkage that he directed his attention in the final four years of his life. Emerson (1986) discusses Vygotsky's critique of Piaget's understanding of egocentric speech and illustrates the way in which he began to analyse the transition between the mediation of social behaviour through speech and the mediation of individual behaviour in Chapter 4 of *Thinking and Speech* (Vygotsky, 1987c).

> Uncomfortable with Piaget's conclusion that this speech is fantasy-talk and generated asocially, Vygotsky ran a series of experiments designed to socialize and complicate the child's environment at precisely the age when the child 'talked to himself'. He demonstrated that a child talks twice as much when presented with obstacles and that this externalized 'conversation with oneself', commenting on and predicting the results of an action is in fact the

natural dynamic of problem solving. Furthermore, this talk turned out to be extremely sensitive to social factors. Piaget had observed similar phenomena: that egocentric speech occurs only in a social context, that the child assumes he is being understood by others, and that such speech is not whispered or abbreviated but spoken as an utterance, that is, as public speech in a specific environment. Vygotsky accepted this data but then devised experiments to detach it from Piaget's conclusions.

(Emerson, 1986, p. 253)

Emerson's discussion proceeds to detail a number of experiments which would doubtless raise the proverbial eyebrows of modern-day ethical scrutiny. For example, Vygotsky used his findings from studies such as those where he witnessed the dramatic drop in egocentric speech when he placed children in a room in which very, very loud music was playing to argue that such speech always emerged with a social orientation.

As Minick (1987) points out, there is an important difference between Chapters 2 and 4 of *Thinking and Speech* in the theoretical account of egocentric speech. In Chapter 4, which was written in 1929, he discusses the transitional nature of such speech. In Chapter 2, which was written in 1932, he becomes more interested in the changing function of such speech. Here he was striving to connect psychological development with transformations in the practices in which the child was participating.

Thus the theoretical move was from a consideration of interfunctional relations in the development of psychological systems to the analysis of the development of such systems with respect to changes in social behaviour. Here he made the direct linkage between changes in the social world and changes in psychological systems. The distinction between Chapters 5 and 6 of *Thinking and Speech* (Vygotsky, 1987c) exemplify this change of direction. In contrast to the understanding of word meaning in terms of abstraction and generalisation seen in Chapter 5, Chapter 6 witnesses an emphasis on the emergent function of words as activities develop. For example, the shift from activities in which communication takes place using words to specific forms of schooling in which communication about words and the meaning systems in which they are located takes place. He was particularly interested in the development that takes place as social behaviour in schooling is directed towards an understanding of systems of meanings.

> [T]he dependence of scientific concepts on spontaneous concepts and their influence on them stems from the unique relationship that exists between the scientific concept and its object ... this relationship is characterised by the fact that it is mediated through other concepts. Consequently, in its relationship to the object, the scientific concept includes a relationship to another concept, that is it includes the most basic element of a concept system.
>
> (Vygotsky, 1987c, p. 192)

He illustrates this with a reference to elementary botany:

> the concept of 'flower' is not actually more general than the concept of 'rose'. When the child has mastered only a single concept, its relationship to the object is different than it is after he masters a second. However, after he masters a second concept, there is a long period during which the concept of 'flower' continues to stand alongside, rather than above, the concept of 'rose'. The former does not include the latter. The narrower concept is not subordinated. Rather, the broader concept acts as a substitute for the narrower one. It stands alongside it in a single series. When the concept 'flower' is generalized, the relationship between it and the concept of 'rose' changes as well. Indeed, there is a change in its relationship with all subordinate concepts. This marks the emergence of a concept system.
>
> (Vygotsky, 1987a, p. 193)

As Minick (1987, p. 27) notes, Vygotsky was now able to link the development of word meaning with development and transformation of practice. Participation in the practices of schooling could be analysed in terms of the development of scientific concepts. Chapter 6 of *Thinking and Speech* provides outline details of a comparative study of the development of scientific and everyday concepts by the Soviet psychologist Zhozefina Il'inichna Shif. Much earlier, Piaget had argued that children's spontaneous concepts reflected their genuine thinking and that they should become the object of study. In Piaget (1924), he presented the results of an investigation in which children were presented with sentences that ended with 'although' and 'because' and asked to complete them. Shif, however, was working on the basis of assumptions that rather than being static, word meanings and scientific concepts develop and that it is impossible to generalise from studies of the development of everyday concepts to the development of scientific concepts. She compared causal (because) and adversative (but, although) relations in everyday and school-based situations. Children were asked to complete sentences which were either concerned with everyday situations or with social science themes in school. This work was designed to assist the development of Vygotsky's distinction between scientific and everyday concepts.

> Subjects were presented with problems that were structurally isomorphic, but which differed in that they incorporated materials based on either scientific or everyday concepts. Using a series of pictures, the experimenter told a story that ended with a sentence fragment broken off at the word 'because' or 'although'. This procedure was supplemented by clinical discussion in order to establish levels of conscious reflection on cause-effect relationships and relationships of implication with both scientific and real-world material.
>
> The pictures illustrated a sequence of events based either on materials from lessons in the social science program or common occurrences in everyday life. Problems based on everyday events required children to complete

sentences such as: 'Kolya went to the movie theatre because...', 'The train left the tracks because...', or 'Olya still reads poorly, although...'. Based on this model, several problems were also constructed using materials from the educational programs of second and fourth grade children.

As a supplementary mode of gathering data, we observed lessons of primary school children that were specially organized for this purpose.

(Vygotsky, 1987a, pp. 167–8)

Other tasks were drawn from the politics of the day such as 'The capitalists prepare for a war against the USSR, because' and 'There are still workers who believe in god, although...'.

As the data in Table 2.1 shows, performance on causal tasks (because) with scientific concepts was much better than on causal tasks with everyday concepts in class II. Performance in class IV witnessed improvement which was attributed to mastery of causal thinking which had been only partially understood in class II, as witnessed by the weak performance with everyday concepts that would not have formed part of the instruction in school. When Shif questioned class II children about their causal answers, they revealed a somewhat fragile understanding in that they seemed to reiterate explanations taught at school in a rather inflexible fashion. There are no such differences with 'although' tasks. Instruction in school was linked by Shif to the development of the strength of understanding of scientific concepts and the emphasis on causal analysis. There is a long and complex account of the interpretation of these findings in Van der Veer and Valsiner (1991, pp. 271–7). The detail of Vygotsky's movement between the interpretation of empirical data and theoretical development is difficult to unravel at this moment in history, so far from the time when reliable first-hand accounts might have clarified the obscurities of the development of his thinking. There is also concern about the over-association of schools, or schooling, with the development of scientific concepts, as though instruction can only take place within institutions.

The major outcome of Shif's work was taken by Vygotsky to suggest that the development of scientific concepts appeared to precede the development of everyday concepts. Vygotsky argued that these two forms of conceptual develop-

Table 2.1 Findings from Shif's experiments on *because* and *although*

Task		Percentage completed	
		Grade II	Grade IV
Sentences with the conjunction *because*	Scientific concepts	79.70	81.80
	Everyday concepts	59.00	81.30
Sentences with the conjunction *although*	Scientific concepts	21.30	79.50
	Everyday concepts	16.20	65.50

ment were both important in the formation of what he termed 'mature' concepts. Scientific concepts are formed on the basis of systematic, organised and hierarchical thinking, as distinct from everyday concepts that were seen to be tightly linked to particular contexts and lacking in an overall system. The latter are seen to bring the embedded richness and detailed patterns of signification of everyday thinking into the systematic and organised structure of scientific concepts. As they meld with everyday referents, scientific concepts come to life and find a broad range of applications. The conscious realisation and deliberate use of the 'scientific rules', or grammars, which underpin the complexities of everyday behaviour were discussed by Vygotsky with reference to the learning of a second language and algebra. Learning a second language through a structured 'scientific approach' provided tools for making choices in the use of a first language. The argument was that instruction introduces children to a scientific way of thinking. Tasks and actions that would be carried out unreflectively could be brought into the child's reflective gaze. The social situation of schooling, with its distinctive approach to instruction, was seen to facilitate a restructuring influence on development. Here again is the hallmark of the later part of Vygotsky's writing: the analysis of development must be that of an analysis of functioning in social practice.

Vygotsky posited the relationship between learning and development as one of dialectical unity, where learning 'leads' and 'is ahead of' development (Vygotsky, 1978, 1987a). He saw learning/instruction (in Russian, there is but one word) as 'completely unnecessary if it merely utilized what had already matured in the developmental process, if it were not itself a source of development' (1987a, p. 212).

> The essential property of scientific concepts is their structure, the fact that they are organised in hierarchical systems (other possible systems would include 'networks', 'groups', 'genealogical trees', etc). When children interiorise a hierarchical structure enables them to carry out a series of intellectual operations (different types of definition, logical quantification operations etc) ... The assimilation of systems of scientific concepts is made possible by systematic education of the type received at school. Organised systematic education is essential for this, unlike oral language acquisition in which teaching has a constructive role but requires no more than the presence of adults with a command of the language to act as partners in shared activities.
>
> (Ivic, 1989, p. 431)

Here Ivic is reaffirming the linkage between the social situation (school) and the type of psychological development. Another social situation which captured Vygotsky's attention was that of imaginative play. As Minick (1987, p. 29) notes, by 1933 he had begun to argue that the social situation of play was one in which imagination frees thought and meanings from the perceptual field. This was a reversal of his earlier emphasis on the power of speech to bring this about.

> Thought is separated from the thing because a piece of wood begins to play the role of a doll, a stick becomes a horse; action according to rules begins to be defined from thought rather than things themselves ... The child doesn't do this suddenly. To tear thought (word meaning) from the thing is a terribly difficult task for the child. Play is a transitional form. At the moment the stick (i.e., the thing) becomes a pivot for tearing the meaning from the real horse ... one of the basic psychological structures that defines the child's relationship to reality is changed.
>
> The child cannot yet tear the thought from the thing. He must have a pivot in another thing ... To think of the horse, he must define his action by this horse in the stick or pivot ... I would say that in play the child operates in accordance with meaning that is torn from things but not torn from real actions with real objects ... This is the transitional character of play. This is what makes it a middle link between the purely situational connectedness of early childhood and thinking that is removed from the real situation.
>
> (Vygotsky, 1978, pp. 69–71)

This central emphasis on the analysis of the social situation of development in connection with psychological development is reaffirmed throughout the writing which Vygotsky undertook in the last two years of his life. Arguably, there are parallels with Gibson's (1986) notion of affordances which are not properties of objects in isolation but of objects related to subjects in activity or putative activities. However, this concept of affordance is open to many interpretations alongside what might be thought of as a post-Vygotskian version (Baerentsen and Trettvik, 2002). It should be noted that Gibson provides an account of person in the environment but does little to progress the analysis of psychological formation within that which is afforded. The latter is Vygotsky's distinctive contribution.

> The social situation of development, which is specific to each age, determines strictly regularly the whole picture of the child's life or his social existence ... Having elucidated the social situation of development that occurred before the beginning of any age, which was determined by the relations between the child and his environment we must immediately elucidate how, new formations proper to (characteristic of) the given age develop from the life of the child in this social setting.
>
> (Vygotsky, 1998b, p. 198)

This linkage between the social situation of development and psychological development pervades his analysis in these crucial final years of his life. Significantly, it informed his understanding of 'word meaning', a term which may too easily be interpreted as 'meaning of the (single) word'. In his hands word meaning becomes not only 'a unity of thinking and speech' but also a 'unity of generalisation and social interaction, a unity of thinking and communication'

(Vygotsky, 1987a, p. 49). He asserts the importance for his method of this understanding in the following manner:

> it reveals the true potential for a causal-genetic analysis of thinking and speech. Only when we learn to see the unity of generalisation and social interaction do we begin to understand the actual connection between the child's cognitive and social development. Our research is concerned with resolving both these fundamental problems, the problem of the relationship of thought to word and the problem of the relationship of generalisation to social interaction.
>
> (Vygotsky, 1987a, p. 49)

The move that Vygotsky made during his work in psychology from the analytic unit of the instrumental act through to the psychological system and on to try and identify a unit compatible with his end-of-career thought on psychological systems in social situations of development was brought to an end at the point at which he was just starting to reflect on another extension to his project. Where in the past he had posited a dialectical unity of thinking and speech he now moved to understand experience as the unity of personality and the environment as represented in development.[1]

> We have inadequately studied the internal relationship of the child to the people around him ... We have recognized in words that we need to study the child's personality and environment as a unity. It is incorrect, however to represent this problem in such a way that on one side we have the influence of personality while on the other we have the influence of the environment. Though the problem is frequently represented in precisely this way, it is incorrect to represent the two as external forces acting on one another. In the attempt to study the unity, the two are initially torn apart. The attempt is then made to unite them.
>
> (Vygotsky, 1998b, p. 292)

Van der Veer (2001) notes that in the last year of his life Vygotsky turned his attention to this new unit of analysis, which in Russian is termed *perezhivanie*.

Vygotsky understood *perezhivanie* as the integration of cognitive and affective elements, which always presupposes the presence of emotions. Vygotsky used this concept in order to emphasise the wholeness of the psychological development of children, integrating external and internal elements at each stage of development. According to Bozhovich (a co-worker of Vygotsky's), for a short period of time Vygotsky considered *perezhivanie* as the 'unity' of psychological development in the study of the social situation of development (Gonzalez-Rey, 2002, p. 136).

This concept, which featured in Minick's (1987) account of the stages of development of units of analysis as 'experience', may be more accurately equated with lived or emotional experience.

> The emotional experience [*perezhivanie*] arising from any situation or from any aspect of his environment, determines what kind of influence this situation or this environment will have on the child. Therefore, it is not any of the factors themselves (if taken without the reference of the child) which determines how they will influence the future course of his development, but the same factors refracted through the prism of the child's emotional experience.
>
> (Vygotsky, 1994, p. 339)

This idea of refraction 'through the prism of the child's emotional experience' has been largely ignored in the development of post-Vygotskian theory. The original Vygotskian conjecture was subsequently reworked in the writing of Vasilyuk (1991), when he introduced the notion of experiencing defined as a particular form of activity directed towards the restoration of meaning in life. He contrasted his activity-theory-based understanding with that of a reflection of a state in the subject's consciousness and with forms of contemplation. In the following statement Ratner (1998), in his introduction to the key text (Vygotsky, 1998a), provides a clarification of the dialectical process which Vygotsky had in mind:

> The experience one has depends upon the perceptions, emotions, ideals, and imagination which mediate an encounter with the physical or social world. Yet these mediations are all internalized from social relations. Social life is not experienced immediately – anew at each moment – but rather is mediated by psychological functions which have been socialized through previous social encounters. Social life works on us from the outside but also from the inside in the form of higher psychological phenomena. This is why Vygotsky concludes that the researcher must make 'a penetrating internal analysis of the experiences of the child, that is, a study of the environment which is transferred to a significant degree to within the child himself and is not reduced to a study of the external circumstances of his life.'
>
> (Ratner, 1998, p. xiv)

On reading the following quotation from Vygotsky (1998a), one is again reminded of the similarity that Gibson's (1986) notion shows with this understanding of experience, and of the limitations of the latter's position when seen in the broader light of cultural-historical theory:

> Experience has a biosocial orientation; it is what lies between the personality and the environment that defines the relation of the personality to the environment, that shows what a given factor of the environment is for the personality. Experience is determining from the point of view of how one environmental factor or another affects the child's development. This, in any case, is confirmed at every step in the teaching on difficult childhood. Any

analysis of a difficult child shows that what is essential is not the situation in itself taken in its absolute indicators, but how the child experiences the situation. In one and the same family, in one family situation, we find different changes in development in different children because different children experience one and the same situation differently.

(Vygotsky, 1998a, p. 294)

This general working hypothesis requires expansion to include notions of experiencing and identity formation within an account that includes a systematic and coherent analysis of the tacit mediation (as in Wertsch, 2007) brought about in the wider social structuring of society (as in Bernstein, 2000) as an inseparable part of the analysis. I will return to this matter in Chapters 5 and 6.

The method of dual stimulation

Vygotsky's cultural-historical psychology created demands for method that could not be met by the existing resources that early twentieth-century psychology offered him. He instigated the development of methods that were commensurate with the challenges that his theoretical programme required.

> The search for method becomes one of the most important problems of the entire enterprise of understanding the uniquely human forms of psychological activity. In this case, the method is simultaneously prerequisite and product, the tool and result of study.
>
> (Vygotsky, 1978, p. 65)

Vygotsky (1978) consistently argued the case for a *historically* based psychology. By this he meant a psychology that is concerned with the process of change. Citing Blonsky, he announced that 'behaviour can be understood only as the history of behaviour' (Vygotsky, 1978, p. 65). He was pursuing a method that allowed for a developmental analysis of process which explained human functioning in terms of dynamic causal relations. As Valsiner notes, 'He advanced the general methodological canon for psychology: Only when psychological phenomena are viewed in their process of change can they be adequately explained' (Valsiner, 1990, p. 61).

It is with respect to this quest that it is possible to see the Vygotskian imagination in full flight. He was borrowing from sources which inspired him to try to create tools for the construction of a new order of psychological thinking. In the quotation given below, he reflects on experimental work undertaken by Lewin in a way which is clearly suggestive of the approach that he intended to adopt:

> In experiments involving meaningless situations, Lewin found that the subject searches for some point of support that is external to him and that he defines his own behavior through this external support. In one set of

experiments, for example, the experimenter left the subject and did not return, but observed him from a separate room. Generally, the subject waited for 10–20 minutes. Then, not understanding what he should do, he remained in a state of oscillation, confusion and indecisiveness for some time. Nearly all the adults searched for some external point of support. For example, one subject defined his actions in terms of the striking of the clock. Looking at the clock, he thought: 'When the hand moves to the vertical position, I will leave.' The subject transformed the situation in this way, establishing that he would wait until 2:30 and then leave. When the time came, the action occurred automatically. By changing the psychological field, the subject created a new situation for himself in this field. He transformed the meaningless situation into one that had a clear meaning.

(Vygotsky, 1987b, p. 356)

He was driven by the desire to escape from what he saw as the methodological stranglehold of Russian reflexology.

This methodology [study of reactive responses based on the S–R formula], which easily establishes the response movements of the subject, becomes completely impotent, however, when the basic problem is the study of those means and devices that the subject used to organize his behavior in concrete forms most adequate for each given task. In directing our attention to the study of specifically these (external and internal) means of behavior, we must conduct a radical review of the methodology of the psychological experiment itself.

(Vygotsky, 1999, p. 59)

Vygotsky developed a 'method of double stimulation', which according to Valsiner and Van der Veer is a sociocultural version of the strictly experimental tradition of Aktualgenese of Friedrich Sander and microgenesis of Heinz Werner (Valsiner and Van der Veer, 2000). As the term 'double stimulation' implies, Vygotsky developed a series of experiments in which subjects were presented with two stimuli: a problem and a second stimulus which offered the possibility of a means to solve that problem.

By using this approach, we do not limit ourselves to the usual method of offering the subject simple stimuli to which we expect a direct response. Rather, we simultaneously offer a *second series of stimuli* that have a special function. In this way, we are able to study the *process of accomplishing a task by the aid of specific auxiliary means*; thus we are also able to discover the inner structure and development of higher psychological processes.

The method of dual stimulation elicits manifestations of the crucial processes in the behavior of people of all ages. Tying a knot as a reminder, in

> both children and adults, is but one example of a pervasive regulatory principle of human behavior, that of *signification*, wherein people create temporary links and give significance to previously neutral stimuli in the context of their problem-solving efforts. We regard our method as important because it helps to *objectify* inner psychological processes.
>
> (Vygotsky, 1978, pp. 74–5)

The double-stimulation method is important in that 'it creates the conditions under which a subject's course of action toward an experimentally given goal makes explicit the psychological processes involved in that action' (Valsiner, 1990, p. 66). His central concern was to study human functioning as it developed, rather than considering functions that had developed. The essence of this approach is that subjects are placed in a situation in which a problem is identified and they are also provided with tools with which to solve the problem *or a means by which they can construct tools to solve the problem*.

> The task facing the child in the experimental context is, as a rule, beyond his present capabilities and cannot be solved by existing skills. In such cases a neutral object is placed near the child, and frequently we are able to observe how the neutral stimulus is drawn into the situation and takes on the function of a sign. Thus, *the child actively incorporates these neutral objects into the task of problem solving*. We might say that when difficulties arise, neutral stimuli take on the function of a sign and from that point on the operation's structure assumes an essentially different character.
>
> (Vygotsky, 1978, p. 74; italics added)

This emphasis on the observing processes through which '*the child actively incorporates these neutral objects into the task of problem solving*' was crucial to this methodological move. His experiments were conceived of as a means of studying development in and through active, creative responses to problems.

> In experimental studies, we do not necessarily have to present to the subject a prepared external means with which we might solve the proposed problem. The main design of our experiment will not suffer in any way if instead of giving the child prepared external means, we will wait while he spontaneously applies the auxiliary device and involves some auxiliary system of symbols in the operation. ... In not giving the child a ready symbol, we could trace the way all the essential mechanisms of the complex symbolic activity of the child develop during the spontaneous expanding of the devices he used.
>
> (Vygotsky, 1999, p. 60)

Wertsch (2007) cites the Forbidden Colours Task as an example of the application of Vygotsky's method of dual stimulation. The second stimulus provides

Wertsch with an example of explicit mediation. The central memory task is one of recalling a list of colours.

> They were given a set of coloured cards and told that these cards could help them remember what colour terms they had already mentioned and, according to the rules of the game, were not to mention again. In this case, the first set of stimuli, which 'fulfill the function of the object on which the subject's activity is directed,' was the set of colour terms used by the subjects as they responded to the experimenter's questions. The second set of stimuli that were to function 'as signs that facilitate the organization of this activity' were the coloured cards introduced by the experimenter.
>
> The basic aim of the Forbidden Colours Task study was to document how children use the signs provided by the experimenter (i.e., the coloured cards) more effectively with age. Most 5- and 6-year-olds did not seem to realize that the signs had anything to do with their performance on the task, whereas 10- to 13-year-olds clearly did. The developmental path involved is one that moves from a point where the stimuli had very little meaning and functional efficacy to a point where subjects came to appreciate their significance for organizing their performance.
>
> (Wertsch, 2007, p. 182)

In his discussion of the findings from studies which used the Forbidden Colours Task, Wertsch (2007) deploys the following quotation to show how Vygotsky was seeking to create a developmental analysis with a specific focus on qualitative transformation:

> We have found that sign operations appear as the result of a complex and prolonged process subject to all the basic laws of psychological evolution. This means that sign-using activity in children is neither simply invented nor passed down from adults; rather it arises from something that is originally not a sign operation and becomes one only after a series of qualitative transformations.
>
> (Vygotsky, 1978, pp. 45–6)

Vygotsky studied the way in which concepts developed and interacted. The so-called 'Vygotsky blocks' were developed through a long series of studies which drew on the work of Ach (1921) and Leonid Sakharov (1994). Sakharov (1994) summarises Ach's methodological assumptions. The following extract witnesses key elements in Vygotsky's approach:

1 One cannot be limited to the study of ready made concepts; the process of formation of new concepts is important.
2 The method of experimental investigation should be genetic-synthetic; during the course of the experiment, the subject must gradually arrive at

the construction of a new concept – hence the need to create experimental concepts with an artificial grouping of attributes that belong to them.
3 It is necessary to study the process by which words acquire significance, the process of transformation of a word into a symbol and a representation of an object or of a group of similar objects – hence the necessity of using artificial experimental words that are initially nonsense to the subject, but acquire meaning for him during the course of the experiment.

(Sakharov, 1994, pp. 82–3)

Van der Veer and Valsiner (1991, pp. 257–83) provide an excellent account of the way in which the 'Vygotsky blocks' experimental method was developed and transformed as Vygotsky struggled to align his theoretical development with the development of method. Much of the early application of these tasks was enacted when Vygotsky was in what Minick (1987) termed his 'second phase', in which the priority was cast in terms of the development of psychological systems. His methods were innovative but not without their limitations.

Vygotsky devised a simple task which revealed some interesting differences between adults' and children's concepts. Wooden blocks differing in shape, colour, size and thickness, are laid out on a table, and one of them is turned over to reveal a nonsense label, such as 'MUR', stuck beneath it. The child (or adult) who is being tested then has to sort together all those blocks likely to have the same label. Very young children tend to lump together an unorganised heap of blocks, often on the basis of subjective criteria or because they make a nice pattern. At a later stage, children make their selections on the basis of objective criteria but not in a stable way: one block suggests another in a chain of responses highly dependent on context. Children next grasp the reference of the concept and sort together an appropriate set of objects, but they have yet to master its sense, ie, its stable relations to other concepts independent of context. Hence, when the experimenter turns over one of the blocks that they have selected revealing that it does not have the label 'MUR', they remove it from the pile but do nothing about other similarly offending selections. Only by interacting with adults, Vygotsky claimed, do children finally infer the sense of a concept. His semiotics yields a plausible account of how children master sense and reference. What modern research has shown is that matters are not quite so uniform as he imagined. George Miller and his colleagues have discovered, for example, that children's grasp of the reference of colour terms does not properly stabilise until they have worked out the basic contrastive relations among the terms.

(Johnson Laird, 1986, p. 879)

Luria (1976) used the double-stimulation method in studies of the people in Uzbekistan and Kirghizia. He considered problem-solving, self-awareness and reasoning in groups of people who lived and worked in strikingly different cultural circumstances. Cole's (1996) criticism of this work for its lack of attention to the ways in which specific cultural formations gave rise to specific patterns of tool or artefact deployment attests to the extent to which Vygotsky was yet to realise the demands of his third phase, in which psychological development was to be analysed in the situation in which that development took place. This matter remains a concern in twenty-first-century developments of his work and it is a major theme for the rest of this book.

Note

1 See Vygotsky, 1998b, pp. 289–96 for an extended discussion.

Chapter 3

The sociocultural tradition

This chapter is concerned with studies that have been located within the category 'sociocultural'. This is a term which takes up different means in different disciplines, locations and historical moments in time. Whilst it remains a diverse collection of accounts, the field is unified in its focus on the development of an understanding of the social formation of mind.

> The relationship between mind and sociocultural setting has concerned scholars for decades, if not centuries, but in recent years it has received renewed attention as dissatisfaction has grown with analyses that limit their focus to one or another part of the picture.
>
> (Wertsch, 1998, p. 3)

A useful historical analysis in phases of the development of the field may be found in Rogoff and Chavajay (1995). They discuss the move from the deployment of cognitive tasks (such as those developed by Piaget (1972) and his colleagues) in cross-cultural studies to the study of psychological functioning in 'real-life' settings and then on to the exploration of the development of different types of literacy (e.g. Scribner and Cole, 1981; Cole et al., 1971) and numeracy (e.g. Lave, 1977, 1988; Nunes et al., 1993) in specific cultural contexts. In the latter, the specificities of a practice were studied in relation to the cognitive processes developed by participants involved in those practices. They draw on the work of Sylvia Scribner (1985) to argue the case for an inseperable form of interrelation between social and individual worlds.

> Vygotsky's analysis of the interrelated roles of the individual and the social world includes individual and environment together in successively broader time frames from momentary learning, to individual life-course development, to generations in a society, to species history (respectively, microgenetic, ontogenetic, sociocultural, and phylogenetic development). Development over the life course takes place within developmental processes occurring over both the course of cultural history and of phylogenetic history. These levels of analysis of development are inseparable: The efforts

of individuals constitute cultural practices that further organize individuals' development, and similarly, human biological development cannot be separated from the cultural institutions and practices that characterize humanity.

(Rogoff and Chavajay, 1995, pp. 871–2)

This account of inseparability takes up a specific position in the framework which Sawyer (2002) helpfully developed in order to try to distinguish between different approaches to sociocultural study. Lantolf (2004) and Wertsch (1995) provide wide-ranging definitions within which there are a multitude of different types of research enquiry based on very different assumptions:

> despite the label 'sociocultural' the theory is not a theory of the social or of the cultural aspects of human existence.... It is, rather ... a theory of mind ... that recognizes the central role that social relationships and culturally constructed artifacts play in organizing uniquely human forms of thinking.
>
> (Lantolf, 2004, pp. 30–1)

> the study of the relationship between human mental functioning, on the one hand, and cultural, historical and institutional setting, on the other.
>
> (Wertsch, 1995, p. 56)

Sawyer (2002) argues that socioculturalists rarely make explicit the differences in the methodological assumptions that underpin their work (Sawyer, 2002, p. 296). He deploys notions of inseparability and process ontology as markers of methodological difference which witness recent debates in sociology. For him, in a process ontology of the social world only processes are real; entities, structures or patterns are ephemeral and do not really exist. In the inseparability thesis individual and social levels of analysis cannot be distinguished methodologically (the analyst cannot meaningfully distinguish between what is internal to the individual and what is external context) or ontologically (distinct entities do not really exist) (Sawyer, 2002, p. 283). He suggests that a high degree of incompatibility exists between theories within the sociocultural field. He draws parallels with the debate in sociology between the methodological assumptions of Giddens (1979) and Archer (1988, 1995). Giddens' (1979) 'third way' resolution of the structure/agency tension which he terms 'structuration' is based on assumptions of both a process ontology and inseparability. Archer (1988, 1995) suggests that Giddens conflates the individual and the social, and proposes a model of analytic dualism between individual action and social context. I will now explore these notions in the sociocultural field.

Separability

A denial of processes of internalisation in the inseparability thesis renders learning as a transformation of the social practices in which individuals participate, within which they appropriate and master specific cultural artefacts or ways of being. Sawyer cites the work of Rogoff (1982, 1990, 1998) as an example of clear adherence to such an inseparability thesis. An important challenge raised to this theoretical position is that found in the sociogenetic question posed by Valsiner and Van der Veer (2000): 'How to construe persons as being social without abandoning their obvious personal autonomy, separateness from any social unit (group, crowd, community), while being members of such units?' (p. 6). The methodological move away from a focus on the individual subject in favour of an analytical focus on actions or events in specific settings demands the development of methods which permit close consideration of action, including communication in microsocial situations. The rejection of two basic tenets of what Sawyer terms 'traditional psychology' (methodological individualism and ecological or 'social influence' models) calls for the refinement of appropriate ethnographic and qualitative methods which allow researchers to attempt to study human functioning as being inseparable from the setting in which it is enacted. As Sawyer notes:

1. Methodological individualism, which among socioculturalists refers to the typical approach in experimental psychology of operationalising variables and constructs associated with individual human subjects. In contrast, the objects of sociocultural study are events, activity and practice, and they are considered to be irreducible to properties of individuals.
2. An ecological or 'social influence' approach that conceives of the individual acting in, and influenced by, an external context or environment. Such attempts to incorporate social context into psychology assume that the individual and the context can be analytically isolated and then the interaction between them studied. Inseparability is incompatible with conceptions of the relation between individual and sociocultural context that assume that the individual acts 'in' a context, or that the individual is 'influenced by' the context; such conceptions implicitly accept the possibility of methodological separability between individual and situation.

(Sawyer, 2002, p. 285)

Archer (1995) writes of her concerns for a self that is purely sociological with no analytical space for the individual in Giddens work. Within sociocultural theory, Saxe (2004) presents a case for a greater degree of separability than Rogoff. He argues that there is a need for co-ordination between epistemic and psychological concerns and social practices and involvement in the production of knowledge:

Taking the individual as an historical subject complicates but also enriches epistemological and psychological analyses of cognitive development. It requires the elaboration of new analytic units to support empirical inquiry, ones that open up opportunities for analysing the interplay between historical and developmental processes in the micro-, socio- and ontogenetic construction of knowledge. My sketch of the work on quantification practices is

> one emerging effort to re-situate the analysis of cognition in a perspective that coordinates not only epistemic and psychological concerns, but also the role of the individual as an actor, participating in, drawing from, and contributing to continuities and discontinuities in forms and functions of knowledge not only in their own developments but in the social histories of communities.
>
> (Saxe, 2004, p. 261)

This is not to say that Saxe (2004) agrees with Archer's (1995) proposal for the analysis of properties at both the collective and the individual level, which are:

> distinct from each other and irreducible to one another.... [T]he different strata are separable by definition precisely because of the properties and powers which only belong to each of them and whose emergence from one another justifies their differentiation as strata.
>
> (Archer, 1995, p. 14, as quoted in Sawyer, 2002)

A similar argument is developed by Valsiner, who seeks to articulate an understanding of interrelated levels of analysis without resorting to complete separation:

> Two issues are at stake in this direction: first, the need to focus on multi-level organization of structured process phenomena; second, how to create systemic accounts of the way culture works within psychological processes. Multi-level hierarchically ordered processes are likely to be part of any theoretical elaboration in cultural psychology. Of course the easiest example of such models is that of Lev Vygotsky's (and Pierre Janet's – see van der Veer & Valsiner, 1991) focus on the hierarchy of higher psychological processes in relation to their lower counterparts (see also Toomela, 2003a, 2003b). The higher processes – of a volitional kind – relate to the lower processes through regulating the flow of the latter. So we have a structure of two levels of processes, which is mediated by another process – their relation.
>
> (Valsiner, 2004, p. 12)

Sawyer proposes a taxonomy of sociocultural approaches informed by the extent to which scholars announce strong or weak separability arguments. Table 3.1 provides examples.

The degree of separability that is theorised gives rise to profound differences in the way that empirical work is discussed. For example, the effects of social factors may only be witnessed in the shaping of individual actions or if an analytical distinction is established, then context and individual are seen as distinct but inherently interrelated levels of analysis (Wertsch, 1994, p. 203). Yet, as Sawyer notes, the field is marked by theoretical espousal of specific theoretical claims (e.g. for

Table 3.1 The inseparability/separability difference between sociocultural theorists

The weak social interaction view, which infers some level of separability	The strong view, which holds to inseparability
Wertsch, 1993, 1994 Cole, 1995, 1996 Valsiner, 1991, 1998a;	Rogoff, 1990, 1997 Lave and Wenger, 1991 Matusov, 1998 Shweder, 1990

strong inseparability) alongside empirical work which does not witness the assumptions of these claims. He makes reference to the work of Rogoff and Hutchins and suggests that they have made analytic distinctions which their own account of inseparability denies.

> By rejecting the inseparability claim in their empirical studies, socioculturalists have been able to study (1) properties of individuals, thus at times connecting their work to cognitive psychology; (2) properties of different contexts, such as different family arrangements, different activity frameworks in classrooms and different peer-group structures; and (3) the forms of microsociological practice that mediate between these two.
>
> (Sawyer, 2002, p. 299)

Doubtless these authors would challenge Sawyer's account. His purpose was to argue the case for a methodology of analytical dualism. My purpose here has been to illustrate the differences that exist within the field with respect to inseparability and to note that the development of methodologies and methods in sociocultural research which celebrates a strong inseparability thesis constitutes a significant challenge for researchers.

Process ontology

The second dimension deployed by Sawyer (2002) is with respect to the degree of affiliation to the notion of a process ontology. He describes this with reference to the work of Hatano and Wertsch (2001, p. 79):

> Developmentalists in some sense are always interested in process, because they focus on change over time. Socioculturalism differentiates itself from this general developmental orientation by making a stronger ontological claim: process is not only a guiding orientation, but is also the fundamental nature of reality. This results in one of the unifying features of the paradigm: the unit of analysis is situated social practice rather than the bounded individual, as in traditional psychology.
>
> (Sawyer, 2002, p. 291)

56 The sociocultural tradition

Sawyer discusses a number of sociocultural theorists with respect to the degree of affiliation to both a process ontology and the non-separability thesis. He argues against the utility of a process ontology on the basis of three claims:

1   The methodological acknowledgement of individuals and groups as 'things' is not incompatible with the study of situated practices.
2   It is not possible to study socially situated practice without analytically distinguishing among individuals and thus being able to study relations between them.
3   A process ontology makes it difficult to theorise difference, heterogeneity, cultural tension and conflict. (Adapted from Sawyer, 2002, p. 293.)

A cline of theorists is set up by Sawyer (2002) with Hutchins (1995a) and Lave and Wenger (1991) taken to represent the relatively strong and explicit advocates of a process ontology and Wertsch (1993) and Cole (1995) portrayed as rather more implicit in their affiliation to the position. The following quotations are taken as evidence of this assertion:

- 'Culture is not any collection of things, whether tangible or abstract. Rather, it is a process ... and the "things" that appear on list-like definitions of culture are residua of the process' (Hutchins, 1995a, p. 354).
- 'Learning is the process of reproduction of the social structure, as embodied in the participatory practices of the community' (Lave and Wenger, 1991, pp. 54–8).
- '[A]gency cannot be reduced further than that of "individual(s)-operating-with-mediational means"' (Wertsch, 1993, p. 170).
- '[A]ny psychological phenomenon emerges from interaction of processes' (Cole, 1995, p. 191).

Sawyer (2002) suggests that there are difficulties with each position in that:

- Hutchins (1995b) is not consistent is his explicit process ontology stance and reverts to entity-based references to individuals, symbols and symbolic structures.
- Lave and Wenger (1991) make reference to the need for an explicit focus on persons through statements such as 'legitimate peripherality provides learners with opportunities to make the culture of practice theirs' and that 'apprentices gradually assemble a general idea of what constitutes the practice of the community' (p. 95), thus referring to related layers of entities (individuals and communities) which are not compatible with the tenets of a process ontology.
- In his account of mediated action, Wertsch (1993, p. 170) argues that '[A]gency cannot be reduced further than that of "individual(s)-operating-with-mediational means"', yet reverts to accounts of individuals appropriat-

ing these means in the absence of an account of the regulation and distribution of these entities. In this, Sawyer claims, Wertsch underplays what may be read as the sociology of mediational means.
- Cole (1995) is seen as providing an account which may be interpreted as one of the interaction of distinct processes which in themselves may be regarded as entities.

Thus, the view taken is that a process ontology presents significant challenges for those concerned with empirical work, albeit that the degree of affiliation to a strong and explicit account of a process ontology is not a constant feature of the work of sociocultural theorists.

Mediated action

I will now move to a discussion of the work of James V. Wertsch, whose work has been central to the movement in sociocultural theory which seeks to understand mediated action in its cultural context. Bruner (1996) captures the essence of the understanding that drives the methodological challenge with his insistence that learning and thinking are always situated in a cultural setting and always dependent upon the utilisation of cultural resources (Bruner, 1996, p. 4). In response to this challenge, Wertsch (e.g. 2002, 1998, 1985a, b) has struggled with the key methodological tensions of separability and process ontology outlined above. He has moved away from Vygotsky's (1978, 1987) early focus on word meaning as a unit for the study of human consciousness by proposing mediated action in its cultural context as an alternative:

> word meaning is not really a unit that reflects the interfunctional relationships that define consciousness. Of course this is the most serious criticism one can raise, since it means that the analytic unit chosen by Vygotsky cannot fulfill the very requirements he assigned to it.... While continuing to accept his claims about the importance of semiotic phenomena in human mental functioning, I have argued that word meaning (or any other semiotic unit for that matter) is a unit of semiotic mediation of mental functioning, not a unit of mental functioning itself. I have also considered, and rejected as incorrect, the possibility that individual mental functions (memory, thinking) could serve as units of analysis in Vygotsky's approach.
>
> (Wertsch, 1985a, pp. 206, 208)

In his earlier work, Wertsch *et al.* (1984) studied the actions of adult tutors (mothers and teachers) as they taught young children to construct a simple three-dimensional puzzle in accordance with a model. He used an activity-theory-based approach to analyse the substantial differences that emerged in the patterns of interaction. In his later work, Wertsch has explored the relationship between social communicative and individual psychological processes, emphasising the dialogicality or multi-voicedness of communication and examining linguistic dimensions of communicative acts. He has developed his approach through an ongoing engagement with Vygtosky's ideas about sense and meaning, Bakhtin's ideas of heteroglossia, voice and dialogicality (Wertsch, 1985a) and Burke's pentadic approach to action (Wertsch, 1998).

In Wertsch's (1991, 1998) hands, the sociocultural emphasis on the use of cultural tools in mediated action is revealed in studies of how humans employ speech in the course of particular forms of action. The Vygotskian heritage is evidenced in the focus on the mediational function and capacity of speech. At the centre of Wertsch's work is the idea of a basic 'irreducible' description of agency as 'individual(s)-acting-with-mediational-means' (Wertsch, 1991) or 'individual(s)-operating-with...' (Wertsch and Tulviste, 1996; Wertsch *et al.*, 1993; Wertsch, 1998). He maintains that a 'focus on mediated action and the cultural tools employed in it makes it possible to "live in the middle" and to address the sociocultural situatedness of action, power and authority' (Wertsch, 1998, p. 65).

It is especially important to him that 'analyses of action not be limited by the dictates of methodological or social individualism' which he defines as follows:

> Methodological individualism assumes that cultural, institutional, and historical settings can be explained by appealing to properties of individuals, and social reductionism assumes that individuals can be understood only by appealing to social fact.... Indeed, one of the reasons for choosing mediated action as a unit of analysis is that it does not carve up phenomena into isolated disciplinary slices that cannot be combined into a more comprehensive whole.
>
> (Wertsch, 1998, pp. 179–80)

The analytical framework focuses on three central considerations: (1) agents and their cultural tools; (2) mediated action or 'agent-acting-with-mediational-means'; and (3) the link between action and broader cultural, institutional and historical contexts. He draws on what Bruner (2005) has referred to as the 'universal arguments of action' in Burke's (1969) pentad which provides him with a method for framing his studies of human action.

Burke (1969) presents his 'pentad' as follows:

> We shall use five terms as generating principle of our investigation. They are: Act, Scene, Agent, Agency, Purpose. In a rounded statement about motives, you must have some word that names the act (names what took place, in thought or deed), and another that names the scene (the background of the act, the situation in which it occurred); also, you must indicate what person or kind of person (agent) performed the act, what means or instruments he used (agency), and the purpose. Men may violently disagree about the purposes behind a given act, or about the character of the person

who did it, or how he did it, or in what kind of situation he acted; or they may even insist upon totally different words to name the act itself. But be that as it may, any complete statement about motives will offer some kind of answers to these five questions: what was done (act), when or where it was done (scene), who did it (agent), how he did it (agency), and why (purpose).
(Burke, 1969, p. xv)

In the terms of Burke's pentad, social reductionism involves an overemphasis on the analysis of what he terms 'scene' at the expense of an acknowledgement of the agent, whereas the methodological individualism of much of the work of traditional psychology tends to prioritise its attention on what Burke calls the 'agent'. Säljö (1994) also reminds his readers that, from a sociocultural standpoint, even methods such as interviews risk decontextualising human action by separating actions from the practice in which they have their origin.

Macdonald (2006) argues that the description of the motives that the participants attribute to each other in a situation is supplied through the turn to Burke in Wertsch (1998) and is missing from Wertsch's (1985a) earlier work which emphasised the creation of intersubjectivity, in and through semiotic mediation. In his attempts to operationalise the work of Burke, Wertsch (1998) directed his attention to the changing relationships of the points of reference within the pentad. This proved to be difficult:

It often seems that we have reached the limits of human understanding when we try to coordinate two or more pentadic elements into a single account of action and motive. For example, some accounts of action that begin with an agent might attempt to incorporate information about the scene as well, but when it comes to extending this account even further by addressing, say, how the purpose or the instruments ('agency') used play a role, the picture gets impossibly complex.
(Wertsch, 1998, p. 16)

In one sense Wertsch (1998) uses this difficulty and the ambiguity as a resource in his attempts to unpack the complexity of what Vygotsky (1987a) would have termed the situation of development of human functioning.

[T]here must remain something essentially enigmatic about the problem of motives, and that this underlying enigma will manifest itself in inevitable ambiguities and inconsistencies among the terms for motives. Accordingly, what we want is not terms that avoid ambiguity, but terms that clearly reveal the strategic spots at which ambiguities necessarily arise.
(Burke, 1969, p. xviii, quoted in Wertsch, 1998, p. 15)

The majority of the questions which drive the research reported by Wertsch may be thought of as attending to the ways in which agents uses particular cultural tools (e.g. discourse) in specific situations. For Wertsch, an important aspect of such agency (or agentic action) is the concept of teleological action: the notion that actors achieve their goals through decisions between alternative courses of action, choosing means that have the promise of being successful in the given situation and applying them in a suitable manner (Wertsch, 1991, p. 9). He maintains that the Bakhtinian construct of ventriloquism is useful 'because it reveals how agency cannot be reduced to an attribute of either the individual or the mediational means in isolation' (Wertsch *et al.*, 1993, p. 346).

Beyond the classic example of the blind man with a stick, he has invoked the performance of the pole vaulter. This account illustrates the ways in which technological changes (the developments in materials from which a pole vaulter's pole is constructed) offer new possibilities for individuals acting with mediational means (ways of vaulting). It is the story of how records increased until the doubling we have today. This increase can be seen as correlated with the introduction of new types of materials. When the poles become more effective, the role of the agent may seem to recede. The pole is experienced as the agent doing the work (the act): 'For my purposes, the major point of interest here is that mediated action can undergo a fundamental transformation with the introduction of new mediational means (in this case, the fiberglass pole)' (Wertsch, 1998, p. 67). From a certain perspective we see 'the reduction of action to motion' (as Burke feared). The relationship of agent and agency changes with the more advanced poles and this creates a tension within the 'agent-acting-with-mediational-means' unit. However, according to Wertsch, we need not systematically take notice of the other terms in the pentad. Elaboration on the scene or on the purpose is always a possibility.

> For example, a pole vaulter may be motivated by the goal of impressing a particular audience, by the desire to overcome a general feeling of failure in life, by an irrational hatred of an opponent, and so forth. In fact, a pole vaulter may have as a goal the desire to let a competitor win for some reason and hence may actually forgo the goal of getting over the cross bar.
> (Wertsch, 1998, p. 33)

Wertsch uses Burke's pentad to think about the local contexts of activity (scene) and the pentad affords the possibility of thinking about and studying meaning in action as it changes over time and space. In some ways, Burke's understanding of human activity in theatrical terms resonates with the dramaturgical influences that led Vygotsky to formulate a principal focus of psychology in personality which, he argued, had the 'character of the drama of life on the social stage' (Yaroshevsky, 1989).

In Chapter 2 of *Mind as Action*, Wertsch (1998) describes ten properties of mediated action that govern the interactions between the elements in the pentad, the understanding of which can aid analysis.

> **Wertsch's ten claims concerning mediation**
>
> 1 There is an irreducible tension between the agent and the mediational means (tools).
> 2 The materiality of mediational means.
> 3 Action has multiple, often conflicting goals.
> 4 Mediated action is historically situated.
> 5 Mediated action provides both affordance and constraints on action.
> 6 New tools transform action because they determine the structure and flow of action.
> 7 Mastery of tools involves following the patterns, the cultural, historical and institutional requirements of a tool.
> 8 Appropriation of tools which refers to making one's own the affordances and constraints inherent in the tool.
> 9 Consumption of tools in ways that are no longer applicable in a given situation and time can impede performance.
> 10 Power and authority are to varying degrees inherent tools.

These claims explicate issues around the material nature of mediational means: their 'affordances' and constraints; the power and authority associated with them; and their use for action not anticipated by the producer. He deals with the multiple goals of action, its developmental paths, the transformation of action by means and the mastery and appropriation by the agent of means (Wertsch, 1998).

Wertsch (1998) argues that mediated action typically serves multiple goals and that these may often come into conflict with each other. For example, in many classrooms children are given what are ostensibly unambiguous tasks, such as problem solving in mathematics or science. However, when such problem solving is enacted it may take place in a context where complex matters of identity formation are in play. In some classrooms girls may not wish to present themselves as too adept at mathematics for fear of being positioned as socially unattractive. Boys may not wish to be seen to be trying too hard lest they be perceived as 'uncool'. However, whilst recognising the dynamic tension among the elements of mediated action, Wertsch also offers a rationale for looking at isolated elements of the system in order to analyse how changes in the mix affect the whole (Wertsch, 1998, p. 27). Wertsch's statement that cultural tools are in themselves powerless and only have impact when agents use them (Wertsch, 1998, p. 30) when presented starkly in this way could appear platitudinous. Nevertheless, the statement carries an important reminder about the focus and methods for research on learning resources. With his concern for the materiality of means (including speech), he underlines the way in which the material properties of tools can illuminate 'how internal processes can come into existence and operate' (Wertsch, 1998, p. 31). He suggests that goals arise as part of the 'background framework' or context within which action is carried out and that there may be conflict between the goals of the agent and the embedded goals of the tools. He is interested also in how new forms of mediated action result from emergence of new means and 'unanticipated spin-offs'. Here he notes that tools can emerge in unpredictable ways through mis-use or borrowing from different contexts or through use for different purposes than designers intended.

Wertsch also considers issues of power and authority in respect of cultural tools and their use. He describes mediational means as 'differentially imbued with power and authority', 'privileging' and, citing Goodnow, imbued with 'cognitive values' (Wertsch, 1998). The notion of cognitive values includes 'why it is that certain knowledge is publicly available and openly taught while other forms or knowledge are not' and why certain types of solutions are more highly regarded than others (Wertsch, 1998, p. 66). He suggests that the 'emergence of new cultural tools transforms power and authority' (Wertsch, 1998, p. 65) and that 'forces that go into the production of a cultural tool often play a major role in determining how it will be used' (Wertsch, 1998, p. 142). He raises questions about how tools are manipulated by users and what tactics are used for employing others' tools. This is an important departure from approaches to sociocultural studies of the formation of mind which neglect the wider situation in which people act. The analysis of relations of power and control as they impact on the production of cultural tools and their use is a vital feature of research which seeks to understand an enriched embedded view of human functioning in the situation in which it develops.

Bakhtin and 'voice'

Wertsch's exploration of Vygotsky's ideas concerning the way in which the inner word extends the boundaries of its own meaning illuminates some of the dilemmas that are inherent in communication. He discusses the difficulties caused by scientific discourse aimed, as it is, at constancy across, and independence of, contexts. In his development of Bakhtin's (1981, 1984, 1986) work, he considers the dynamic tension between the dialogic and univocal functions of texts and the difference between monologic and dialogic models of communication, describing the transmission model (or conduit) as unidirectional and based on monologic assumptions. There is a shared understanding in the work of both Bakhtin and Vygotsky that meaning is dependent on the social and historical contexts in which it is made.

> Our thought itself – philosophical, scientific, and artistic – is born and shaped in the process of interaction and struggle with others' thought, and this cannot but be reflected in the forms that verbally express our thought as well ... The utterance proves to be a very complex and multiplanar phenomenon if considered not in isolation and with respect to its author (the speaker) only, but as a link in the chain of speech communication and with respect to other, related utterances.
>
> (Bakhtin, 1986, pp. 92–3)

He draws on Lotman (1990, 1994) in suggesting that this function is fulfilled best when the codes of the speaker and the listener most completely coincide, which, however, he makes clear is rare. In comparison, he returns to Bakhtin's idea of intermediation and Lotman's notion of the text as generative of new meaning, that is, as a 'thinking device' (Wertsch, 1991).

Wertsch and Toma (1995) also provide a critique of the conduit model of communication and suggest that either one of the univocal and dialogic functions of texts may tend to become dominant in certain forms of interaction (Lotman, 1994, 1990). They draw attention to the way in which the dialogic function involves the generation of new meanings. In extracts from classroom discourse, Wertsch and Toma illustrate the role of the dialogic function by showing how pupils reformulate and reword the words and comments of others as they reject, incorporate or take further other utterances. They use the term 'interanimate' to refer to the way in which one voice can transform the voice of another in a dialogic encounter. For them, this ambiguity of meaning is never finalised and this unfinished character is what Alexandrov (2000) sees as a creative resource rather an irritant noise in the system, arguing that it should be seen as a resource for communication and of collaboration.

In Wertsch's examination of the practice of reciprocal teaching, he supports the notion that 'reading involves active, dialogic engagement' (Wertsch, 1998, p. 130). Like Bakhtin and Vygotsky, his work assumes that the addressee 'may be temporally, spatially, and socially distant' (Wertsch, 1991, p. 53). In his later work, Wertsch examines agency from the point of view of the roles that constituents play, as revealed through their linguistic expression. His idea of 'discourse referentiality' is helpful in pointing to methods for investigation of communicative acts. This involves consideration of the 'relationship between unique, situated utterances and the contexts in which they occur' and 'how utterances function to presuppose the context of speech in which they occur, on the one hand, or act in a 'performative' capacity to create or entail the context, on the other' (Wertsch, 1998, p. 95). Specifically, he addresses issues to do with the presence/accessibility of the writer/reader in the text and reference to characters where their presence is assumed in the text (Wertsch, 1998).

> Sociocultural studies of the formation of mind – derived from the work of Vygotsky and Bakhtin – have explored the way in which historicity enters into the organisation of human action. Such work takes as central the assertion that human consciousness is organised within the appropriation, use and generation of culturally evolved resources. These include systems of symbolic representation and communication, artefacts and institutionalised practices for the generation and distribution of knowledge systems.
> (Middleton and Brown, 2005, p. 102)

Wertsch considers voice and multi-voicedness as important dimensions of the sociohistorical context for communication. He explores ideas about given and new information; about knowledge that is not held in common between speakers/writers; and about alterity, intersubjectivity and individual perspectives and how they help to explain how speakers understand or fail to understand each other (Wertsch, 1991, 1998).

> The general point to be made about intersubjectivity and alterity, then, is not that communication is best understood in terms of one or the other in isolation. Instead, virtually every text is viewed as involving both univocal, information-transmission characteristics, and hence intersubjectivity, as well as dialogic, thought-generating tendencies, and hence alterity.
> (Wertsch, 1998, p. 117)

Wertsch transcribes several dialogues within teacher–child dyads in an attempt to reveal something of the process whereby the latter appropriates speech genres from the former. Wertsch's (2002, 1998, 1991) research is extremely important, not only for the many concrete illustrations it provides but for the way in which it extends the idea of semiotic mediation to include this notion of 'voice' (Farmer, 1995). I shall return to alternative conceptions of 'voice' in Chapter 7. At this point, it is important to note that this account of voice is a profoundly dialogical notion in which it should be possible to understand the workings of relations of power and control as some voices predominate and others are marginalised and silenced. This is also a historical analysis in that it seeks to understand the evolution of consciousness through the struggles that are played out in dialogue.

> The importance of struggling with another's discourse, its influence in the history of an individual's coming to ideological consciousness, is enormous. One's own discourse and one's own voice, although born of another or dynamically stimulated by another, will sooner or later begin to liberate themselves from the authority of another's discourse. This process is made more complex by the fact that a variety of alien voices enter into the struggle for influence within an individual's consciousness (just as they struggle with one another in surrounding social reality).
> (Bakhtin, 1981, p. 348)

The questions of legitimacy of 'voice' concerning how utterance may be recognised as legitimate and how that utterance signifies and shapes a social position in a field are not always addressed. Wertsch does consider the range of semiotic options open to a speaker and the reasons for choice of one over another and draws on linguistic theories in his examination of how the use of deictic, common and context-informative referents are associated with levels of intersubjectivity (Wertsch, 1985a).

One feature of Vygotsky's theory that is seldom mentioned is that social speech, especially as it occurs within the zone of proximal development, is rhetorical speech. It is not supplanted by the development of inner or written speech, nor does it vanish on its own once other speech forms develop. To state the obvious, social speech remains a constant and necessary staple of human existence. For that reason, voice, in a rhetorical sense, is realised only in its relationship to, and difference from, other voices that it must address and answer. The quality of voice, in some measure, always presupposes other voices (Farmer, 1995, p. 309).

Dialectical or dialogical models?

In a critique of Wertsch and Kazak (2007), Wegerif (2007) argues that Vygotsky was a dialectical thinker rather than a dialogical thinker. His concern is that neither Vygotsky nor Wertsch can provide an account of creative thinking. He cites Bakhtin (1986) as part of his attempt to clarify the distinction:

> Take a dialogue and remove the voices (the partitioning of voices), remove the intonations (emotional and individualizing ones), carve out abstract concepts and judgments from living words and responses, cram everything into one abstract consciousness – and that's how you get dialectics.
>
> (Bakhtin, 1986, p. 147)

The core of his argument involves the questioning of the suggestion that dialogues in education can be adequately studied through a focus on mediation by tools. He calls for an extension of the Wertsch position in order to obtain a greater sophistication in the understanding of dialogic relations in education. In what amounts to a strong version of the process ontology argument, he suggests that uses of the term 'dialogic', as shown below, could have been developed without specific reference to dialogic methods:

- Dialogic as pertaining to dialogue suggests the promotion of dialogue as chains of questions in classrooms both through teacher–pupil dialogues (Alexander, 2004) and through establishing communities of enquiry (Wells, 1999).
- Dialogic as being about the open and poly-vocal properties of texts brings in the need for intertextuality in classrooms (Maybin, 1999; Kozulin, 1996) and the appropriation of social discourses as a goal in education (Hicks, 1996; Wertsch, 1998).
- Dialogic as an epistemologic framework suggests an account of education as the discursive construction of shared knowledge (Mercer, 2000).

His predilection is with the dialogic as an ontological principle:

> the most important thing to be learnt is learning itself and, to achieve this, teachers need to be even more teachable than their students (Heidegger,

1978, p. 380)...: dialogue is not primarily a means to the end of knowledge construction, but an end in itself, the most important end of education (Sidorkin, 1999). In my view the ideal of 'teaching' learning to learn through promoting dialogue as an end in itself is the most distinctive and important contribution that a dialogic perspective brings to the debate about education.

(Wegerif, 2007, p. 145)

This debate appears to me to witness the way in which this body of theory is open to a wide range of interpretations. Thus, when a particular philosophical perspective (e.g. a fraction of post-structuralist or postmodern theory) is brought to bear on a body of writing which does not share its epistemological and ontological assumptions, then critical attention is directed and deflected according to different priorities. Vygotsky was concerned with creativity within his overall account of mediation, however, his interpretation of the phenomena did not share Wegerif's (2007) assumptions.

Appropriation and mastery

In a seminal article, Vygotsky (2004) recognised the importance of the development of creativity through schooling and also rejected the notion of creativity as the product of sudden inspiration. He argued that the active promotion of creativity was a central function of schooling. He provides an account of the development of creativity which rests heavily on his notion of tool/artefact-mediated action.

Learning and development are dealt with by Wertsch and collaborators by building on an interpretation of Vygotsky's work on internalisation and externalisation and Bakhtin's notions of ventriloquism, alterity, resistance, mastery and appropriation (Wertsch and Stone, 1985; Wertsch, 1991; Wertsch et al., 1993; Wertsch and Tulviste, 1996; Wertsch, 1998). Wertsch and Stone (1985) differentiate cognitive mastery from appropriation and use both terms in preference to internalisation, a concept which, they argue, implies a Piagetian model of transmission, assimilation and accommodation. Mastery is characterised as 'knowing how to do' particular actions, whereas appropriation is characterised as 'making something one's own'. They see the process of learning as involving construction, rather than copying, and being dependent upon mastery of the cultural system of symbolic representation (Wertsch and Stone, 1985). Appropriation can involve resistance to the social setting which includes the cultural tool and Wertsch suggests that 'development often occurs through using a cultural tool before an agent fully understands what this cultural tool is or how it works' (Wertsch, 1998, p. 132). He carried out narrative analyses of accounts given by citizens of the former Soviet republic of Estonia, who mastered the 'official' historical accounts of their region's annexation when in public settings, but resisted and rejected such accounts in private settings. Thus, there may be situations of mastery without appropriation as in Wertsch's Estonian work or appropriation without mastery. He regards conscious reflection as an important element in development within mediated action. Middleton and Brown (2005, p. 144) note that Wertsch argues that mediation is never completely transparent. Although mediational means typically facilitate and enlarge the scope of what the subject is able to achieve, this comes at some cost.

> [M]ediational means are often used with little or no conscious reflection. Indeed, it is often only when confronted with a comparative example that one becomes aware of an imaginable alternative. This conscious awareness is one of the most powerful tools available for recognising and changing forms of mediation that have unintended and often untoward consequences.
> (Wertsch, 1991, p. 126)

However, he also argues that appropriation of the tool does not depend upon reflection, though the degree and types of conscious reflection and voluntary use characterise particular instances of appropriation. Wertsch reminds us that individuals' histories with regard to cultural tools are an element in the development of mediated action. He argues that when Vygotsky uses the term 'mental function' he does so with reference to social interaction and to individual processes. In this sense mental functions may be seen to be carried by groups as well as individuals. Mind is thought of as being socially distributed, belonging to dyads and larger groups who can think, attend and remember together (Wertsch, 1991, 1998). '[T]he microdynamics of appropriation in this case draws on at least three pentadic elements: agent, instrument (i.e., cultural tools), and scene (i.e., context)' (Wertsch, 1998, p. 176).

Remembering

Wertsch's examination of speech genres includes discussion of the privileging of ways of thinking in certain settings (Wertsch, 1991); the emergence of particular sets of discourse and cognitive skills through 'exposure to the patterns of speaking and reasoning in formal instructional settings' (Wertsch and Tulviste, 1996); and the silence and distance that authoritative texts induce, compared with the dialogue and contact of internally persuasive discourse (Wertsch, 1998). He considers instructional contexts and the way in which questioning presupposes questions about 'the mastery, possession, and communication of knowledge' (Wertsch, 1998, p. 122). He cites Bruner when considering the importance of narrativity in organising and representing interrelationships of different kinds and as a key to the retention of information through integration of textual information in a coherent schema. Specifically, he sees narrative as a means for 'reflection', 'selection' and 'deflection' of reality (Wertsch, 1998).

Wertsch and O'Connor (1994) provide an account of voicing and historical narrative which sets an important backdrop for the seminal text entitled *Voices of Collective Remembering* (Wertsch, 2002). Here he develops an analysis of narrative, particularly in the context of constructions of national history, as semiotic mediated action which carries, and can be used to construct, representations of the past. He argues that the development of shared perspective (intersubjectivity) and productive alternatives (alterity) plays an important part in the social practice of remembering.

> Wertsch argues for an understanding of collective remembering where mediated action constitutes the basic unit of analysis. By this, he intends to draw attention to the range of 'cultural tools' that people employ in accomplishing remembering activities. What counts as a tool, for Wertsch, is quite broad – language qualifies, as do written texts and technologies such as electronic search agents. These tools are always relative to the cultural and historical settings in which they are fashioned and produced.... Control over mediational resources is a means of ensuring that what can be collectively remembered is shaped to fit official, state-sponsored versions of the past.
> (Middleton and Brown, 2005, pp. 30–1)

Wertsch (2002) retains a focus on the narrative templates deployed by Russians as cultural tools in order to shape and represent their historical development in terms of contemporary circumstances (see Middleton and Brown, 2005, p. 30). Wertsch (2002) compares these templates to the text patterns in folk tales discussed by Vygotsky's formalist contemporary, Vladimir Propp. Through comparative analyses of textbooks and memories in Soviet and post-Soviet times, Wertsch (2002) identifies collective narrative templates and the transformations that took place in these artefacts after the radical changes that took place during the demise of the Soviet system.

> What Wertsch offers is an innovative way of analysing the relationship between individual lived experience and historical times as defined by the state-sanctioned 'grand narratives' of Soviet history. Soviet citizens necessarily drew on such mediational means and, as a consequence, patterned their experience in part around these narratives, but, at the same time, avoided subsuming their individual biographies. There is, however, more that we can say about the resulting 'irreducible tension'. The widespread sense among Soviet citizens that counternarratives could not be publicly voiced was founded on the operation of a massive system of monitoring, recording, reporting and archiving information of individuals that was formalised in a party administrative apparatus. This colossal system of surveillance acted as an 'archontic infrastructure'. To be a Soviet citizen was, then, to be 'attached' (in the sense described in Chapter 8 and 9) to this infrastructure.
> (Middleton and Brown, 2005, p. 207)

Wertsch positions his work against the background of a debate within activity theory about the relative importance of the individual and the collective, and the relative emphasis on the historical, cultural and social, and choices that are made between the discourses and practices of the disciplines which make an impact on the theory itself. He argues that notions of dialogicality, speech genre and social language help 'make it possible to examine concrete intermental and intramental functioning without losing sight of how this functioning is situated in historical, cultural and institutional settings' (Wertsch, 1991, p. 122). Elsewhere he says:

> One of the most important characteristics of an activity is that it is not determined or even strongly circumscribed by the physical or perceptual context in which humans function. Rather, it is a sociocultural interpretation or creation that is imposed on the context by the participant(s).
> (Wertsch, 1985a, p. 203)

Transformation of theories

Although perhaps introduced at a different level of specificity, Griffin and Cole (1984) caution their readers against a popularisation of Vygotskian theory which in some sense would subsume it within the tradition of transmission and determinism. They criticise specific versions of the scaffolding model arguing that it often appears to embody a form of pedagogic control and remains monological in character. They argue a case for a dialogical interpretation of what Wertsch would term 'mediated action' within a zone of proximal development in which the learner always brings a creative response to instruction or information given. The process which Griffin and Cole (1984) refer to as 'popularization' may be seen as part of a much wider and larger process of cultural and historical transformation. These processes have affected and continue to affect interpretations and developments of Vygotsky's work. Pablo del Río and Amelia Álvarez have done much to foreground Vygotsky's emphasis on the functioning of emotion. This is witnessed in their studies of the impact of television (del Río, 1996; del Río and Álvarez, 1995). They also lay great emphasis on the way in which cultural artefacts carry history through time. These two directions may be seen as part of the general concern about reductionism which they draw directly from Vygotsky. They set an agenda through, first, setting out what they regard as the dangers of methodological reductionism:

1   Reduction to the rational. The mind of the psychologist, believing that it reflects the mind of the subject, has left abandoned in its wake all that is considered animist or irrational and has neglected emotion and action (or has made it subject to cognitive calculation or to raw psychological mechanisms).
2   Reduction to the individual. The psychological mind and subject are self-contained and self-explanatory. Despite the acceptance of social and situationally distributed processing, the glass-bell isolation of the subject remains immutable.

3 Reduction to the internal. Mental and psychological phenomena should be attributed only to internal processes. That which is external is not psychological but physical; it is the context.
4 Reduction to the innate. Psychological functions, both basic (at 'animal level') and 'higher' (exclusively human), are explained by biological heredity – or are not explained. Construction and development are supposed to be biologically or logically caused from inside. Cultural construction is lacking. (Adapted from del Río and Álvarez, 1995, p. 385.)

They then set out a case for the development of an agenda driven by Vygotsky's response to the errors of reductionism:

1 In the face of rationalistic reductionism, Vygotsky emphasised the importance of the development and cultural construction not only of meaning, but of emotion and directivity.
2 In reply to individualist reductionism, he proposed the social genesis of the higher functions and consciousness ('all that is individual was first social').
3 Internalist or mentalist reductionism he countered with the systematic and neural relationship with the cultural environment, the network that he called 'extracortical connections' ('all that is internal was first external').
4 And finally, he met innatist reductionism with the postulate of the sociocultural-historical construction of higher functions and the correlated formation of new internal neural structures (so-called neoformations). (Adapted from del Río and Álvarez, 1995, p. 386.)

They are keen to progress development on three frontiers that they identify in Vygotsky's work: the evolutionary and historical frontier (change and evolution of the child and individual, of the species, of cultures); the identity frontier (the view of the functional system as shared, of functions as socially distributed); and the ecological frontier between the internal and external, the mental and the material, the organism and the medium (del Río and Álvarez, 2007). The historical aspect of this work echoes the earlier writing of Wertsch and Tulviste:

> In order to explain the highly complex forms of human consciousness one must go beyond the human organism. One must seek the origins of conscious activity.... In the external process of social life within the social and historical forms of human existence.
> (Wertsch and Tulviste, 1992, p. 548)

In a recent study, del Río and Álvarez (2007) extend their previous analyses (del Río and Álvarez, 1995, 1994) of extracortical connections in which they seek to make psychological connections between the inner and outer without resorting to reductionism. They apply this argument directly to its logical educational conclusion. They do this on the basis of some despair about the cultural-historical work that is engendered by modern media and they call for more 'human' forms of mediation that can shape the operation of personal directivity (which is at the same time a cognitive and affective function).

> It is the classical educational endeavour. But we also need a strong and functional external, social, cultural network, a solid cultural construction, both for allowing a more social, relevant, critical, and ecological education and for supporting in the everyday agency our 'internal directive brain'. This is a most pressing cultural-educational task.
>
> (del Río and Álvarez, 1995, p. 405)

Del Río and Álvarez provide one example of the way in which a methodological position such as that established and developed by Wertsch has itself been developed and shaped according to cultural and historical specificities of a particular research agenda. In one sense, the theoretical and methodological developments that are taking place in the sociocultural field constitute an example of the dialogic function of text outlined by Lotman, Wertsch and Bakhtin. Space does not permit a full consideration of the range of such creative developments within the field. A good example is to be seen in the work of Ana Smolka (2005) in Brazil, who argues for a view of authoring as a historically instituted and instituting social practice. In this dialect of sociocultural theory Foucault (1979, 1982, 1992) is deployed in order to theorise notions of power in the constitution of the subject.

In sum, the analysis of mediated action is concerned with how humans employ cultural tools in social and individual processes. Because of its focus on the irreducible tension between agents and cultural tools which defines mediated action, this analysis stands in contrast with others that focus on individuals or on instruments in isolation. Many studies of mediated action are grounded in the ideas of Vygotsky, with the result that analyses of sociocultural situatedness and of language as a cultural tool have been particularly important. Contemporary analyses of mediated action are beginning to go beyond Vygotsky's formulation to examine issues such as the conditions that have given rise to cultural tools, and the constraints as well as affordances associated with them.

The wider situation of development

I will draw this chapter to a close with a discussion of two groups of researchers who have a shared interest in talk and who both struggle to understand the talk that they study in the setting in which it is spoken. Candela (e.g. 1995) has directed her attention to the construction of meaning in science classrooms. This work shares an intellectual lineage with that undertaken by Rojas-Drummond on independent problem solving (e.g. Rojas-Drummond and Alatorre, 1994). This group, based in Latin America, have links with a UK-based team who have developed a creative and compelling series of intervention-based studies.

The two extracts shown below reveal a concern to both 'include information about the educational content and practices' and 'analyz[e] the local features of cultural processes' whilst studying talk. In this way, the researchers are keen to study talk in its contexts.

> But rather than studying several turns between two or three participants in mundane settings as the more traditional ethnomethodological studies do, I have analyzed the interaction of approximately 40 participants, in a particular institutional setting. This has required the analysis of relatively long sequences (20 to 40 turns), in order to include information about the educational content and practices as well as to identify the conversational rules being used. This analysis deals with the participants' constructed meaning of the educational activities as revealed in the interactional discourse structure.
> (Candela, 1995, p. 461)

> [V]ery few ethnographic studies have analyzed talk in as much detail as conversation analysis has – this is a powerful instrument for analyzing the local features of cultural processes, as long as the external context of those processes – in which history, meaning, and intention can be found – is not lost.
> (Candela, 1995, p. 471)

I will return to the discussion that Makitalo and Säljö (2002) provide of the tensions between conversation analysis-based research and sociocultural approaches in Chapter 6. Suffice it to say at this point that the history of social science is riven with tensions concerning a kind of chicken-and-egg debate about whether culture, history and context may be seen through the study of interaction or whether the possibilities for interaction have to be studied within a clear articulation of the material conditions in which interaction including communication is enacted. This important body of Mexican work strives to keep the analysis of history and place in the analytical frame, albeit that the methodology trains its eye primarily on the mediational means. For example, Rockwell (1999) studied three intersecting planes (the *longue durée*, relative continuity, and everyday co-construction) in order to try to integrate both the historicity and cultural diversity of school environments, and the profound subjectivity of school experience.

Mercer et al. (2004) report one example of research which reveals a commitment to improving the quality of talk in classrooms (e.g. Mercer, 1995). This body of work counts the writing of Douglas Barnes (1975) as one its underpinning influences. The focus on language in classrooms and the 'work' that it does has found expression in interventions which are designed to promote what they term 'exploratory talk' which they see as a basic tool in the practices of reasoning (for a full account, see Mercer and Littleton, 2007). Mercer (1995) reports a set of ground rules which were developed as a way of making explicit the basis on which desired forms classroom talk should proceed. Examples of such ground rules are: the views of all participants are sought and considered and that explicit agreement precedes decisions and actions. The aim is to help children both share and explore ideas and learn to work with conflicting views. Science lessons have often been the target of these intervention studies and they aim to change the ways in which teachers work on and with children's talk in classrooms, arguing that increases in practices of exploratory talk will lead to increases in measures of verbal reasoning. They sought to bring pedagogic and didactic principles to bear on the design of their programme in order that the teachers would be able to combine guidance on subject knowledge (science) with guidance on the use of language in the science classroom. They reported changes in the quality of talk and levels of collaborative activity, along with the predicted increases in measures of non-verbal reasoning and performance on assessment tasks in science. They illustrated the difference that their programme (entitled 'Thinking Together') engendered with the following representative samples of classroom talk. The first transcript is from a non-intervention control classroom and the second is from a Thinking Together intervention classroom which had been in place for two school terms.

Transcript 1: Control school group: Keep it Quiet (working on a Science Explorer investigation into the effectiveness of materials for providing soundproofing)

HANNAH: [Reads from screen] Keep it Quiet. Which material is the best insulation? Click 'measure' to take a sound reading. Does the pitch make a difference?
DARRYL: No we don't want clothes. See what one it is then. [Points to screen]
HANNAH: No it's cloth.
DARRYL: Oh it's cloth.
HANNAH: Go down. This is better when Stephanie's in our group.
DARRYL: Metal?
HANNAH: Right try it.
DEBORAH: Try what? That?
HANNAH: Try 'glass'.
DARRYL: Yeah.
DEBORAH: No one.
HANNAH: Now.
DARRYL: (interrupts) Measure.
HANNAH: Now measure. Hold. [Turns volume control dial below screen]
DARRYL: Results, notes.
HANNAH: Results. We need to go on a different one now. Results.
DARRYL: Yeah, you need to go there so you can write everything down.
HANNAH: I'm not writing.

74 The sociocultural tradition

Transcript 2: Target school group: Blocking out light (working on a science Explorer activity about the effectiveness of materials for blocking out light)

ROSS: OK. [Reads from screen] Talk together about a plan to test all the different types of paper.
ALANA: Dijek, how much did you think it would be for tissue paper?
DIJEK: At least ten because tissue paper is thin. Tissue paper can wear out and you can see through, other people in the way, and light can shine in it.
ALANA: OK. Thanks.
ALANA: [To Ross] Why do you think it?
ROSS: Because I tested it before!
ALANA: No, Ross, what did you think? How much did you think? Tissue paper. How much tissue paper did you think it would be to block out the light?
ROSS: At first I thought it would be five, but second –
ALANA: Why did you think that?
ROSS: Because when it was in the overhead projector you could see a little bit of it, but not all of it, so I thought it would be like, five to block out the light.
ALANA: That's a good reason. I thought, I thought it would be between five and seven because, I thought it would be between five and seven because normally when you're at home if you lay it on top, with one sheet you can see through but if you lay on about five or six pieces on top you can't see through. So that's why I was thinking about five or six.

(Mercer et al., 2004, pp. 368–9)

Transcript 1 shows weak knowledge sharing and low, almost trivial levels of cooperation through an impoverished pattern of communication, in which no attempt is made to provide a rationale for suggestions or seek a consensus through debate. They do not appear to be interested in or concerned about or perhaps listening to what their classmates have to say. Mercer et al. (2004) suggest that, sadly, this is all too typical of the talk to be found in many primary classrooms and argue that this desultory state of affairs provides a strong argument for what is essentially a sociocultural intervention. In contrast, the exploratory talk to be seen in Transcript 2 reveals relatively high levels information exchange and exploration of reasons and opinions. Ideas are shared, challenged and evaluated in a positive and purposeful manner. Mercer et al. (2004) argue that a sociocultural intervention such as theirs, which intervenes at the level of interaction and communication, has a direct impact on reasoning and attainment. Mercer and Littleton (2007) affirm the validity of this claim with reference to a number of similar interventions in different contexts. The argument is that intervention at the sociocultural level provides a powerful and robust approach to effective education:

> the results provide support of other kinds for the sociocultural perspective on education, and hence for the validity of sociocultural theory as the basis for

an applied psychology of education. By showing that children's increased use of certain ways of using language leads to better learning and conceptual understanding in science, we have provided empirical support for the conception of science education as induction into a community of discourse or practice.

(Mercer *et al.*, 2004, p. 375)

The challenging questions about this important body of work and that of Candela and colleagues is, on the one hand, whether for the non-intervention work it is really possible to keep 'the analysis of history and place in the analytical frame albeit that the methodology trains its eye primarily on the mediational means'. Conversely, for Mercer's interventionist studies the question is reversed and asks whether the intervention has an impact on the broader 'context'. The relation between setting and development lies at the heart of the Vygotskian account of mediation and yet it continues to provide us with profound methodological challenges. My reading is that Wertsch, Mercer and Candela and many of the other researchers mentioned in this chapter have engaged with determination and vigour to the challenge set by Vygotsky and stated bluntly by Veresov and Hakkarainen:

Mediation by sign, mediators, the social nature of consciousness, and object-related activity are the 'minimal' set of primary ideas without which it is impossible to imagine a contemporary cultural psychology of development. But the *ideas* about these processes and their role in the development of human consciousness must not, and cannot, be an object of thoughtless acceptance 'on faith,' but should be an object of discussion. Otherwise, they simply cease to 'work' as explanatory principles; and science becomes the worst variety of mythology – an endless repetition of adjurations, empty forms that express nothing *of content.*

(Veresov and Hakkarainen, 2001, p. 5)

Chapter 4

Researching distributed cognition

Vygotsky (1987a) argued that the human mind must be understood as the emergent outcome of cultural-historical processes. In Vygotsky (1997a), he showed how cultural-historically developed tools mediate the individual's relation to the world and that the competence to handle such tools is acquired in social settings through guidance from other persons. He was concerned to develop an account in which humans were seen as active in 'making themselves from the outside' as they used, produced and modified culturally produced artefacts (tools, signs and symbols). It was suggested that through acting on things in the world they engage with the meanings that those artefacts embodied and acquired within social activity. Humans both shape those meanings and are shaped by them. The concept of Zone of Proximal Development (ZPD) was created by Vygotsky as a means of explaining the way in which such social and participatory learning takes place (John-Steiner and Mahn, 1996).

This emphasis on the mediational function of artefacts which are produced in and through human activity brings with it questions about the situation in which development takes place and the organisation of the activity itself. In this and the following chapter I will explore the implications of two areas of research which engage with these questions. These two approaches suggest that learning, and cognition more generally, is either or both situated and distributed across people and things. These arguments are sketched in the following extract:

> There is a reason to suspect that what we call cognition is in fact a complex social phenomenon. The point is not so much that arrangements of knowledge in the head correspond in a complicated way to the social world outside the head, but that they are socially organized in such a fashion as to be indivisible. 'Cognition' observed in everyday practice is distributed – stretched over, not divided among – mind, body, activity and culturally organized settings which include other actors.
>
> (Lave, 1988, p. 1)

This chapter will commence with an introduction to the central themes within the emergent research field that is usually understood as being concerned with distributed cognition. I will then move in Chapter 5 to a consideration of situated accounts, whilst recognising the overlap between the two and the somewhat unsatisfactory nature of the categories themselves.

Distributed cognition

The origins of this branch of social theory may be found in sociology and cognitive science, along with Vygotsky's writing. Within this body of work there is a concern for co-ordination between individuals and artefacts. It is preoccupied with the way in which knowledge is represented and the way in which those representations are transformed, as well as the processes through which representations are co-ordinated with each other. The unit of analysis deployed in research within the field of distributed cognition is usually discussed in terms of a cognitive system which is understood as a system comprising individuals and the tools or artefacts that are used when particular tasks are undertaken. Salomon (1993a) identifies two conceptions of distributed cognition: a radical tradition (e.g. Cole and Engeström, 1993) which downplays the analysis of individual cognition but, following Luria, recognises the neuropsychological distribution of cognition across the brain; and a less radical tradition which retains a focus on the dynamic interaction between solo and distributed cognitions (e.g. Salomon, 1993b). The term 'cognitive system' is avoided by some researchers who wish to avoid too strong an association with the basic assumptions and limitations of traditional cognitive psychology. For example, Hutchins (1995) uses the term 'functional system' to emphasise the way in which tasks are shared between people and the things that they use as they carry out particular functions. The key elements of this argument are summarised by Hollan *et al.* (2000):

- Cognitive processes may be distributed across the members of a social group.
- Cognitive processes may involve co-ordination between internal and external (material or environmental) structure.
- Processes may be distributed through time in such a way that the products of earlier events can transform the nature of later events.

This approach argues that processes that may rightly be termed cognitive are not straightforwardly to be understood as happening just in the brain and that they can equally well be understood and thus researched as happening between brains or between brains and other things such as physical elements of a laboratory or a classroom, or indeed any setting in which humans act with artefacts. This approach is therefore profoundly social in its orientation in that it does not revert to the necessity of understanding cognition as a facet of individual functioning. Hence the following statement by Hollan *et al.* (2000):

> it extends the reach of what is considered *cognitive* beyond the individual to encompass interactions between people and with resources and materials in

the environment – distributed cognition refers to a perspective on all of cognition, rather than a particular kind of cognition – looks for cognitive processes, wherever they may occur, on the basis of the functional relationships of elements that participate together in the process. A process is not cognitive simply because it happens in a brain, nor is a process noncognitive simply because it happens in the interactions among many brains. Whereas traditional views look for cognitive events in the manipulation of symbols inside individual actors, distributed cognition looks for a broader class of cognitive events and does not expect all such events to be encompassed by the skin or skull of an individual.

(Hollan et al., 2000, pp. 175–6)

Shared or distributed models

Much of the work has focused on the way in which technology is deployed in complex work settings. For example, Hutchins (1995a, b) is well known for his studies of 'cognition in the wild', in which he tries to understand the way in which cognition works across people and technology in real-life settings, such as the distributed cognitive system necessary to navigate a large military naval vessel or fly a large modern civil aircraft. Wertsch (2007) cites such work as an example of explicit mediation which, he notes, continues to be a topic of study in contemporary psychology and cognitive science.

[I]n his analysis of 'how a cockpit remembers its speeds,' Edwin Hutchins (1995b) examines human agents' uses of various 'sociotechnical systems' to organize their memory and cognitive processes. As part of his argument he makes an explicit call for cognitive science to go beyond its focus on isolated individuals and to take into account the role of cultural tools such as airplane gauges and instruments in remembering and human action more generally.

(Wertsch, 2007, p. 180)

The cockpit of a plane was analysed as one sociotechnical system comprising pilot, co-pilot and aeroplane and it was argued that the function of system memory was fulfilled by the dials to which they referred whilst flying the aircraft. It was also argued that the navigation of a US Navy ship is achieved as an act of distributed functioning with several individuals working with specific tools, each of which contribute to the collective achievement. Hutchins (1995a, p. 117) argues that the completion of this task involves the 'propagation of representational states across a series of representational media'. The argument here is that the cognitive system is distributed both amongst and between individuals and the technology with which they work which, in the case of the work on navigation, includes instruments and artefacts such as charts. Importantly, the analysis also includes the social structures which facilitate task completion and in so doing connects inter- and intrapersonal functioning with the ordering of social relations. In this way, he is also invoking the need for an understanding of processes of implicit mediation conceived in terms of the everyday communicative action that takes place in a particular form of social order as discussed in Chapter 3. Hutchins' formulation of a unit of analysis shifts the notion of subject away from the individual and towards a group or grouping. His approach may be contrasted with one in which the emphasis is on the acquisition of a shared mental model rather than a distributed cognitive system as in Banks and Millward (2000).

> These findings justify the adoption of a distributed cognition approach to studying shared mental models. The distributed cognition approach allowed the possibility that using the mental model required a process undertaken by the whole team rather than the cognitive processes being solely undertaken by the individual and then the team performance being solely determined by the similarity or dissimilarity of the individual processes. Once the possibility of a team process had been considered, the nature of such a process could be hypothesized from the underlying form of a model. Finally, from this hypothesized process a series of predictions could be formed which were more specific about the role of planning in shared mental models.
>
> (Banks and Millward, 2000, p. 515)

This approach reveals some similarity with that developed through the ethnographic studies carried out by Shore (1996), in which the major preoccupation is with the conceptualisation of the relationship between culture and mind. The intersubjective sharing of a model by a group is seen as 'glue' which brings coherence across individuals and thus ties individuals to cultures. The argument is that the transformation of cultural representations or models into cognitive representations is carried out through a process of analogical schematisation. The resulting cognitive models can act to conserve prior understanding but can also serve to act on new information to transform what, in effect, are thought of as models in the guise of cultural memories or repositories. There are, of course, strong echoes here of the later works of Piaget (1995). There are clear differences between this approach and that developed by Hutchins and that described by Cole and Engeström (1993) as being in the radical tradition. The shared mental model approach understands distribution in terms of something that is distributed and shared amongst all members of a group. The alternate form is where the component functions of a cognitive system are distributed across people and things.

Cognitive ethnography

Together with his colleagues Hollan and Kirsh, Hutchins has formulated a map of integrated research activity by way of an agenda for the development of the field of distributed cognition. They suggest that there are three fundamental tenets on which the development of a new form of cognitive ethnography for the investigation of the functional properties of distributed cognitive systems will be based (Hollan et al., 2000). These are socially distributed cognition, embodied cognition and culture and cognition. With regard to socially distributed cognition, they argue that cognitive processes involve trajectories of information (transmission and transformation), so the patterns of these information trajectories, if stable, reflect some underlying cognitive architecture. Since social organisation – plus the structure added by the context of activity – largely determines the way information flows through a group, social organisation may itself be viewed as a form of cognitive architecture (Hollan et al., 2000, p. 177). Their suggestion is that researchers should use the conceptual apparatus and models derived and developed in studies of social groups to describe distributed cognitive functioning. They direct attention to the way in which what have been thought of as 'individual' cognitive processes in fact operate across a group of individuals and further try to identify the ways in which group cognitive functioning differs from the functioning of individuals who make up such groups. The latter leads to the development of questions concerning the way in which participation in group functioning affects the ways in which individuals may themselves come to function. They draw from Andy Clark's (1997) account of the embodied mind in their incorporation of notions of embodied cognition in their proposals for novel approaches to design.

> To thus take the body and world seriously is to invite an emergentist perspective on many key phenomena – to see adaptive success as inhering as much in the complex interactions among body, world, and brain as in the inner processes bounded by the skin and skull.
>
> (Clark, 1997, p. 85)

From this perspective, the tools of work become tools of the mind and thus are integral elements of an integrated cognitive system. The tools or artefacts of work are thus seen as part of the way that cognitive systems perceive, think and exercise control. They cite examples of the blind person's cane or a cell biologist's microscope. Through a similar line of argument but in the context of language, Spurrett and Cowley (2004) draw on Clark and Chalmers' (1998) account of the 'extended mind' as they seek to develop an object of study which they term 'utterance-activity', which refers to kinetic and prosodic features of communicating humans. They suggest that utterance activity is best thought of in terms of embodied activity, the complex joint control of which contributes to the learning of some features of language. In this frame, the cognitive powers of young children are augmented by the cognitive powers of those with whom they interact.

In his epistemology of cybernetics, Gregory Bateson also proposes an account of a way in which mind comes together in brain, body and environment. He illustrates his suggestion of the immanence of mind in the person plus the environment through an example of the felling of a tree with an axe in which the total system of 'tree-eyes-brain-muscles-axe-stroke-tree' 'has the characteristics of immanent mind' (Bateson, 1972, p. 317).

> The cybernetic epistemology which I have offered you would suggest a new approach. The individual mind is immanent but not only in the body. It is immanent also in the pathways and messages outside the body; and there is a larger Mind of which the individual mind is only a subsystem.
>
> (Bateson, 1972, p. 467)

Cole and Engeström (1993) also emphasise the way in which external artefacts become tools which function as part of us. This position draws on Vygotsky's (1987, 1978) emphasis on tools as mediators and leads Cole and Engeström (1993) to argue that:

> The ways in which mind is distributed depend crucially on the tools through which one interacts with the world and these in turn depend on one's goals. The combination of goals tools and setting constitutes simultaneously the context of behaviour and the ways in which cognition can be said to be distributed in that context.
>
> (Cole and Engeström, 1993, p. 13)

In a similar vein, Bateson calls for an understanding of co-adaptive complex systems of the human individual, the society and the ecosystem, and in so doing notes the need to reconceptualise the relationship between thought and emotion. This ecosystemic notion leads to the third of Hollan et al.'s tenets: that of culture and cognition in which an inseparability position is maintained (Sawyer, 2002). In a way that echoes Cole's (1996) account of the mutual shaping of person and culture, and Sawyer's (2002) outline of the inseparability thesis, Hollan et al. (2000) assert that:

> the study of cognition is not separable from the study of culture, because agents live in complex cultural environments. This means, on the one hand, that culture emerges out of the activity of human agents in their historical contexts, as mental, material and social structures interact, and on the other hand, that culture in the form of a history of material artifacts and social practices, shapes cognitive processes, particularly cognitive processes that are distributed over agents, artifacts, and environments.... Permitting the boundary of the unit of analysis to move out beyond the skin situates the individual as an element in a complex cultural environment.... We find that cognition is no longer isolated from culture or separate from it where cognitive science traditionally views culture as a body of content on which the cognitive processes of individual persons operate, in the distributed cognition perspective, culture shapes the cognitive processes of systems that transcend the boundaries of individuals.
>
> (Hollan et al., 2000, p. 178)

Guided by the assertions of these three tenets, Hollan et al. (2000) propose significant methodological developments in the guise of a new kind of cognitive ethnography in which attention is directed towards events and on studying 'not only in what people know, but in how they go about using what they know to do what they do' (p. 176). In order to carry out such research work, they note that there is a need for the development and design of research methods along with a creative approach to the incorporation of methods that are legacies from other fields of enquiry. As should always be the case, the selection of methodologies and methods should always be driven by the nature of the research questions. Sadly, this basic maxim is not always observed. There is also a parallel case for the forms of theoretically driven descriptions of events or activities that are the object of study. Such descriptions must be developed at a level of delicacy which is commensurate with the research questions in hand. As I will argue in Chapter 6, this calls for a language of description which is capable of generating such descriptions. My suggestion is that much of the research that is carried out under the label of distributed cognition struggles to identify a language of description which is capable of generating appropriate accounts of the events/practices/activities that are so central to the notion of a distributed cognitive system.

In the new forms of cognitive ethnography advocated by Hollan *et al.* (2000), video and audio recording and the analysis of recordings of events (Goodwin and Goodwin, 1996; Suchman, 1987) is used as it is in the recent developments in activity-theory-driven research which is discussed in Chapter 5. Much of the research conducted under the banner of distributed cognition tends to focus on events in which humans used machines whether these machines are very large and complex such as naval vessels and aircraft or smaller personal machines with which individuals carry out complex tasks. Increasingly, such machines automatically make records of events and these records of histories of interaction can become important sources of data (cf. Hill and Hollan, 1994). That such data are becoming available not only points to new ways of gaining insight into complex cognitive systems, but also points to more general matter in that it directs our attention to the ways in which information is stored, displayed and arranged in the social world in which events take place. The challenge for research is to 'see' the ways in which such data are deployed, specifically as to how actors engage with and use such data and arrange sources of data as they engage in complex forms of distributed cognitive work. The concept of cognitive 'offloading' is relevant here in that it refers to the ways in which actors co-ordinate material things and others during events in order to minimise the cognitive demands of complex tasks. The dynamics of the ways in which such offloading is orchestrated thus becomes an important aspect of the observational field in research.

As shown in Figure 4.1, Hollan *et al.* have developed a map which seeks to integrate all the key aspects of the research activity which they argue should constitute a new approach to research, specifically research concerned with Computer–Human Interaction. This map shows that distributed cognition, ethnography and experiment can together help to inform the design of work materials which themselves transform the workplace and the way in which cognition is distributed in the course of events. The introduction of an experimental

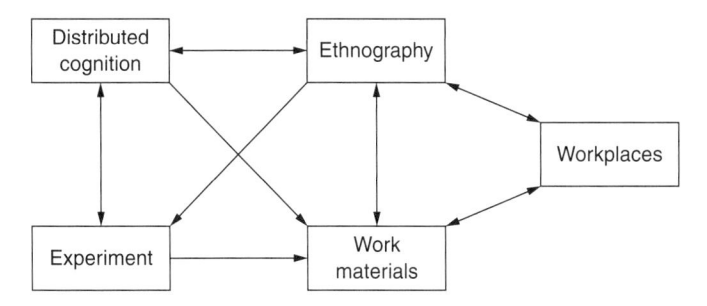

Figure 4.1 Integrated research activity map (source: Hollan et al., 2000, p. 181).

element into research is seen as an important adjunct to the observational practices of cognitive ethnography which is oriented to the meanings that arise, whereas experiments can be used as a means for developing and testing theory and thus give rise to the design of new work materials that in turn can be made open for study.

> [C]ognitive ethnography is an observational field, the inferences we would like to draw are at times underconstrained by the available data. The richness of real-world settings places limits on the power of observational methods. This is where well-motivated experiments come in. In these cases, the findings of cognitive ethnography may suggest 'ethnographically natural' experiments to enrich our data.
>
> (Hollan *et al.*, 2000, p. 181)

Dynamics of historical change

Thus, an iterative approach to the design of new forms of machine interfaces is enhanced through the incorporation of experimental methods into cognitive ethnography. This map of mixed methods constitutes an advance in the field but it is clearly not the 'end of the story' of development in this field. Geoffrey Saxe and Indigo Esmonde (2005) point to an important omission in the gaze of such research, in that it does not engage with the 'dynamics of historical change'.

> In studies of dairy workers loading crates (Scribner, 1984), navy personnel operating a ship (Hutchins, 1995), and street children engaged with the sale of goods (Nunes, Schliemann, & Carraher, 1993; Saxe, 1988), investigators showed how the cognitive activities of individuals draw on properties of artifacts and the activities of others in structuring and solving local tasks. Though such studies pointed to the importance of historically situated activities in cognitive analyses, they did not focus on the dynamics of historical change itself and its relation to the conceptual activities of individuals.

> Further, many of these studies are not developmental. That is, they do not offer ways of understanding processes of people's developmental trajectories as they engaged with historically situated practices.
>
> (Saxe and Esmonde, 2005, p. 173)

They discuss Luria's (1976) attempt to incorporate history during the expedition to Uzbekistan which was planned with Vygotsky. The sampling of people with different levels of engagement in the newly emergent practices of collectivised agriculture and the examination of responses to specific cognitive tasks (such as syllogisms) allowed him to consider the ways in legacy cognitions may be brought in to play with large-scale shifts in practice (e.g. from a so-called peasant agrarian economy to the practices of state-owned collective farming). Whilst this study was less than clear about the culturally specific nature of privileged and privileging forms of thinking and reasoning, it did attempt to incorporate a historical dimension into the research design. It was much later in the last century that Michael Cole and colleagues brought forward a less eurocentric account of such phenomena on the basis of studies conducted in Liberia (e.g. Cole *et al.*, 1971; Scribner and Cole, 1981; and as reported in Cole, 1996).

Greenfield's studies of shifts in pedagogic practices in the work of Mexican weavers pointed to developmental effects of changing historical circumstances again as the economy was transformed under commercial pressure (e.g. Greenfield, 1993, p. 99; Greenfield *et al.*, 1997). However, as Saxe and Esmonde (2005) point out, this body of work does not demonstrate how individuals act to shape and transform practice as history is made. Cast in terms of the way in which individuals shape and are shaped by cultural practice, the caution advanced by Saxe and Esmonde is that research should show how individuals shape historical change and how historical change affects individuals' practices. As noted by Saxe (2004):

> Taking the individual as an historical subject complicates but also enriches epistemological and psychological analyses of cognitive development. It requires the elaboration of new analytic units to support empirical inquiry, ones that open up opportunities for analysing the interplay between historical and developmental processes in the micro-, socio- and ontogenetic construction of knowledge.
>
> (Saxe, 2004, p. 261)

Situated cognition, situated learning and communities of practice

A much-cited debate between the respective positions occupied by Greeno (1991, p. 97) and Anderson *et al.* (1996) concerning situative versus cognitive perspectives is often used as a device to denote a complex and convoluted history of difference within social science. DeCorte *et al.* (1996) summarised the central tensions as follows:

from a concentration on the individual to a concern for social and cultural factors; from 'cold' to 'hot' cognition; from the laboratory to the classroom as the arena for research; and from technically to humanistically grounded methodologies and interpretive approaches.

(DeCorte *et al.*, 1996, p. 491)

In so doing, they suggest that the Anderson *et al.* (1997) argument, that the differences were largely a matter of terminology, was misplaced or underestimated the extent of the difference beween traditional cognitive psychology and the later distributed and situated accounts. DeCorte's distinction echoes Norman's (1993) earlier account of the cognitive/situated divide. In the following statement he expands on the idea of the lone individual as cognitive processor:

All the action is inside the head, yielding a natural distinction between the stuff out there and the processes taking place inside here. What could be more natural than to study the human by recognizing that the brain is the computational engine of thought, and thereby concentrating one's efforts upon understanding brain mechanisms and mental representations? Seems pretty obvious. Sure, there is a lot of action in the world at large and within sociocultural groups, but cognitive processing occurs within the heads of individuals. So, all we have to do is understand the internal mental processes and the nature of the input/output transformations of individuals, and we will have covered everything that matters.

(Norman, 1993, pp. 3–4)

In contrast, he offers this account of what he terms the field of 'situated cognition':

Human knowledge and interaction cannot be divorced from the world. To do so is to study a disembodied intelligence, one that is artificial, unreal, and uncharacteristic of actual behavior. What really matters is the situation and the parts that people play. One cannot look at just the situation, or just the environment, or just the person. To do so is to destroy the very phenomenon of interest. After all, it is the mutual accommodation of people and the environment that matters, so to focus upon only aspects in isolation is to destroy the interaction, to eliminate the role of the situation upon cognition and action.

(Norman, 1993, p. 4)

He casts his contrast in ways that echo Sawyer's (2002) methodological divide, analysed in terms of the separability thesis that he draws from scrutiny of writings within sociology but that also serve to order the sociocultural field.

Socioculturalists who accept inseparability reject two approaches to the study of human action associated with traditional psychology:

1 Methodological individualism ... the objects of sociocultural study are events, activity and practice, and they are considered to be irreducible to properties of individuals.
2 An ecological or 'social influence' approach that conceives of the individual acting in, and influenced by, an external context or environment.... Inseparability is incompatible with conceptions of the relation between individual and sociocultural context that assume that the individual acts 'in' a context, or that the individual is 'influenced by' the context; such conceptions implicitly accept the possibility of methodological separability between individual and situation (see Rogoff, 1982, 1990, 1998).

(Sawyer, 2002, p. 285)

Whilst Vera and Simon (1993a, b) have complained about the lack of 'operational definitions' in the situative approach, it remains the case that there is little consensus about what precisely is meant by terms such 'situated cognition', 'situated action' or 'situativity', let alone the methodological assumptions that underpin particular examples of such research in the literature. Sawyer (2002) and Sfard (1998) both point to a central methodological difference between cognitivist and situative approaches as that of the distinction between a process ontology and 'things' or entity ontology: 'Entities and objects are not the fundamental categories of being; rather, process is fundamental, and entities are derivative of or based in process: "[T]he ultimate atoms of social reality are *events* ... they are the only elementary ontological objects"' (Sawyer, 2002, p. 286). However, as Sawyer (2002) notes, this distinction also has some organising force within the 'situative' or 'situated' field itself, in that 'we could accept the traditional "entity" view that individuals and groups both exist and nonetheless argue that it is methodologically necessary to study situated practices'. Wertsch and Cole take this approach, whereas Rogoff and Lave and Wenger adopt the stronger stance of a process ontology (Sawyer, 2002, p. 293).

The situated development of theory

It would appear that the personal academic histories and trajectories of personal participation within academic domains of individuals or groups have exerted some considerable influence on the shaping of the field. Anthropologists like Lave (1988; and Wenger, 1991) and Suchman (1993), who often deploy the terms 'situated action' or 'situated learning' as descriptors of their work, have drawn on anthropology, critical and post-Vygotskian theory. Their research tends to focus on meaning as it arises in specific forms of cultural practice and in so doing tends not to announce itself with terms like cognition. This is unlike those researchers whose backgrounds lie more in cognitive science, systems design and psychology, such as Norman (1993) and Clancey (1995a, p. 97), whose central focus is cognition itself, albeit at individual and social levels. However, it is important to note that Clancey (2007) himself views situated cognition as having developed instrumentally, not simply within Artificial Intelligence, psychology or educational technology, but as a 'way of thinking' or seeing challenges within psychology, biology, ethology, sociology, psychiatry and philosophy. This position on new ways of seeing and thinking is commensurate with the view of cognition itself which emerges from the literature on situated cognition. Rather than being considered and studied as form of high-level 'expertise', it is conceived of and studied as 'ability to find one's way around the world, to learn new ways of seeing things, and to coordinate activity' (Clancey, 1997, p. 1).

There are a number of writers who retain a focus on cognition but who maintain a marked theoretical distance from those whose work is associated with traditional cognitive science. On the one hand, Agre (1997) and Brooks (1991, 1999), amongst others, have pointed to the need to study persons co-ordinating activity, acting and interacting with the environment and the physical activity that they undertake in such interactions as part of the process of studying cognition. This incorporation of the physical bodily, indeed, biological mechanisms that are involved in interaction with the environment and its artefacts stretches the gaze of research and brings with it a critique of traditional within-person cognitive science. There is again a marked difference between this approach to the study of cognition and that which strives to show how social identification and academic learning are intertwined. Although writing from the perspective of linguistic anthropology of education, Wortham (2006) has added another dimension to the field through his demonstration that 'even apparently pure academic discourse is thoroughly interwoven with allegedly irrelevant processes like social identification, power relations and interpersonal struggles' (Wortham, 2006, p. 283). In Wortham (2001), he focused on the interactional functions of speech that can facilitate the cognitive accomplishments speakers make through that speech. In a general argument about the interrelation between cognition and interaction, he argues that, in institutions such as schools, cognition cannot be extricated from enduring social structures and the construction of social identity (Wortham, 2001, p. 39). Accordingly, and in line with Sawyer's (2002) depiction of a process ontology, knowledge is seen as arising dynamically. That is, it is constructed, remembered, and reinterpreted and articulated within a social context which is regulated by social relations of power and control. It is therefore distributed across a population according to the ways in which the ecology or social situation of that population is structured, and within which it is socially reproduced, shaped and transformed by individuals and groups, in part by the same formative influences that maintain social positions in the ordering of populations.

This work demonstrates the 'flakiness' of some of the categories that are used to organise the field. My criteria for inclusion in this section have been related to a clear focus on cognition rather action. Arguably, Wortham's work could be equally well placed within the next chapter which is concerned with situated action models such as those developed by Lave. The key distinction is with the extent to which cognition and situation are seen as separable. Thus, as one would perhaps predict, despite a near-consensus within the situated cognition field on the limitations of traditional cognitive theory, there is clearly much less agreement as to the exact nature of the new alternative.

External representations

There is certainly considerable overlap between research in the field of situated cognition and that which resides within the framework of distributed cognition, which is witnessed in the attention that is directed to both situatedness and embodiment. For example, Greeno and Moore (1993), amongst many others, study the role of specific local external representations in cognition. In line with the assertions of distributed cognition, external representations are taken as part of cognitive systems. Scaife and Rogers (1996) considered the way in which internal and external representations are integrated into such cognitive systems and in so doing proposed a framework for investigating what they termed 'external' cognition. This emphasis on the importance of studying the interaction between internal and external structures has frequently been applied to the study of the way in which a web page may be read. The notion of external cognition carries with it the notion of 'computational offloading', a term which attempts to capture the way in which external representations support or exacerbate cognitive demands (Scaife and Rogers, 1996). These are:

- re-representation – how different external representations, with the same abstract structure, make problem-solving easier or more difficult and how different strategies and representations, showing variability in efficiency for solving a problem, are selected and used by individuals.
- graphical constraining – the way graphical elements in a graphical representation are able to constrain the kinds of inferences that can be made about the underlying represented concept.
- temporal and spatial constraining – this refers to the way different representations can make relevant aspects of processes and events more salient when distributed over time and space. (Adapted from Scaife and Rogers, 1996.)

Clancey argues a case for the study of situated cognition in terms of the way it relates social, behavioral/psychological and neural perspectives of knowledge and action (Clancey, 1997, p. 343). His arguments concerning stored representations and symbolic processing have fluctuated over the years. In 1993, he asserted that 'every act of deliberation occurs as an immediate behavior' (Clancey, 1993, p. 111), thus eliminating them from his thesis. In Clancey (1995a and 1997) he gradually acknowledged a more inclusive model. It is perhaps Greeno and the Middle School Mathematics Through Applications Projects Group (1998) who have made the clearest statement of the way in which this dialect of psychology has developed through the incorporation of increasingly sophisticated accounts of cognitive processes within and without the head following the early-days nihilism of behaviourism. Their case is one of progressive incorporation into models of situated cognition:

> Behaviorist principles tend to characterize learning in terms of acquisition of skill. Cognitive principles tend to characterize learning in terms of growth of conceptual understanding and general strategies of thinking and understanding. Situative principles tend to characterize learning in terms of more effective participation in practices of inquiry and discourse that include constructing meanings of concepts and uses of skills. We argue here that the situative perspective, focused on practices, can subsume the cognitive and behaviorist perspectives by including both conceptual understanding and skill acquisition as valuable aspects of students' participation and their identities as learners and knowers. Both the behaviorist skill-oriented and cognitive understanding-oriented perspectives have informed the development of educational practices significantly, but they are often portrayed, in research literature and the popular press, as diametrical opposites, where learning according to one view precludes learning according to the other. We argue here that important strengths and values of behaviorist and cognitive practices can be included in practices on the basis of the situative principles of valuing students' learning to participate in inquiry and sense-making. Situative principles can provide a useful framework for evaluating the contributions of behaviorist and cognitive practices in a larger context.
>
> (Greeno et al., 1998, pp. 14–15)

The essence of this argument, that the situative can subsume cognitive and behaviourist perspectives, preserves the assumptions of the earlier work and wraps them in a new situative cloak, marking out a significant difference with the situated action and community of practice perspectives. The work of the situation is often seen to be brought about by the vector of external representations that load and offload the cognitive and behavioural mechanisms. The gaze of the researcher is directed in many directions within and without the head. Before rushing to assumptions of criticality of this kind of research work, I will invoke Sfard's (1998) warnings concerning the dangers of narrowly applying a single theory to practice, which in this case is educational practice, although the cautions are of more general application:

> When a theory is translated into an instructional prescription, exclusivity becomes the worst enemy of success. Educational practices have an overpowering propensity for extreme, one-for-all practical recipes. A trendy mixture of constructivist, social-interactionist, and situationist approaches is often translated into a total banishment of 'teaching by telling,' an imperative to make 'cooperative learning' mandatory to all, and a complete delegitimization of instruction that is not 'problem-based' or not situated in a real-life context. But this means putting too much of a good thing into one pot. Because no two students have the same needs and no two teachers arrive at their best performance in the same way, theoretical exclusivity and didactic single-mindedness can be trusted to make even the best of educational ideas

fail.... Dictatorship of a single metaphor, like a dictatorship of a single ideology, may lead to theories that serve the interests of certain groups to the disadvantage of others.

(Sfard, 1998, pp. 10–11)

With this thought in mind, I will now move to the related field of accounts of situated action and learning in the next chapter.

Chapter 5

Situated action and communities of practice

This chapter is concerned with a move from research that takes its major preoccupation as being that of cognition to a more concerted interest in action. Alongside this move there comes a more detailed analysis of social practices and social processes, rather than a primary focus on the investigation, description and analysis of cognitive processes. This is associated with a change in the 'driving discipline' from psychology to anthropology and also a shift in research topic from external systems (that of late have often been in the form of web designs or computer-based artefacts of some description) to historically more established forms of human activity – often that of traditional work. As Bredo (1994) notes, situated cognition may be seen as 'shifting the focus from individual *in* environment to individual *and* environment' (Bredo, 1994, p. 29), whereas theories of situated action and learning, as Lave (1988) notes, are more concerned with the 'everyday activity of persons acting in [a] setting' (Lave, 1988, p. 1); the latter's emphasis being on the study of the 'emergent, contingent nature of human activity, the way activity grows directly out of the particularities of a given situation'.

Transfer from situation to situation

Those who emphasise the situated character of learning often affirm that knowledge is situated or grounded in particular activities and social contexts. It emphasises the sociocultural nature of learning. However, there is a deeper interpretation of situated learning:

> It is a theory about the nature of human knowledge, claiming that knowledge is dynamically constructed as we conceive of what is happening to us, talk and move. Especially, our *conception of our activity* within a social matrix shapes and constrains what we think, do, and say. That is, our action is *situated in our role* as a member of a community.
>
> (Clancey, 1995a, p. 16)

The interest of those who take this view of learning is in the interactions of the individual with the situation. The unit of analysis is thus the individual and the situation and not merely the mind of the individual.

As Suchman (1987) points out, the emphasis is on the often temporary and moment-by-moment activity that takes place in and with a particular situation. In her strong account of inseparability, the notion of what counts as a 'situation' becomes almost elusive given its ongoing reformulation. The calibration of 'situation' is not only unachievable, it is a task which is incommensurate with the fundamental assumption of the approach. Similarly, durability over time and persistence or even transfer across contexts are either discounted or not placed in a prioritised position in the researcher's analytic lens. To the extent that some models of situated action privilege the emergent and that which is improvised, they consequently downplay a consideration of features, both of the situation and the person acting in the situation, that are routine and predictable. I am making a strong case here and it should be noted that not all adherents of situated action take this position. Suchman (1987), for example, appears to show more concern for routines of one type or another. Greeno (1997, 2006) posits the existence of common or recognisable patterns of participation in various sites as an explanation of transfer. Also with regard to situation specificity, Beach (1995) and Bowers (1996) discuss a theoretical position which they use to explain instances of transfer in situated terms. Beach (1999) argues against both 'within the head' and simple 'within the context' notions of transfer. He seeks to develop an account of the interweaving of mind and context over time and that human beings purposively cut transects across settings and shape and are shaped by them: 'Any sociocultural reconceptualization of transfer should be true to the premise that underlies all sociocultural approaches to learning and development: that learners and social organizations exist in a recursive and mutually constitutive relation to one another across time' (Beach, 1999, p. 111). Tuomi-Grohn *et al.* (2003) provide a well-researched and important review of the tension between constructivist/cognitivist and situated accounts of transfer which concludes with an analysis drawn from activity theory, which will be discussed in Chapter 6.

Beyond 'within the head' models

The important common factor which links the writing of researchers such as Suchman (1987) and Lave (1988), amongst many others, is that they take up a methodological stance which challenges the within person, insulated 'in the head' that either ignores the situation or context in which it is enacted or downplays the understanding of situated action. Suchman, Lave and others are directly challenging the insulated view of cognition that ignores these contextual factors. The social and individual are not connected in a mechanical manner by some device which acts much like the lead in an electronic system, as a conduit of data from the outside to the inside, nor are the person and the situation simply different levels of analysis. The mutual constitution of person and situation in an ongoing, emergent dialectical interplay of inseparable co-formation is posited. As Lave and Wenger (1991) note: '"Situated" ... implies that a given social practice is multiply interconnected with other aspects of ongoing social processes in activity systems at many levels of particularity and generality' (p. 84). These arguments that have been promulgated by Lave and Wenger (1991) in terms of situated learning, or indeed by sociologists such as Giddens (1974, 1984, 1989) who shares a phenomenological influence in theorising human action which may be attributed to Heidegger (1978a). The assumption is that much social action is pre-reflexive and embedded in the specificities of the local rhythms and routines of ongoing activity. The ongoing negotiation of meaning arises as a dialectical ricochet between the way in which the world is locally defined and the recreation of those definitions and understandings as personal meaning struggles with, acts upon and is shaped by collective understanding. This is witnessed in Suchman's (1987) statement that 'the organization of situated action is an emergent property of moment-by-moment interactions between actors, and between actors and the environments of their action'. An account of situated learning posits 'learning as a social and cultural activity and success is not focused upon the cognitive attributes that individuals possess, but upon the ways in which those attributes play out in interaction with the world' (Boaler, 1999, p. 260). It is Sawyer (2002) who develops a cautionary note on the unrealised methodological demands of such ontological and epistemological aspirations.

Methods for situated accounts

Rogoff and Chavajay (1995) provide a very useful discussion of the evolution of methods for the investigation of the cultural basis of cognitive development. Their discussion starts with an account of the deployment of cognitive tasks developed in Europe and North America (such as those associated with Piaget) in other cultural settings in the 1970s. It then moves to a consideration of the way in which researchers took account of arguments concerning the cultural specificity of both educational practices and the capacity to solve specific tasks that at one time would have been designed to assess some form of universal developmental feature. Examples are to be found in the field of literacy in the writing of Olson (1976), Scribner and Cole (1981) and Goody and Watt (1968), and numeracy through the work of Lave (1977) and Carraher *et al.* (1985). As they note:

> The research of the late 1970s and early 1980s demonstrated the importance of not assuming generality of ability on the basis of experience with any particular practices. It also drew attention to the roles of values and practices involved in cognitive performances in the test situation as well as outside it.
> (Rogoff and Chavajay, 1995, p. 865)

Vygotskian theory was deployed (albeit in slightly different ways) to argue this case. Rogoff and Chavajay (1995) point to the work of Goodnow (1976) and the challenge it mounts to the idea that a test can be deployed without due consideration of the immediate cultural context in which it is administered. This research was further developed by scholars such as Mehan (1979), who discussed an approach to studying the institutional contexts of learning, teaching and testing.

With admirable clarity, Rogoff and Chavajay (1995) show how a move has taken place from regarding 'culture as an independent variable affecting cognition to regarding cognitive processes as inherently cultural' (p. 873). They also point to the then future which they understood as developing:

> questions of how participation by individuals in certain cultural practices relates to participation in others, how cognition involves communication in the context of institutional and cultural practices, how learning involves transformations not only of skills but of identity, how development involves creation of new forms as well as use of given forms, and how communities and individuals manage diverse practices across overlapping or separate institutions and communities.
>
> (Rogoff and Chavajay, 1995, p. 873)

The struggle to articulate the notion of context or situation has been approached in a number of ways. Lave's (1988) formulation, which flows from the argument sketched above, is that the focus of research must be the relations between the individual and the context or situation. Early-day research such as Lave *et al.* (1984) had demonstrated the situation-specific nature of 'cognitive processes' in everyday situations. Consequently, Lave argued for a focus on what people were actually doing in a particular situation. This anthropologically driven demand still calls for definitions of what counts as context or situation. Lave's (1988) answer is to distinguish between the stable institutional framework or 'arena' in which activity takes place and the way in which that arena is acted upon by participants in that activity and thence becomes the 'setting'. This shows a marked difference from the approach adopted by Scribner and Cole (1981), who acknowledged knowledge, skills and technologies as the components of practices in a formulation which appears to reveal a more avowedly cognitive background. From Sawyer's (2002) point of view, the cognitive essence of this work positions it as a methodological assumption of separability. This early work, which appears to be grounded in a psychological model, has been replaced in a development from the social as context to a cultural-historical account which argues for a much less separable understanding of social and cultural influences from an understanding of individual functioning, as in Cole (1996) and Scribner (1985). I will pursue these developments in the context of the influence of activity theory in Chapter 6.

Community of practice

My turn at this point is to consider the hugely influential notion of a 'community of practice' which grew out of the work on learning that researchers such as

Seely Brown, Duguid, Lave and Suchman initiated in the 1980s. A number of terms have been put in circulation by such work: the 'participation metaphor' and 'enculturation' (Brown *et al.*, 1989); 'guided participation' (Rogoff, 1990), or 'legitimate peripheral participation' (Lave and Wenger, 1991); and 'improved participation in interactive systems' (Greeno, 1997). Perhaps the best known is the introduction that a reader may gain through a reading of Lave and Wenger (1991). From the argument for a focus on 'the activity of persons acting in setting', set up by Lave (1988), flows the distinction between arena and setting mentioned above. The roots of much of this work are to be found in the shift in focus made by anthropologists to study learning which had, until relatively recently, remained absent from their research agenda. Lave (1988) discusses emergent improvisation in the situated action of workers as they respond to the fluctuations and regularities in their environment. Problem solution is seen as a response which is, in part, structured and supported by features of that environment. Meanings are 'indexicalised' by the shared context in which they are used and in this way conversation is made possible in an emergent and intertwined coalescence of persons and context. This was shown very clearly in Suchman's (1987) account of the use of a help system attached to a sophisticated photocopier. As a consequence, forms of competent functioning are in many ways 'locked' into the context in which they take place, thereby undermining traditional notions of transfer.

As noted above, critics have raised concerns regarding the transferability of learning in the situated approach. However, the question of 'transfer' takes on a new meaning as compared to the traditional understanding. Successful transfer here denotes improved participation:

> Portability of knowledge is less important than whether everyone knows at least something relevant to the mission of the group. How can marginal individuals (e.g. children) find a legitimate place in the group's activities, and gradually become able to participate more centrally (Lave & Wenger, 1991; Sfard, 1998)? And if knowledge is indeed situated in particular activities or roles, then the very term transfer is a misnomer, since it implies movement of an intact object from one container of knowledge (e.g. my brain) to another (e.g. your brain). When social constructivists engage the problems of participation and transfer, they frame them not in terms of transfer, but of recontextualizing experience: what was learned previously is not transported to new situations, like a suitcase full of tools, but rather combined with new experiences into broader, more enriched knowledge and skills.
> (Seifert, 2002, p. 202)

The idea of transfer depends on how a situation is transformed. Knowledge transfer may be taken to refer to the way in which knowledge travels across barriers or boundaries that are maintained within and between contexts. Sfard (1998) explains that the idea is meaningless when there are no boundaries to be crossed, because in the situated perspective neither knowledge nor contexts are viewed as clearly demarcated. The situation and the role of the learner within the situation are important factors from this perspective.

At the centre of the community of practice initiative is the idea of participants being, in some way, brought together and sustained in relation to a particular common practice within which shared understandings and a common language develop. Lave and Wenger (1991) define a community in terms of such participatory learning processes:

> In using the term community, we do not imply some primordial culture-sharing entity. We assume that members have different interests, make diverse contributions to activity and hold varied viewpoints. In our view, participation at multiple levels is entailed in membership in a community of practice. Nor does the term community imply necessarily co-presence, a well-defined, identifiable group or socially visible boundaries. It does imply participation in an activity system about which participants share understandings concerning whatever they are doing and what that means.
> (Lave and Wenger, 1991, p. 171)

Learning as a process is linked with identity formation as in Brown and Duguid (2000), who see learning as demand driven, a social act and as identity formation. Lave and Wenger argue that persons 'become' as they progressively involve themselves with the activities of a community. In this way, learning means to move from peripheral participation to full membership within a knowledge community (Lave and Wenger, 1991). This theme is also pursued by Holland *et al.* (1998) and Wenger (1998), who theorised identity as a 'way of talking about how learning changes who we are and creates personal histories of becoming in the context of our communities':

> We have attempted to articulate the relation of person and society in a way that makes light of neither social life nor the world of the psyche. At the same time, we reject a dichotomy between the sociological and the psychological. 'Person' and 'society' are alike as sites, or moments of the production and reproduction of social practices. But there is a substantiality to both sites. ... Forms of personhood and forms of society are historical products, intimate and public, that situate the interactivity of social practices. It is in this doubly historical landscape that we place human identities. We take identity to be a central means by which selves, and the sets of actions they organize, form and re-form over personal lifetimes and in the histories of social collectivities.
> (Holland *et al.*, 1998, p. 270)

Clearly Holland *et al.* (1998) bring a historical dimension into the analysis, perhaps more strongly than do Lave and Wenger (1991). Both groups struggle to provide an account of identity which is grounded in the material organisation of world.

Power, conflict and history in communities of practice

Hodkinson (2004) reminds his readers, in a way that echoes Vygotsky, that the rational and emotional are part of each other. Both are located in our sometimes deeply held and often largely tacit beliefs about the world, education, research and writing. Arguing from his base in educational research he deploys the notion of 'field' from Bourdieu (1988, 1998) and Bourdieu and Wacquant (1992) to assert that learning is embodied, being emotional, social, cultural and partly tacit (Hodkinson, 2004, p. 23). These views are, to some extent, acknowledged in the idea of 'legitimate peripheral participation', as suggested by Lave and Wenger (1991), in that participants acquire the knowledge and values they need to be full members of, and competent within, a community. Participants start out as newcomers on the periphery of the community and gradually, through observation and incremental participation with the established community members, the so-called old-timers, acquire the understandings and values along with the way of speaking that constitutes the community. In this way, they gradually move to the centre of the community and newcomers become old-timers equipped with the knowledge, understanding, language and identities of full community members; 'learning, thinking, and knowing are relations among people engaged in activity *in, with, and arising from the socially and culturally structured world*' (Lave, 1997, p. 67). Jay Lemke makes this explicit when he links activity, modes of participation, processes of learning, and individual identities:

> Our activity, our participation, our 'cognition' is always bound up with, codependent with, the participation and the activity of others, be they persons, tools, symbols, processes, or things. How we participate, what practices we come to engage in, is a function of the whole community ecology ... As we participate, we change. Our identity-in-practice develops, for we are no longer autonomous Persons in this model, but Persons-in-Activity.
>
> (Lemke, 1997, p. 38)

Lemke extends this 'within a moment of time' analysis to incorporate or at least place particular emphasis on the need for a historical perspective. His argument is that a particular situation can only be understood and analysed by reference to the history of participants and associated groups:

> We interpret a text or a situation in part by connecting it to other texts and situations that our community or our individual history has made us see as relevant to the meaning of the present one. Our community, and each of us, creates networks of connections (and disconnections) among texts, situations

and activities. These networks of connections that we make, and that are made in the self-organizing activity of the larger systems to which we belong, extend backwards in time as well [as] outwards into the social-material world.

(Lemke, 1997, p. 50)

Hodkinson (2004) also notes that, whilst Lave and Wenger (1991) are clear that there are significant issues of power and conflict in this process of becoming a full member of a community of practice, in that tensions arise between newcomers and full participants:

> unequal relations of power must be included more systematically in our analysis.... It would be useful to understand better how these relations generate characteristically interstitial communities of practice and truncate possibilities for identities of mastery [p. 42] ....
> Any given attempt to analyze a form of learning through legitimate peripheral participation must involve analysis of the political and social organization of that form, its historical development, and the effects of both of these on sustained possibilities for learning [p. 64] ....
> Thus, participation in the cultural practice in which any knowledge exists is an epistemological principle of learning. The social structure of this practice, its power relations, and its conditions for legitimacy define possibilities for learning (i.e., for legitimate peripheral participation) [p. 98] ....
> In addition to forms of membership and construction of identities, these terms and questions include the location and organization of mastery in communities; problems of power, access, and transparency; developmental cycles of communities of practice; change as part of what it means to be a community of practice; and its basis in the contradiction between continuity and displacement [p. 123].
>
> (Lave and Wenger, 1991)

From my point of view these tensions are acknowledged but remain under-theorised. These are themes to which I will return in Chapters 6 and 7.

Barab and Duffy (2000) provide their own summary, as shown in Table 5.1, of the characteristics of a community which captures many of the points outlined above.

Knowledge in a community of practice

Within the community of practice approach, knowledge is understood, in a way that echoes Dewey, 'not as a mental state; rather, it is an experienced relation of things, and it has no meaning outside of such relations (Dewey, 1981, p. 185). Brown and Duguid (1991) argue that such knowledge is characterised by a low degree of codification: 'Learners are acquiring not explicit, formal "expert know-

Table 5.1 Characteristics of a community (after Barab and Duffy (2000))

Common cultural and historical heritage	Communities go beyond the simple coming together for a particular moment in response to a specific need. Successful communities have a common cultural and historical heritage that partially captures the socially negotiated meanings. This includes shared goals, meanings, and practices. However, unlike the social negotiation of practice fields that primarily occurs on the fly, in communities of practice new members inherit much of these goals, meanings and practices from previous community members' experiences in which they were hypothesised, tested and socially agreed upon.
Interdependent system	Individuals are becoming a part of something larger as they work within the context and become interconnected to the community, which is also a part of something larger (the society through which it has meaning/value) This helps provide a sense of shared purpose, as well as an identity, for the individual and the larger community.
Reproduction cycle	It is important that communities have the ability to reproduce as new members engage in mature practice with near peers and exemplars of mature practice. Over time, these 'newcomers' come to embody the communal practice (and rituals) and may even replace 'old timers'.

ledge," but the embodied ability to behave as community members' (p. 48). Brown *et al.* (1989) argue that knowing and doing are reciprocal – knowledge is situated and progressively developed through activity and that one should abandon the notion that concepts are *self-contained entities*, instead conceiving them as *tools*, which can only be fully understood through use. Learning is understood as a process which is often tacit and takes place through shared or joint action and has a generative effect on the pattern activities in which it occurs.

> The notion of situated learning now appears to be a transitory concept, a bridge, between a view according to which cognitive processes (and thus learning) are primary and a view according to which social practice is the primary, generative phenomenon, and learning is one of its characteristics. There is a significant contrast between a theory of learning in which practice (in a narrow, replicative sense) is subsumed within processes of learning and one in which learning is taken to be an integral aspect of practice (in a historical, generative sense). In our view, learning is not merely situated in practice – as if it were some independently reifiable process that just happened to be located somewhere; learning is an integral part of generative social practice in the lived-in world.... Legitimate peripheral participation is proposed as a descriptor of engagement in social practice that entails learning as an integral constituent.
> (Lave and Wenger, 1999, p. 86)

100 Situated action and communities of practice

Table 5.2 Focus of psychological and anthropological views of situativity theory (after Barab and Duffy (2000))

	Psychological views	*Anthropological views*
Focus	Cognition	Individuals' relations to community
Learners	Students	Members of communities of practice
Unit of analysis	Situated activity	Individual in community
What is produced from interactions	Meaning	Meanings, identities, and communities
Learning arena	Schools	Everyday world
Goal of learning	Prepare for future tasks	Meet immediate community/ societal needs
Pedagogical implications	Practice fields	Communities of practice

These views are captured in elements of Table 5.2, also produced by Barab and Duffy (2000), in which they contrast what they term psychological and anthropological views of situativity theory.

Developments of the community of practice idea

There are many alternatives, extensions and, to some extent, parallel dialects of the community of practice argument. For example, in his later writing Wenger (1998) has offered the view of communities of practice as having three dimensions: mutual engagement; joint enterprise; and a shared repertoire of actions, discourses and tools. Brown and Duguid (1991) extend the discussion to incorporate the notion of a superordinate organisation characterised as a 'community of communities':

> The gap between espoused and actual practice may become too large for noncanonical practices to bridge. To foster working, learning, and innovating, an organization must close that gap. To do so, it needs to reconceive of itself as a community-of-communities, acknowledging in the process the many noncanonical communities in its midst. It must see beyond its canonical abstractions of practice to the rich, full-blooded activities themselves. And it must legitimize and support the myriad enacting activities perpetrated by its different members. This support cannot be intrusive, or it risks merely bringing potential innovators under the restrictive influence of the existing canonical view.
>
> (Brown and Duguid, 1991, p. 53)

Lindkvist (2005) introduces a distinction between the notions of a 'community-of-practice' and a 'collectivity of practice'. He associates the use of the descriptor community-of-practice with groups that have been working together long enough to develop into a cohesive community with relationships of mutuality and shared understandings. In contrast, he deploys collectivity of practice with the ways in which temporary organisations or project organisations operate.

> These are groups which consist of diversely skilled individuals, most of whom have not met before, who have to solve a problem or carry out a pre-specified task within tightly set limits as to time and costs ... operating on a minimal basis of shared knowledge and understandings.
> (Lindkvist, 2005, p. 1189)

The distinction between a 'knowledge community' and a 'knowledge collectivity' is invoked and aligns the community and collectivity with ideal-type notions of epistemology. Albeit in an exploratory manner, he begins to draw distinctions between the different modalities of organisation, as shown in Table 5.3.

As shown in Table 5.4, in her later writing Rogoff (1995) proposes a view of learning and development within a community in terms of three 'inseparable, mutually constituting planes comprising activities that can become the focus of analysis at different times, but with the others necessarily remaining in the background of the analysis' (p. 139). Her suggestion is one of three planes of analysis

Table 5.3 Comparison between the knowledge community and the knowledge collectivity: some important dimensions on which they differ (after Lindkvist (2005))

		The knowledge community	The knowledge collectivity
1	General type of knowledge base	Decentred knowledge	Distributed knowledge
	Type of memory	Blackboard memory	Network memory
	Main repository	Knowledge-as-practice Communal activity and narratives	Individual knowledge and competences
	Integration principle	Knowledge base similarity	Well-connectedness of knowledge bases
2	The individual members' way of learning	Socialization	Problem solving
	Operating basis	Dispositional knowledge	Articulate knowledge
	Type of knowledge worker	Enculturated	Free agent (within limits set)
3	Type of knowledge-development process	Paradigm-driven/normal-science process	Goal-directed trial-and-error/market-like process
4	Epistemological maxim	'We know more than we can tell'	'We tell more than we can know'

Table 5.4 Rogoff's inseparable, mutually constituting planes

Plane of analysis	Developmental process
Personal	Participatory appropriation
Interpersonal	Guided participation
community processes	Apprenticeship

which are: apprenticeship (community/institutional); guided participation (interpersonal); participatory appropriation (personal). This is not to say that one cannot focus on individuals and individual change, but rather that one should strive always to conduct such analysis in relation to features of the system of which they are a part (Rogoff, 2003). In so doing, she flags the need to supplement the notion of participation as the sole focus of analysis.

However, the relationships between the planes of analysis are not made clear. The means by which transformation between levels may occur is not fully explicated, although implicit in the outline. In introducing these planes, it would seem that she softens the somewhat hard line on separability established in Lave's work. Cobb and Bowers (1999) suggest that Hatano's (1993) call to synthesise constructivist and Vygotskian perspectives and Saxe's (1991) discussion of the intertwining of cultural forms of cognitive functions show methodological similarities with the position adopted by Rogoff. Sawyer (2002) notes a discrepancy between a theoretical acceptance of a strong separability thesis and the empirical/methodological stance that she adopts. He also notes the development of her ideas from her view of the context and individual as 'jointly producing psychological events' (Rogoff, 1982, p. 132), which tacitly accepts separate elements or aspects of an occurrence, to a strong 'mutual constitution' view in Rogoff (1990) and the Rogoff (1997) argument that 'the boundary between individual and environment disappears' (p. 267). Sawyer (2002) argues that with the introduction of the analytic distinction between individual, group and community which were termed 'angles', 'windows' (Rogoff, 1990, p. 26) and 'lenses' or 'planes of analysis' (Rogoff, 1997, pp. 267–8) there comes a suggestion of analytic separability:

> although they avoid the ontological connotations of the conventional term 'levels of analysis'. Although 'the three planes cannot be isolated', the analyst can nonetheless examine individual or social as a 'current focus of attention' (1997, p. 269). In referring to these three as 'perspectives' rather than entities, individuals and cultural contexts 'can be considered separately without losing sight of the inherent involvement in the whole' (Rogoff, 1992, p. 317). These perspectives are separable in practice and are in principle not reducible to each other (Rogoff, 1997, p. 269 n. 3). This acceptance of analytic separability is difficult to reconcile with theoretical claims for analytic inseparability.
>
> (Sawyer, 2002, pp. 294–5)

Sawyer (2002) is also dubious about the extent to which claims for a process ontology are actually realised in the work of Lave and Wenger (1991), arguing that a definition of 'person' as a member of community implies a stratified ontology with progressive membership of larger and larger entities as exemplified in the following statement by Lemke:

> Talking physics and writing criticism are *social practices*. They are parts of larger social activities. They are learned socially, function socially, and are socially meaningful. Spoken and written language are social resources for making social meaning. And the specific *genres* and *semantic patterns* of physics, or of literary criticism, are institutionalized social formation, patterns of language *use*, and patterns of *deployment* of the social resources of language in particular communities and subcommittees.
>
> (Lemke, 1988, p. 82)

These arguments point to the gaps and challenges that exist within both sociological and sociocultural theory. The important point is that we should try and at least be aware of the methodological weaknesses when seeking to deploy such understandings. Alternatively, one can revert to Gadamer (1979), who argued that method cannot ensure truth, for truth and knowledge formation entail interpretation, by individuals and by wider research communities collectively (Hodkinson, 2004, p. 23).

Implications of the situated learning approach

With this caution in mind, I will continue to explore some of the implications of the situated learning approach. Lave's analyses of everyday workplace settings such as tailor shops and everyday practices such as a Weight Watchers™ class has given rise to discussions about the practice of school teaching. Given the difficulty that has been experienced with the over-association of Vygotsky's scientific concepts with schooling, it is worth remembering that, despite the fact that all their examples are of fairly close-knit groups of practitioners, Lave and Wenger insist that communities of practice can be dispersed, even virtual (Hodkinson, p. 2004, p. 13). However, Lave did describe how formal learning environments (i.e. schools) tend to commodify knowledge and learning:

> The products of human labour are turned into commodities when they cease to be made for the value of their use in the lives of their maker and are produced in order to exchange them, to serve the interests and purposes of others without direct reference to the lives of their maker.
>
> (Lave, 1993, p. 75)

She also discusses the encapsulation of school learning and offers a radical critique of much of what counts as instruction in schools.

> The way we conceptualize teaching must be rethought within the perspective that takes learners learning, as the fundamental phenomena of which teaching may (or may not) be a part. Learning, taken here to be first and principally the identity-making life projects of participants in communities of practice: The powerful, multiply structured processes of learning in school-settings encompass and subsume what is generally assumed to be the more dominating agenda of school classroom teaching ... Whether and how classroom 'instruction' results in the incorporation of class activities into the life project of students (and all others in schools), depends on the ways they are taken into those life projects.
>
> (Lave, 1996, p. 157)

Suchman (1993) takes up this point when discussing Lave's research in relation to classroom environments:

> [T]he very premise that schools constitute some neutral ground apart from the real world, in which things are learned that are later applied in the real world, is fundamentally misguided ... [A]ll learning is learning in situ ... [S]chools constitute a very specific situation for learning with their own cultural, historical, political, and economic interests: interests obscured by the premise that schools are asituational. Schools prepare students not for some generic form of transfer of things learned in schools to other settings, but to be students, to succeed or to fail, to move into job markets or not, and so forth.
>
> (Suchman, 1993, p. 72)

Not surprisingly, this argument is not without its detractors who, in response to the introduction of the notion of a community of learners working on real-life problems in classrooms, argue that 'learning' the culture of workplaces is not the function of schooling:

> The type of cognition and learning favored by the cognitive apprenticeship approach is primarily connected to unreflected social practice in everyday life activities with no qualitative differentiation between knowledge and practice of different communities – tailors, mathematicians, classrooms, and so forth. Adults' activities in different communities of practice are regarded as unquestioned standards for the goals of development. This approach has no reflected goal for development, and it does not have a theory of the relation between learning and development. However, other ways of conceptualizing the relation between subject-matter concepts and student's everyday knowledge and between learning and development could be promoted in school, for which the cultural-historical tradition of Vygotsky and his followers (Davydov, 1977, 1982, 1989; Hedegaard, 1990, 1995; Lompscher, 1984, 1985) provide a theoretical foundation.
>
> (Hedegaard, 1998, p. 117)

Hedegaard (2007) has further distinguished between different knowledge forms as part of analysis which insists that there is no one-to-one relation between such knowledge forms and institutional practice. She identifies three knowledge forms:

- *Empirical knowledge* which is reflected in abstract concepts that are attained through observation, description, classification, and quantification (Bruner *et al.*, 1956). This knowledge form circulates in everyday life and in many western classrooms.
- *Narrative knowledge* which may be characterized by: (a) changeableness in intentions, (b) possible mutual perspectives and goals which interact, and (c) involvement of feelings and emotions (Bruner, 1986, pp. 16–25). Narrative knowledge and thinking forms can also be seen in 'folk theories' about daily life events.
- *Theoretical – dialectical knowledge* which is related to forms of systematic knowledge. This kind of knowledge can be found in theories and models that can be used to understand events and situations and to organize and experiment with actions (concrete life activities). This type of knowledge can also be found in all professional work where persons have a theory and models for their work. (Adapted from Hedegaard, 2007, pp. 251–2.)

Bernstein's (2000) work on discursive practice and knowledge structures and Hedegaard's enrichment of tools for the analysis of knowledge forms provide important starting points for the development of the original Vygotskian thesis on concept formation. They are clearly at odds with the assumptions of the community of practice theorists. Thus, although Hedegaard and Lave may share an interest in Vygotsky's work, there are great differences in their positions that in this case are conditioned by their views on the nature of knowledge and knowledge structures.

Similarly, a shared interest in the notion of 'habitus' may be witnessed in the work by Wenger (1999), yet there is an acknowledged tension between Bourdieu's use of the concept and that which is found in some of the communities of practice literature. For Bourdieu, habitus constitutes a generative infrastructure which is antithetical to Wenger's notion of 'an emerging property of interacting practices' (Wenger, 1999, p. 96). Where one holds an understanding of that which is formative, the other speaks of that which is formed. This issue is handled somewhat differently in Lave's earlier work, which is:

> concerned with dialectical synthesis, and assume[s] the partially determined, partially determining character of human agency ... Their work recommends the study of social practice in spatial and temporal context. For the synthetic character of these theories makes it difficult to argue for the separation of cognition and the social world.
>
> (Lave, 1988, p. 16)

However, it is possible to point to differences in epistemological and ontological assumptions which serve to create significant divides in the post-Vygotskian field. Their existence is not always made clear and yet they carry with them such important implications for research and the development of theory. This situation would appear to call for two forms of action: that readers of these texts should be encouraged and supported in their efforts to understand the methodological and theoretical lens through which Vygotsky's work is interpreted; and that writers should be encouraged to be much more explicit in their articulation of the assumptions which guide their work.

Applications of the community of practice approach

With these thoughts in mind, I will continue to discuss the application of the community of practice idea. Before doing so, I would wish to point out that that there are many intermediary positions between those I have discussed above. My selection has been guided by a desire to illustrate difference rather than provide a comprehensive overview of the rapidly expanding literature. As an example of research which appears to recognise some of the challenges concerned with the nature of knowledge, I have taken a quotation from recent writing in the field of mathematics education. Despite what I read as some confusion with terms such as situated cognition, Boaler (1999) takes the theoretical position on knowledge boundaries adopted by Lave and places it within a framework which at least recognises an institutional constraint on the perceptions of students, albeit with an interesting comparison between the perceptions of students and 'real' human cognition!

> Lave has moved away from the idea of boundaries that exist between formal and informal knowledge in order to recognise the overlapping and mutually constituting nature of cognition, but the notion of boundaries or barriers may retain some use, not as a means of separating formal and informal knowledge, but as recognition that the unnatural systems and structures we impose on students in schools – the constraints and affordances to which they become attuned – create perceptions of boundaries and barriers amongst students, even if human cognition is naturally more flexible and dynamic.
>
> (Boaler, 1999, p. 280)

Vann and Bowker (2001) offer a radical and trenchant critique of the later stages of the development of the community of practice idea. They suggest that the groundbreaking work undertaken by Lave (1988) on notions of practice has been 'reinstrumentalized and reconfigured as a commercial object with special uses' in the later work of Wenger (1998): ' "practice" is configured first as an instrument of a dereifying critical theory, and then as an instrument of economic value creation' (Vann and Bowker, 2001, p. 248). Their suggestion is that the powerful critique of functionalism which Lave (1988) outlined has been eroded as the community of practice approach has been enveloped by commercial concerns.

There have been similar critiques of the development of Vygotsky's original work. For example, Burmenskaya (1992), a developmental psychologist working in the department of developmental psychology that Gal'perin used to lead, argues that many Western attempts to interpret Vygotsky have been marked more by enthusiasm for Western pedagogical preoccupations than for the concern to understand the range and depth of the arguments. This has been compounded by a marked tendency to ignore the work of more recent Russian writers (see Kozulin *et al.* (2003) for a recent exception). Valsiner (1988) analysed the dissemination of Vygotsky's idea through citations made in journal articles and books. He refers to the 'canalized nature' of references to Vygotsky's writing. Of the 1,373 citations, he identified 1,129 that were made to either 'Thought and language' (*Thinking and Speech*) or *Mind in Society*. Both these texts, he argues, suffer from translation difficulties and, in the case of the original translation of 'Thought and language', severe truncation. For example, almost all references to Marx were expunged from the first English-language translation of 'Thought and language'. As a consequence, the version of neo-Vygotskian Psychology that is being developed in the West is regarded as, at best, partial, if not inaccurate by those concerned with Developmental Psychology in present-day Russia. Yaroshevsky (1989, 1990) and Petrovsky (1990) do provide English-language versions of Russian views of the history of Psychology in general and of Vygotsky's work in particular. Chaiklin (2003) has delved into the some of the more obscure elements of the Vygotskian opus to produce a significant challenge to much of the received understanding of the much-bowdlerised concept of Zone of Proximal Development (ZPD). A key element of his argument is that Western interpretations have subsumed the original intentions within their own culturally situated academic priorities. In a way, this could be argued as an example of a community of practice as a transformer of knowledge and a vehicle of developing values.

This effect may be witnessed in the different approaches to the theorisation and application of the community of practice and community of learners ideas. The examples I will now discuss are but two perspectives among many.

From the perspective of discursive psychology, Linehan and McCarthy (2001) criticise Greeno *et al.* (1998) and Rogoff *et al.* (1996) as paying insufficient attention to the complex relations between individuals and between individuals and communities:

> Taking more account of individual responsiveness to community discourses suggests that as people engage in joint activity they not only appropriate but also create or reconstruct the context in which they participate. This approach leads to a reading of individual-community relations quite different than that produced by Rogoff, Lave, and others. Discursive events are

portrayed as acts in which multiple centers of emotional, valuational, and cognitive consciousnesses meet (Hicks, 1999). This perspective gives full weight to the sense of lived dilemmas and conflicts faced by individuals engaged with practices. Thus, we can think of individual and community as mutually emerging from particular relations, which entail the sociocultural and personal historical contexts from which they emerge. Relations in which conflict and control may necessarily emerge as part of the process of negotiating who you may become in a community.

(Linehan and McCarthy, 2001, p. 146)

From the perspective of constructivist pedagogy, Brown and Campione (1996) have discussed an approach entitled Fostering Communities of Learners (FCL) with classroom teachers in upper elementary and middle school science classrooms in urban settings in the United States. The same principles have been applied in social studies classrooms (Mintrop, 2004), English language arts classrooms (Whitcomb, 2004) and mathematics classrooms (Sherin *et al.*, 2004).

[W]e will argue that this reform exemplifies many of the learning-centred efforts of contemporary school improvement that would be characterized as constructivist, learner-centred, oriented toward the development of higher-order understanding and skills, and emphasizing collaborative efforts by students in learning communities engaging in complex, 'authentic' tasks through 'distributing their expertise'.

(Shulman and Sherin, 2004, p. 136)

These ideas are also witnessed in many other areas such as medical education (e.g. Hoffman and Donaldson, 2004) and management (e.g. Thompson, 2005) and in online settings (e.g. Thomas, 2005). I will conclude this section with a warning note from James Paul Gee, where he counsels against the application of the community of practice idea within an unreflective framework.

The new capitalism is bringing new social formations to workplaces, such as project-based communities of practice. In turn, it is reshaping classrooms, where things like communities of practice become popular forms of school reform. Won't this just mean that schools will, once again, as in the old capitalism, simply produce 'fit,' ideologically quiescent workers – in this case, flexible, proactive, self-reliant knowledge workers? Worse yet, given the need for lots of service workers, might not schools use one curriculum (e.g., scripted skill and drill) to produce fit service workers and another (communities of practice) to produce fit knowledge workers and symbol analysts? These dilemmas are real, and there is no easy way out. However, my own tentative answer is this: classrooms as what I will call reflective communities of practice. In reflective communities of practice, students learn the core knowledge for which the community exists, as well as ways of thinking about knowledge, language, discourses, and their relationships and distribution in society. They engage in both subject-centered design knowledge and world-building design knowledge through which they imagine and enact new, more moral worlds and futures.

(Gee, 2000, p. 521)

From my point of view, the research community, or the research field, or the practices of research, or research activity (or what you will) must retain the critical edge (which is most definitely present in Lave and Rogoff's writing) as it seeks to develop and refine ideas such as the community of practice or learners. This critical edge must surely be used to pare and parse the methodological and theoretical underpinnings of such development.

Funds of knowledge and third spaces

I will now discuss, albeit briefly, a body of work which also takes up specific views on the situated nature of learning and the knowledge which is developed and acquired. Within this discussion is a commentary on the implications of acknowledging or discounting the possibilities of different knowledge structures and/or, in Vygotsky's term, the differences between scientific and everyday concepts.

Luis Moll has made an important contribution to that fraction of the post-Vygotskian research field which also draws on the methodologies and imaginations of anthropology. His classroom-based and home-based studies of language and literacy (see Moll and Whitmore, 1993) focus on the social distribution of knowledge, understood as a cultural resource for thinking, within Latino homes (Moll et al., 1993). In this way, he considers both situated and distributed features of learning. In order to gain access to the understandings that have been acquired and developed in different settings, he sought the help of classroom teachers as researchers who carried out ethnographies of practices of literacy within children's communities, the intention being to recognise value and build on the funds of knowledge which are specific to the social, economic and productive activities of people living in specific settings.

> Households in our sample share not only knowledge regarding repair of homes and automobiles, home remedies, planting and gardening, as mentioned, but funds of knowledge specific to urban living, such as access to institutional assistance, school programs, transportation, occupational opportunities and other services. In short, households' funds of knowledge are wide-ranging and abundant.
>
> (Moll and Greenberg, 1990, p. 323)

This work has been influential on researchers in many settings. For example, Martin Hughes and colleagues (Hughes et al., 2003; Hughes and Pollard, 2006) have explored how children's attainment and learning disposition, including attitudes to school and to learning, could be enhanced through a process of exchanging knowledge and information exchange between home and school in the United Kingdom. This work can be read as a counter to many parent involvement projects in the United Kingdom which are seen to operate 'as a form of cultural imperialism' (Dyson and Robson, 1999).

Moll argues that schools should draw on the social and cognitive contributions that parents and other community members can make to children's development. Through these anthropologically driven studies of learning in clusters of households much has been learned about the ways in which knowledge is built and acquired in such settings. After-school clubs are used as settings in which the richness of the community knowledge funds can be brought together with the academic purposes of the teaching. The after-school clubs were designed so that multiple goals could be pursued. The children engaged in meaningful activities in which valued outcomes were achieved. Teachers ensured that academic progress was facilitated in the context of these activities.

Rowlands presents a strident critique of this approach, arguing that it fails to incorporate an understanding of Vygotsky's position on epistemology which he attributes to Marx:

> Survival strategies (or 'funds of knowledge') of the oppressed cannot be used to facilitate a scientific and objective understanding of the world (this is a Marxist position despite how 'politically incorrect' it may sound)!... A scientific understanding has to be developed from 'above' in school; it cannot come from 'below', in the everyday experience of having to survive in the world.
>
> (Rowlands, 2000, p. 558)

Moll and Greenberg (1990) suggest that scientific concepts (after Vygotsky) *are* to be found in the funds of knowledge that are developed in communities:

> Vygotsky (1987) wrote that in 'receiving instruction in a system of knowledge, the child learns of things that are not before his eyes, things that far exceed the limits of his actual and even potential immediate experience' (p. 180). We hardly believe that rote instruction of low-level skills is the system of knowledge that Vygotsky had in mind. We perceive the students' community, and its funds of knowledge, as the most important resource for reorganizing instruction in ways that 'far exceed' the limits of current schooling. An indispensable element of our approach is the creation of meaningful connections between academic and social life through the concrete learning activities of the students. We are convinced that teachers can establish, in systemic ways, the necessary social relations outside classrooms that will change and improve what occurs within the classroom walls. These social connections help teachers and students to develop their awareness of

how they can use the everyday to understand classroom content and use classroom activities to understand social reality.

(Moll and Greenberg, 1990, pp. 345–6)

Davydov (1988, 1990, 1995) and, following him, Hedegaard (1998) as outlined above, insisted that the tradition of teaching empirical knowledge should be changed to a focus on teaching theoretical knowledge. He developed a 'Developmental Teaching' programme which pursued this goal. The connection between the spontaneous concepts that arise through empirical learning and the scientific concepts that develop through theoretical teaching is seen as the main dimension of the ZPD. The process of 'ascending from the abstract to the concrete' which formed the core of Davydov's early work has been extended by Hedegaard into a conceptualisation of teaching and learning as a 'double move' between situated activity and subject matter concepts. When working within this approach, general laws are used by teachers to formulate instruction and children investigate the manifestations of these general laws in carefully chosen examples that embody core concepts. These core concepts constitute the 'germ cell' for subsequent learning. In practical activity, children grapple with central conceptual relations which underpin particular phenomena. In this way, the teaching focuses directly on the scientific concepts that constitute the subject matter.

Hedegaard (1998) suggests that 'the teacher guides the learning activity both from the perspective of general concepts and from the perspective of engaging students in "situated" problems that are meaningful in relation to their developmental stage and life situations' (Hedegaard, 1998, p. 120). Her account makes it clear that successful applications of this approach are possible, whilst indicating the enormous amount of work that will be required if such practices are to become both routine and effective. In this way, Davydov is associated with the formulation of an approach to teaching and learning within which the analysis of theoretical knowledge is central. Davydov and his group, along with the now 2,500-school-strong Association for Developmental Instruction, have done much to pursue the 'Marxist epistemologist' interpretation of Vygotsky's work to which Rowlands alludes:

> any consideration as to the conditions necessary to evoke development must have, as its starting point, the content of the body of knowledge (and by content I mean logical structure, its theoretical objects and the way these theoretical objects speak of the world). This ... is Vygotsky as 'marxist epistemologist' and the ZPD ought to be seen in the context of this epistemology.
>
> (Rowlands, 2000, p. 541)

As Hedegaard (2007) reminds us, this body of work identifies the general developmental potential of particular forms of teaching as well as its specific microgenetic function. The assertion is that teaching should promote general mental development as well as the acquisition of special abilities and knowledge. Karpov (2003) contrasts Russian approaches such as those developed by Davydov with North American guided discovery pedagogies that he claims serve only to promote empirical learning rather than the theoretical learning that leads to the acquisition of scientific knowledge comprising scientific concepts and relevant procedures.

In contrast, Moll (1990) suggested that the focus of change within the ZPD should be on the creation, enhancement and communication of meaning through the collaborative use of mediational means, rather than on the transfer of skills from the more to less capable partner. Thus, even within the 'scaffolding' interpretation there are fundamental differences. A rigid scaffold may appear little different from a task analysis produced by teaching which has been informed by applied behaviour analysis. A negotiated scaffold would arise in a very different form of teaching and may well be associated with collaborative activity as discussed by Moll. From the perspective of Developmental Teaching it is very unclear as to whether the content of scaffolded instruction would serve a developmental function.

Griffin and Cole (1984) mount a strong criticism of instructional approaches in which the child's creativity is underplayed. They draw on the work of the Russian physiologist Nicholas Bernstein and A.N. Leontiev. From Bernstein they borrow an emphasis on essential creativity in all forms of living movement and from Leontiev they pursue the notion of 'leading activity'. The argument is that different settings and activities give rise to 'spaces' within the ZPD for creative exploration rather than pedagogic domination: 'Adult wisdom does not provide a teleology for child development. Social organization and leading activities provide a gap within which the child can develop novel creative analyses' (Griffin and Cole, 1984, p. 62). There have been a number of recent attempts to both recognise and value the knowledge that develops in homes and communities and to make connections with the knowledge that is valued in schools and other official pedagogic sites. This 'third space pedagogy' been developed by researchers such as Kris Gutiérrez (Gutiérrez et al., 1999) and it resonates with the literacy and discourse studies undertaken by Carol Lee and James Paul Gee (e.g. Lee, 2007; Gee, 1996). The move has been to find ways to connect the 'first space' of learning, knowledge and understanding in the home, community and social networks with the 'second space' of formal pedagogic practice and its discourses. This is done through the creation of a 'third space' in which connections are made between the two that may, for example, involve classroom instruction which engages with and then re-positions forms of literacy that have often been regarded as marginal or irrelevant in schools. Lee's (2007) Cultural Modeling Project has been trialled in a school where most of the pupils bring African American English Vernacular (AAEV) from their 'first space' to the 'second space' of schooling. Lee (2007) seeks to engage these young learners with literary reasoning through a 'third space' in which the AAEV practice of signifying that entails the use of figurative language, persuasion and double entendre to engage in insult is recognised and valued. Here there is a theoretical acknowledgement of different forms and structures of knowledge, along with a political recognition of power of different discourses in different contexts. I understand such attempts in terms of what I take to be an appropriate and reasonably correct translation of the Russian term *obuchenie* (often translated as 'instruction') which was used by Vygotsky (1987a, 1978) to signify the process of teaching and learning in which to learn one has to teach (communicate one's understanding with the teacher) and to teach one has to learn (about the understandings of the pupil/learner). Thus, there is a need for dialogue or at least connection across the knowledges that to a greater or lesser extent may be situation-specific. It is here that the questions of separability and knowledge boundaries discussed above condition the theorisation and methodology of pedagogic practice and research. Despite Matusov's (2007) scepticism about the prevalence of Bakhtinian dialogues which seem to him to be 'accidental rather than essential to pedagogy and education' (Matusov, 2007, p. 236), I find the following statement about learning from otherness to be an important starting point in the consideration of situated and distributed understanding:

> In the realm of culture, outsideness is a most powerful factor in understanding. It is only in the eyes of *another* culture that foreign culture reveals itself fully and profoundly ... A meaning only reveals its depths once it has encountered and come into contact with another, foreign meaning: they engage in a kind of dialogue, which surmounts the closedness and one-sidedness of these particular meanings, these cultures. We raise new questions for a foreign culture, ones that it does not raise itself; we seek answers to our own questions in it; and the foreign culture responds to us by revealing to us new aspects and new semantic depths.
>
> (Bakhtin, 1986, p. 7)

Matusov (1998) had earlier argued the case for differing socio-political orientations on the part of Vygotsky (who he sees as advocating a separability thesis and thus a model of internalisation) and placed the non-separability thesis (linked a model of learning through participation) firmly in the domain of Bakhtin's work.

> Vygotsky shaped and gave the major impetus for the internalization model of development. He ethnocentrically considered Western societies as the historically most progressive and advanced (Rogoff, 1990; Wertsch, 1985). His life project [using Sartre's term] seemed to be how to facilitate people's connection with the network of Western sociocultural practices of mass production, formal schooling, vast institutional bureaucracy, and alienated labor. That is why, in my view, Vygotsky mainly focused on studying children, people with disabilities, and people from 'primitive' cultures. In contrast, his contemporary Russian theoretician Bakhtin, whose scholarship was deeply literary, had a very different life project. Bakhtin seemed to be concerned

with how people constitute each other in their diversity, agency, and dialogue. According to Bakhtin, people need each other not so much to successfully accomplish some goal in their cooperative efforts but because of their 'transgradience' (it literally means 'the outsideness'), which allows them to be participants of never-ending dialogue. Bakhtin's project was much closer to the participation worldview than Vygotsky's.

(Matusov, 1998, pp. 237–8)

I will close this chapter with a quotation from Jaan Valsiner, whose work may be thought of in terms of the development of analytic dualism. He distinguishes dualisms from dualities, arguing that the denial of dualism (inner, outer) in appropriation models leads to a denial of the dualities which are the constituent elements in dialectical or dialogical theory. As such, he occupies a very different position on the interpretation of Vygotsky from that developed by Rogoff and Lave. However, there is no necessary refutation of Bakhtin's argument on meaning and dialogue here. The following statement Diriwächter and Valsiner (2006) surfaces and, for me, reaffirms one of the central claims of this book:

Methodology is not a 'toolbox' of different methods from which the researcher selects some on the basis of personal or social preferences! Instead, it is an integrated structure of the epistemological process (Branco & Valsiner, 1997) that can equally and easily reveal and obscure the empirical reality in the knowledge construction process of social scientists.

(Diriwächter and Valsiner, 2006, p. 8)

This calls for clarity of purpose and belief in research. As I and others have argued (notably Sawyer (2002)), the post-Vygostkian field is populated by a number of epistemological and ontological positions, not all of which are made clear in publications. The clarification of such positions would appear to be an important part of the development of the field. As Vygotsky, in what may arguably have been his preferred role as a methodologist, remarked: 'The search for method becomes one of the most important problems of the entire enterprise of understanding the uniquely human forms of psychological activity ... the method is simultaneously prerequisite and product, the tool and the result of the study' (Vygotsky, 1978, p. 65).

Chapter 6

Activity theory and interventionist research

In this chapter I will discuss activity theory. This highly influential body of writing is seen as a product of the reworking and extension of the original Vygotskian ideas on the social formation of mind by A.N. Leontiev (1978) and colleagues who had initially worked as part of Vygotsky's group in Moscow and departed for a new setting with new theoretical emphases in Kharkov (see Kozulin, 1998, 1996). At a very general level of description, activity theorists seek to analyse the development of consciousness within practical social activity. Their concern is with the psychological impacts of activity and the social conditions and systems that are produced in and through such activity. I will open this chapter by outlining some of the distinctions, fissures and cleavages that have formed in the field since the original early twentieth-century body of work became widely available in the West. I will then provide a brief outline of the methodology developed by Engeström and his colleagues in Helsinki and finally move to an example of research which has sought to apply this approach. I will conclude the chapter by outlining a number of issues which feature in current debates.

Sawyer (2002) suggests that, as a field, activity theory has still to come to (methodological) terms with the inseparability thesis it celebrates. For example, he argues that Cole (1996) provides an example of an approach to psychology which retains an acceptance of analytical distinction and causal relation between context and the individual, whilst developing a theory of mutual constitution. Just as Sawyer (2002) has complained that sociocultural theorists spend too little time explicating the methodological assumptions that underpin their work, so Roth (2007a) has argued that activity theorists should spend more time trying to understand and articulate the differences that exist between different conceptualisations of the relationships between mind, culture and activity.

Early twentieth-century Russian activity theory

I will start with the differences that emerge from readings of the early twentieth-century Russian writers. Thorne (2005) points to the essence of a primary distinction between a focus on word meaning as the central mediational means and a focus on the systems of activity as appropriate units of analysis in the writings of Vygotsky and Leontiev:

> Despite certain divergences from Vygotsky's work, *activity theory*, as it became known, is considered part of Vygotsky's lineage (Frawley, 1997; van der Veer & Valsiner, 1991). Although Vygotsky and Leontiev both proposed that participation in culturally organized activity generates higher mental functions, their emphases differed significantly. Vygotsky's writings argued for the genesis and mediation of mind by cultural tools (semiosis). This focus on cultural mediation was constructively contested in Leontiev's (1981) formulation that emphasized the genesis and mediation of mind through *sensuous human activity* (to paraphrase Marx, 1972, p. 144). Activity in this sense refers to social relations and rules of conduct that are governed by cultural, political, and economic institutions (Ratner, 2002). Leontiev and subsequent activity theorists elaborated this shift by more formally operationalizing the roles of communities, the rules that structure them, and 'the continuously negotiated distribution of tasks, powers, and responsibilities among the participants of an activity system' (Cole & Y. Engeström, 1993, p. 7).
>
> (Thorne, 2005, p. 395)

Cole and Gajdamaschko (2007) provide an important political perspective on the origins of these differences and also make the suggestion that the two contributions can be seen as complementary contributions to a common theme:

> Leontiev's writings have been seen as a repudiation of Vygotsky, the substitution of activity for mediation. It is certainly plausible that Leontiev, like many others, seek to distance themselves from ideas and association that had been the death of their colleagues and friends. However, I prefer to see it as an effort to place mediation in its cultural context, extending culture's actual presence in human life. From a contemporary point of view, not only mediational means but the cultural practices of which they are a part constitute culture.
>
> (Cole and Gajdamaschko, 2007, p. 205)

Holzman (2006) opens a very general question concerning the kind of theory that is activity theory and suggests that no unified perspective exists on the matter. It is most certainly not an easy question to answer, as the emergence of the theory itself has been clouded by difficulties in translation and several levels of difference and disagreement. For example, whilst Davydov (1990, 1995) reminds us that the Russian term *deyatelnost'* refers to activity of long duration which has some developmental function and is characterised by constant transformation and change, Roth points to translations and consequent associations that have resulted in differences in the use of and the understanding of the term 'activity': 'Leont'ev

(1978, p. 46) likened it to the German term *Tätigkeit* (which has the synonyms *work, job, function, business, trade,* and *doing*) and distinguishes it from *Aktivität* (which has the synonyms *effort, eagerness, engagement, diligence,* and *restlessness*)' (Roth, 2007a, p. 145). There are also tensions within the Soviet and subsequent post-Soviet Russian school. As Cole notes in a discussion of the work of Rubinshtein, Vygotsky and Leontiev:

> I found it very difficult to work out the empirical implications of Rubinshtein's ideas that I could link to my work. I also failed to understand the academic value of the strong polemical character of exchanges between those who preferred to follow Rubinshtein and those who followed the Vygotsky/Leontiev line. I am not alone among non-Russian psychologists in failing to find value in intra-Russian arguments among adherents of these different schools.
>
> (Cole, 2001, p. 98)

Both Engeström (1987) and P. Hakkarainen (2004) suggest that there is a clear difference between Western interpretations (commonly referred to as Cultural Historical Activity Theory (CHAT), as in Cole (1996)) and the Russian approach to activity theory: 'The Western CHAT and Russian activity approach have different functions. The former defines activity more as an object of scientific study and management and the latter as an explanatory principle. The approaches aim at solving different problems' (P. Hakkarainen, 2004, p. 10). There are undoubted tensions between contributions to the development of activity theory at the time of its inception, in its migration to the West and in its subsequent development within Russia. These are important issues that should be understood and acknowledged, but not allowed to distract attention from the fundamental contribution to social science that is being made by this field.

In his discussion of the concept of activity in Soviet Psychology, Kozulin (1998) considers the importance of the article written by Vygotsky under the title 'Consciousness as a problem of psychology of behaviour'. In was in this article that Vygotsky sought to restore the concept of consciousness as a legitimate and necessary element of psychology. It had been the subject of study through introspectionism and was deposed by the Russian behaviourists and reflexologists of the late nineteenth and early twentieth centuries. Vygotsky's distinction between 'subject of study' and 'explanatory principle' is central to his methodological oeuvre.

> If consciousness is to become a subject of psychological study, it cannot simultaneously serve as an explanatory principle.... Vygotsky suggested that sociocultural activity serves as such an explanatory source. He thus broke the vicious circle within which the phenomena of consciousness used to be explained through the concept of consciousness, and similarly behaviour

through the concept of behaviour, and established premises for a unified theory of behaviour and mind on the basis of sociocultural activity.

(Kozulin, 1998, p. 11)

Kozulin suggests that, in part, under the influence of philosophical trends which were dominant at the time, Vygotsky came to adopt and subsequently develop the concept of historically concrete human praxis as the explanatory principle. The development of this explanatory principle became one of the politically contested elements of his thesis in the years that followed Vygotsky's death. At times, it appeared that the very concept of mediation itself was to be ripped from the framework of ideas which Vygotsky had struggled to put into place. In the hands of the command/control ideologues of the Stalinist era it appeared as though what was left of Russian Psychology would become a theory of determination rather than mediation. Thankfully, the essence of Vygotsky's thoughts on mediation survived, even if they had to be handled covertly at times. The heritage is, as Cole reminds us, of an activity theory within which mediation is a central concept, thus removing the possibility of an account of 'heavy handed' determinism: 'The central thesis of the Russian cultural-historical school is that the structure and development of human psychological processes emerge through culturally mediated, historically developing, practical activity' (Cole, 1996, p. 108). Leontiev 'focused on those activities that eventually lead to the internalisation of external human actions in the form of inner mental processes' (Kozulin, 1996, p. 112). The search for the appropriate unit of analysis, the 'minimal unit that preserves the properties of the whole' (Davydov and Radzihovskii, 1985, p. 60) gave impetus to the divergence of opinion on what is the most appropriate focus for study between the various theorists working in activity theory and other sociocultural approaches. Leontiev's work on activity involved an elaboration of the notions of object and goal and the centrality of the object to an analysis of motivation:

> A basic, as sometimes said, a constitutive characteristic of activity is its objectivity. Properly, the concept of its object (Gegenstand) is already implicitly contained in the very concept of activity. The expression 'objectless activity' is devoid of any meaning. Activity may seem objectless, but the scientific investigation of activity necessarily requires discovering its object. Thus, the object of activity is twofold: first, in its independent existence as subordinating itself and transforming the activity of the subject; second, as an image of the object, as a product of its property of psychological reflection that is realized as an activity of the subject and cannot exist otherwise.
>
> (Leontiev, 1978, p. 52)

These ideas have been highly influential on contemporary researchers who have sought to develop and refine the original thesis. For example, Engeström has noted that the object of activity has evolved culturally and historically and carries, therefore, collective meanings and motives with it (Engeström, 2000b). Whilst Leontiev established the idea that their objects distinguish different activities and that it is the transformation of the object/goal that leads to integration of elements of the activity system, Miettinen and Peisa (2002) argue for the notion of object-oriented mediation and also surface the issue of object-relatedness of activities. As Märtsin (2007) notes, different sociohistorically created collective motivating possibilities are embedded in the object, making it possible for different individuals to relate to the object. When met with individual needs and goals, these motivational possibilities become actualised in individual actions as they engage with the object. Similarly, the motivating possibilities of an object can create a state of need on a collective level that allows for individual engagement with the object (P. Hakkarainen, 2004). Märtsin (2007) also notes that questions such as why people decide to engage with certain objects and why they ignore other activities or refuse to deal with specific contradictions in the activity system need to be addressed (Langemeyer, 2005). The latter strand of research may be especially important in relation to the new kinds of objects and related activities that have emerged under contemporary societal circumstances (Engeström, 2006).

As shown in Figure 6.1, Leontiev (1978) also developed a distinction between the concepts of 'activity' and 'action' which were underdeveloped by Vygotsky and which, as Roth (2007a) and P. Hakkarainen (2004) note, still constitute a challenge for many researchers and constitute a marker between different traditions within activity theory.

> A classical dispute regarding Leontiev's theoretical model involves the origin of needs in human activity. It has been easier to carry out technological analyses of activity and construct goal-directed processes aimed at end products than to analyze the revealing motivational dynamics of human activity. This technological analysis A.N. Leontiev called action-level analysis. He

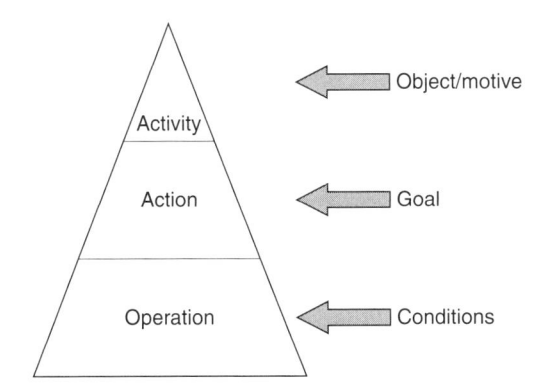

Figure 6.1 The hierarchical structure of activity.

defined the second type of analysis as being at the level of sense. The main role in this analysis is played by motivation and its relation to the goals of the participants in an activity. The problem is that the same process can be an activity for one participant and an action for another depending on motivation and goals.

(P. Hakkarainen, 2004, p. 5)

For Engeström (1987), activity is a collective, systemic formation that has a complex mediational structure. An activity system produces actions and is realised by means of actions. However, activity is not reducible to actions. Actions are relatively short-lived and have a temporally clear-cut beginning and end. Activity systems evolve over lengthy periods of sociohistorical time, often taking the form of institutions and organisations. This explanation has been slightly nuanced by Roth (2007a), who draws attention to the way in which activity as a whole 'mediates the sense of the actions that realize goals':

> Goals, however, which are realized in and through *actions*, constitute a different level of analysis, subordinate to that of activity. However, goals are bound rather than free because they stand in a mutually constitutive (i.e., dialectical) relationship with the motives that drive activities: Goals realize motives, but motives give rise to goals, each presupposing the other. The activity as a whole therefore mediates the sense of the actions that realize goals. Actions are not the outcome of subjectivist singularity but rather, because they realize collective activity, inherently are shared and intelligible: An 'action has a double significance not only because it is directed against itself as well as against the other, but also because it is indivisibly the action of one as well as of the other' (Hegel, 1807/1977, p. 112).
>
> (Roth, 2007a, p. 145)

Thus Leontiev distinguished between the material objective and affective motives of activity, seeing the objective purpose as translating motive into a physical act, transforming the internal plane to the external world and driving activity through the formation of goals. After Hegel, he maintained that goals are determined in the course of activity (Engeström, 1999a). Engeström (2000b) notes a dual function in that an object can give coherence and continuity to the activity, but by virtue of its societal and historical nature it is also internally contradictory and thus a source of instability. 'The object is a heterogeneous and internally contradictory, yet enduring, constantly reproduced purpose of a collective activity system that motivates and defines the horizon of possible goals and actions' (Engeström, 2004a, p. 17). Leontiev saw operations as the external method used by individuals to achieve goals (Glassman, 1996, p. 323). Automatic operations are driven by the conditions and tools available to the action, that is the then prevailing circumstances. Engeström (1999a) argued that motive can be collective but that goals are individual, and he explored the idea of partial and overall goals.

The shifting and developing object of an activity is related to a motive which drives it. Individual (or group) action is driven by a conscious goal. 'Although actions are aroused by the motive of the activity, they seem to be directed towards a goal ... the one and the same action can serve different activities' (Leontiev, 1978, p. 64).

> [A]part from its (the action's) intentional aspects (what must be done) the action has its operational aspect (how it can be done), which is defined not by the goal itself, but by the objective circumstances under which it is carried out ... I shall label the means by which an action is carried out its operations.
>
> (Leontiev, 1981, p. 63)

Leontiev illustrates his proposed structure of activity with well-known examples of the activity of hunting, in which to understand why separate actions are meaningful one needs to understand the motive behind the whole activity (Leontiev, 1978, pp. 62–3), and of learning to drive a car that illustrates the movement from one level of the structure of an activity to another as actions become automatic operations such as gear changing when learning to drive (Leontiev, 1978, p. 66).

There have been many dialects of activity theory which have flowed from its inception in Russia, both within the country itself and beyond. In the next section I will discuss one of the more influential interpretations, developments and empirical applications of the theory.

Engeström's development of activity theory

As we noted in Daniels and Warmington (2007), Engeström (1999a and b) has explained the genealogy of his conceptual tools by outlining the development of three generations of activity theory. This development may be viewed as a process whereby the account given of the setting of development (Vygotsky, 1987a) is progressively finessed. It starts from a view of mediation abstracted from context and then moves to the modelling of a single activity in a setting which is articulated in terms of rules, community and the division of labour. The third generation posits networks of activities and this is currently being developed to take account of some of the complexities of the boundaries that are created and transgressed between multiple activities in practice.

The first generation of activity theory drew heavily upon Vygotsky's concept of mediation. Vygotsky, in turn, predicated his notion of mediation upon Marx's (1976 [1883]) transhistorical concept of labour (or 'activity'), which states that: 'The simple elements of the labour processes are (i) purposeful activity, that is work itself, (ii) the object on which that work is performed, and (iii) the instruments of that work' (Marx, 1976, p. 284). Engeström's (1999a) second generation of activity theory refers to the work of Leontiev (1978). Here Engeström (1999a) advocates the study of tools or artefacts 'as integral and inseparable components of human functioning' and argues that the focus of the study of mediation should be on its relationship with the other components of an activity system. The now very familiar depiction of an activity system as developed by Engeström (1987) is shown in Figure 6.2.

Figure 6.2 represents the social/collective elements in an activity system through the elements of community, rules and division of labour, whilst emphasising the importance of analysing their interactions with each other. The object is depicted with the help of an oval, indicating that object-oriented actions are always, explicitly or implicitly, characterised by ambiguity, surprise, interpretation, sense-making and potential for change (Engeström, 1999a).

Recent developments have witnessed increased emphasis on the multivoicedness of activity systems and the way in which individual actors bring in their own histories from the social positions that they take up in the division of labour that obtains within the activity. Following in the Vygotskian 'genetic' tradition, a historical developmental analysis of activity is adopted in which contradictions are thought of as sources of change and development. Engeström sees the construction and redefinition of the object as related to the 'creative potential' of activity (Engeström, 1999b, p. 381). He maintains that it is important to extend beyond the singular activity system and to examine and work towards transformation of networks of activity. To this end, he sees potential in the exploration by some activity theorists of 'concepts of boundary object, translation, and boundary crossing to analyze the unfolding of object-oriented cooperative activity of several actors, focusing on tools and means of construction of boundary objects in concrete work processes' (Engeström, 1999a, p. 7). The third generation of activity theory outlined in Engeström (1999a) takes *joint activity* or practice as the unit of analysis for activity theory, rather than individual

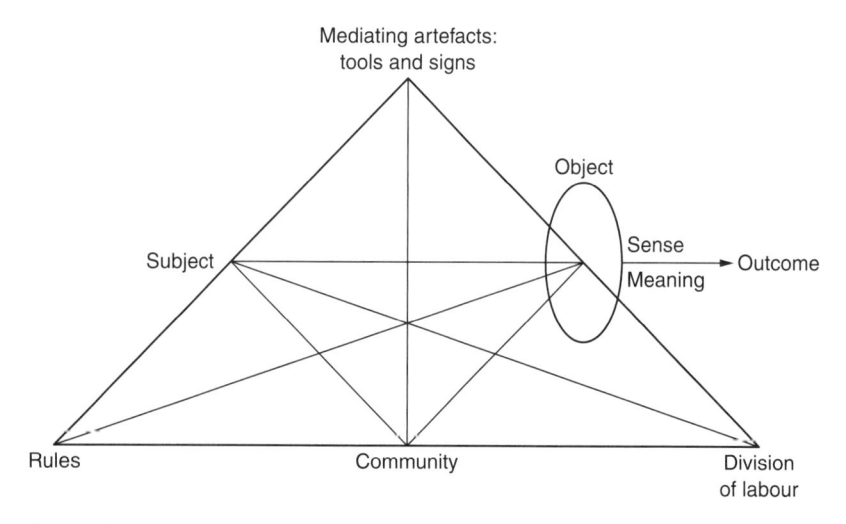

Figure 6.2 The structure of a human activity system (source: Engeström, 1987, p. 78).

activity. Engeström's (1999a) analysis is concerned with the process of social transformation and incorporates the structure of the social world, with particular emphasis upon the *conflictual* nature of social practice. Instability and contradictions are regarded as the 'motive force of change and development' (Engeström, 1999a, p. 6) and the transitions and reorganisations within and between activity systems as part of evolution. The third generation of activity theory aims to develop conceptual tools to understand dialogues, multiple perspectives and networks of interacting activity systems.

The minimal representation that Figure 6.3 provides shows two of what may be myriad systems exhibiting patterns of contradiction and tension.

> Third-generation activity theory endorses the fact that all activity systems are part of a network of activity systems that in its totality constitutes human society. Diverse activity systems are the result of a continuous historical process of progressive job diversification and collective division of labor at the societal level (Marx, 1867/1976). Thus, during societal development,... the network is formed as activity systems lose their self-containment and exchange entities, including objects, means of productions, people, and various forms of texts. The first activity system is understood as a concrete universal, which particularizes itself into many mutually constitutive activity systems.
>
> (Roth and Lee, 2007, p. 201)

Five principles of cultural historical activity theory

Overall, Engeström (1999a) suggests that activity theory may be summarised with the help of five principles. The first of these is that a collective, artefact-mediated

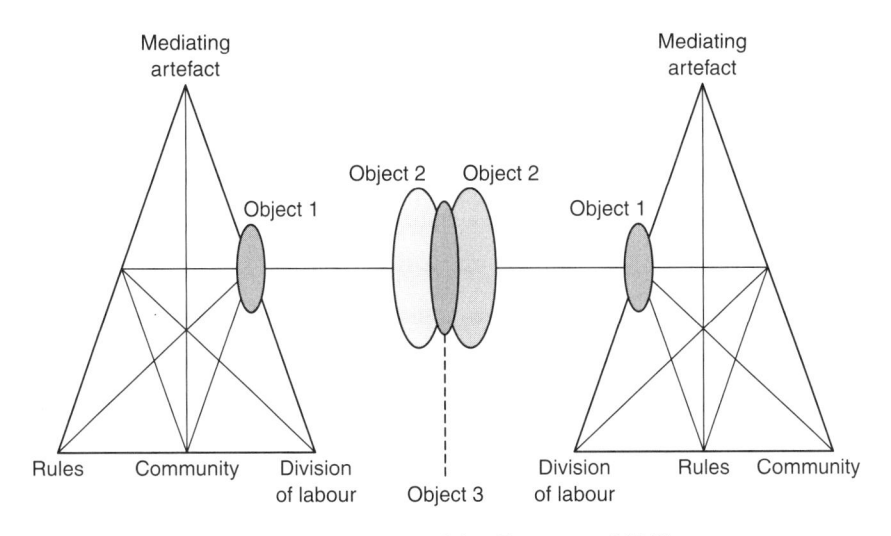

Figure 6.3 Two interacting activity systems (after Engeström (1999)).

and object-oriented activity system, seen in its network relations to other activity systems, is the prime unit of analysis. The second principle is the multi-voicedness of activity systems. An activity system is always a nexus of multiple points of view, traditions and interests. The division of labour in an activity creates different positions for the participants; the participants carry their own diverse histories and the activity system itself carries multiple layers and strands of history engraved in its artefacts, rules and conventions. This multi-voicedness increases exponentially in networks of interacting activity systems. It is a source of both tension and innovation, demanding actions of translation and negotiation. The third principle is historicity. Activity systems take shape and are transformed over lengthy periods of time. Their problems and potentials can only be understood against their own history. Engeström (1991a) bemoans the absence of historical analysis in some fractions of social science which espouses a Vygotskian root:

> It is surely appropriate to avoid rigid, one-dimensional sequences being imposed on social reality. But especially among Anglo-Saxon researchers adhering to the ideas of Vygotsky, the standard alternative seems to be to avoid history altogether. Differences in cognition across cultures, social groups and domains of practice are thus commonly explained without seriously analyzing the historical development that has led to those differences. The underlying relativistic notion says that we should not make value judgments concerning whose cognition is 'better' or 'more advanced' – that all kinds of thinking and practice are equally valuable. While this liberal stance may be a comfortable basis for academic discourse, it ignores the reality that in all domains of societal practice those very value judgments and decisions have to be made every day. People have to decide where they want to go, which way is 'up'. If behavioural and social science wants to avoid that issue, it will be unable to work out useful, yet theoretically ambitious intellectual tools for practitioners making those crucial decisions.
>
> (Engeström, 1991a, p. 10)

History needs to be considered in terms of the local history of the activity and its objects, but also as the history of the theoretical ideas and tools that have shaped the activity.

> It is important to note that any material entity is not fixed but can take different functions within an activity system. For example, signs can switch functions and become tools in the process of reading texts that further generate new texts and meanings that are culturally and historically situated (Smagorinsky, 2001). By the same token, mundane objects such as textbooks can continue their lives in other roles and assume diverse functions within the same or other activity systems.
>
> (Roth and Lee, 2007, p. 200)

The central role of contradictions as sources of change and development is the fourth principle. Engeström drew on Ilyenkov (1977, p. 82) to emphasise the importance of contradictions within activity systems as the driving force of change and thus development.

Contradictions are not the same as problems or conflicts. Contradictions are historically accumulating structural tensions within and between activity systems (Engeström, 2001a, p. 137). Activities are open systems.

> When inner contradictions are conscious, they become the primary driving forces that bring about change and development within and between activity systems. Generally overlooked is the fact that contradictions have to be historically accumulated inner contradictions, within the things themselves rather than more surface expressions of tensions, problems, conflicts, and breakdowns.
>
> (Roth and Lee, 2007, p. 203)

Engeström defines the 'primary inner contradiction' of use and exchange value as a 'Level 1 contradiction': one that exists within each constituent component of the central activity. When an activity system adopts a new element from the outside (for example, a new technology or a new object), it often leads to an aggravated secondary contradiction, where some old element collides with the new one. Such contradictions not only generate disturbances and conflicts but also drive attempts to change the activity. For Engeström, a tertiary contradiction is apparent when a more sophisticated external object attempts to supplant an existing object within an activity system. Intersystemic quaternary contradictions are also envisaged. Contradictions within activity become 'a guiding principle of empirical research' (Engeström, 2001a, p. 135).

The Center for Activity Theory and Developmental Work Research (2007) website summarises this account of contradiction as follows:

> Level 1: Primary inner contradiction (double nature) within each constituent component of the central activity.
> Level 2: Secondary contradictions between the constituents of the central activity.
> Level 3: Tertiary contradiction between the object/motive of the dominant form of the central activity and the object/motive of a culturally more advanced form of the central activity.
> Level 4: Quaternary contradictions between the central activity and its neighbour activities.

Engeström's fifth principle proclaims the possibility of expansive transformations in activity systems. Activity systems move through relatively long cycles of qualitative transformations. As the contradictions of an activity system are aggravated, some individual participants begin to question and to deviate from its established norms. In some cases, this escalates into collaborative envisioning and a deliberate collective change effort. An expansive transformation is accomplished when the object and motive of the activity are reconceptualised to embrace a radically wider horizon of possibilities than in the previous mode of the activity.

Expansive learning

In many theories of learning, the learner or learners acquire some identifiable knowledge or skills in such a way that a corresponding, relatively lasting change in the behaviour of the subject may be observed. It is assumed that the knowledge or skill to be acquired is itself stable and open to reasonably unambiguous definition and articulation. The assumption is that in the practice of learning there is a teacher who knows what has to be learned. The situation we are studying is one in which subjects are learning something that is not known. The knowledge that has to be learned is being learned as it is being developed. Therefore there is no one in the role of teacher.

In the original formulation of expansive learning, Engeström (1987) acknowledges the importance of this form of learning and draws on Bateson's (1972) formulation of levels of learning. Down (2004) provides a summary of Bateson's levels as shown in Table 6.1.

Engeström draws attention to Learning III. He argues that this form of learning involves reformulation of problems and the creation of new tools for engaging with these problems. This ongoing production of new problem-solving tools enables subjects to transform the entire activity system and potentially create, or transform and expand, the objects of the activity (Engeström, 1987, pp. 158–9).

Expansive learning and enhanced professional practice occurs in activity settings which enable expansion of the object of activity. Expansive learning involves the creation of new knowledge and new practices for a newly emerging activity; that is, learning embedded in and constitutive of qualitative transformation of the entire activity system. Such a transformation may be triggered

Table 6.1 Bateson's levels of learning

	Description	Example
Level I	Conditioning through the acquisition of responses deemed correct within a given context	Learning the correct answers and behaviours in a classroom
Level II	Acquisition of the deep-seated rules and patterns of behaviour characteristic to the context itself	Learning the 'hidden' curriculum of what it means to be a student
Level III	Radical questioning of the sense and meaning of the context and the construction of a wider alternative context	Learning leading to change in organisational practices

by the introduction of a new technology or set of regulations, but it is not reducible to it. This type of learning may be seen as distinct from that which takes place when existing knowledge and skills embedded in an established activity are gradually acquired and internalised as in apprenticeship settings or when existing knowledge is deployed in new activity settings, or even when the new knowledge is constructed through experimentation within an established activity. All three types of learning may take place within expansive learning, but these gain a different meaning, motive and perspective as parts of the expansive process. A full cycle of expansive transformation may be understood as a collective journey through the zone of proximal development of the activity (Engeström, 1999a). His argument is that expansive learning involves the creation of new knowledge and new practices for a newly emerging activity: that is, learning embedded in and constitutive of qualitative transformation of the entire activity system. Such a transformation may be triggered by the introduction of a new technology or set of regulations but it is not reducible to it. This type of learning may be seen as distinct from that which takes place when existing knowledge and skills embedded in an established activity are gradually acquired and internalised, as in apprenticeship models, or when existing knowledge is deployed in new activity settings, or even when the new knowledge is constructed through experimentation within an established activity. All three types of learning may take place within expansive learning but these gain a different meaning, motive and perspective as parts of the expansive process.

Dialogicality and multi-voicedness

As noted above, the third generation of activity theory, as proposed by Engeström, intends to develop conceptual tools to understand dialogues, multiple perspectives and networks of interacting activity systems. He draws on Bakhtin's (1986, 1984, 1981) ideas on dialogicality and multi-voicedness in order to move beyond the limitations of the second generation of activity theory, which was concerned with the analysis of single activity systems. The idea of networks of activity within which contradictions and struggles take place in the definition of the motives and object of the activity calls for an analysis of power and control within developing activity systems. Engeström (1999a) provides the following example:

> [Object] moves from an initial state of unreflected, situationally given 'raw material (object 1; e.g. a specific patient entering a physician's office) to a collectively meaningful object constructed by the activity system (object 2; e.g. the patient constructed as a specimen of a biomedical disease category and thus as an instantiation of the general object of illness/health), and to a potentially shared or jointly constructed object (object 3; e.g. a collaboratively constructed understanding of the patient's life situation and care plan). The object of activity is a moving target, not reducible to conscious short-term goals.
>
> (Engeström, 1999a, p. 136)

Boundary objects, translation, and boundary-crossing

In Engeström (2000a), he also argues that it is important to extend beyond the singular activity system and to examine and work towards the transformation of networks of activity. He advocates the 'exploration of the concept of boundary crossing to analyze the unfolding of object-oriented cooperative activity of several actors, focusing on tools and means of construction of boundary objects in concrete work processes' (Engeström, 1999b, p. 391). The concept of boundary-crossing offers a potential means of conceptualising the ways in which collaboration between workers from different professional backgrounds might generate new professional practices (Engeström *et al.*, 2003; Engeström *et al.*, 1995). Standard notions of professional expertise imply a vertical model, in which practitioners develop competence over time as they acquire new levels of professional knowledge, graduating 'upwards' level by level in their own specialisms. By contrast, boundary-crossing suggests that expertise is also developed when practitioners collaborate *horizontally* across sectors.

Engeström *et al.* (1999) developed the concept of knotworking to describe the 'construction of constantly changing combinations of people and artefacts over lengthy trajectories of time and widely distributed in space' (p. 345). They described knotworking as follows:

> Knotworking is characterized by a pulsating movement of tying, untying and retying together otherwise separate threads of activity. The tying and dissolution of a knot of collaborative work is not reducible to any specific individual or fixed organizational entity as the center of control. The center does not hold. The locus of initiative changes from moment to moment within a knotworking sequence. Thus, knotworking cannot be adequately analyzed from the point of view of an assumed center of coordination and control, or as an additive sum of the separate perspectives of individuals or institutions contributing to it. The unstable knot itself needs to be made the focus of analysis.
>
> (Engeström *et al.*, 1999b, pp. 346–7)

They pointed out the difference between knotworking which operates at the individual and collective levels. Thus 'intersubjectivity is not reducible to either the *inter*action between or the *subjectivity* of each participant. Both are needed' (Engeström *et al.*, 1999, p. 354). Boundary zones allow practitioners to express multiple alternatives, challenge the concepts that are declared from above by using their own experienced concepts, and through these debates create a new negotiated model of activity (Engeström *et al.*, 2005). In this respect, expansive learning is dialogical; it helps to tie knots between different activity systems and find a common perspective by moving sideways using the existing knowledge and practitioners' experiences, as well as their visions for the future (Engeström,

2004a). Taken together, the concepts of boundary-crossing and knotworking are attempts to theorise the actions that place as networks of activity are transformed.

Cognitive trails

Engeström has also drawn on Cussins' (1992) theory of cognitive trails, which he and Kerosuo suggest serve as anchors and stabilising networks that make divided activity networks and their multi-organisational terrains knowable and livable (Engeström and Kerosuo, 2007). Cognitive trails are constantly created and recreated in the flow of a person's experiences (Engeström, 2006). They are a form of embodied cognition created as people move through space and time.

> Trails are both person-made and world-made, and what makes persons and worlds. Trails are in the environment, certainly, but they are also *cognitive* objects. A trail isn't just an indentation in a physical surface, but a *marking* of the environment; a signposting for coordinating sensation and movement, an experiential line of force. Hence the marking is both experiential and environmental.
>
> (Cussins, 1992, pp. 673–4)

Cognitive trails 'mark' the landscape in which people have acted and they act as a means of support for future action. Although it is not an entirely correct analogy, when I was first trying to understand this concept I thought about 'Songlines' or dreaming tracks described in the novel by Bruce Chatwin (1987) that are remembrances that support navigation through what might ostensibly be seen as a featureless landscape in rural Australia. Cussins' description emphasises the way in which, once created, cognitive trails functions as guides for future action.

> Each trail occurs over time, and is a manipulation or a trial or an avoidance or capture or simply a movement. It is entirely context-dependent ... Yet a trail is not transitory (although a tracking of a trail is): the environmental marking persists and thereby the ability to navigate through the feature-domain is enhanced.
>
> (Cussins, 1992, p. 674)

These inscriptions facilitate development of new forms of action in the relatively unknown territory that is developed when boundaries as crossed. In Engeström (2006), he extends this notion when he deploys the metaphor of mycorrhizae, the invisible subterranean structure of fungus, to describe the emergence and functioning of knotworking. Once developed, mycorrhizae can lie dormant for lengthy periods but is able to grow mushrooms, i.e. unite successfully heterogeneous partners in order to work together symbiotically when the conditions are right (Engeström, 2006). Similarly, cognitive trails required for knotworking may stay unused for periods but become re-activated by different innovatively collaborating and improvising actors when new contradictions and new learning challenges for the activity system occur. The subterranean structure has a meaning only in relation to the plants it grows, but the growing of plants (i.e. transformation of activity systems) cannot be understood without taking into account the mycorrhizae-like base (Märtsin, 2007). It is through this kind of metaphorical discussion that Engeström seeks to theorise and understand what might be happening when subjects cross the boundaries that are created in complex activity system networks as they seek to develop and promote new ways of working and being.

Labour power

In Daniels and Warmington (2007), we suggested that cognitive trails, knotworking and boundary-crossing could be regarded as tools for reconfiguring collective labour power. We argued that the notion of labour power may also prove to be a useful addition to the activity theory model of the 'setting of development' with specific reference to the notion of 'subject'.

The categories of use- and exchange-value that Engeström (2001a, p. 137) identifies as 'the primary contradiction of activities in capitalism' derive from Marx's depiction of commodification. In offering an explanation of the internal relationship between use- and exchange-value, Engeström customarily invokes Leontiev's example of a medical practitioner's work. However, this example of a commodity is only partly helpful, since Marx, in *Capital* (Marx, 1976/1883) and its precursor, *Grundrisse* (Marx, 1973/1858), posits *two* categories of commodity: the 'general class of commodities', of which Leontiev's medicines are an example and the 'other great class of commodity', which he terms *labour-power*. The latter is described as a potential force: a resource residing in the subject (and in the subject's tool appropriation). It includes an array of qualities: not just skills and knowledge forms but also attitudes, motivation and self-presentation. The definition of 'labour-power' might include the potential or the disposition to form those intersubjective resources such as 'cognitive trails', 'confidence pathways' and 'trust cohorts' (Cussins, 1992; Knorr Cetina, 1999).

Education, training and work-related learning are forms of social production of labour-power potential. This has implications for the practical application of activity theory in work-related research, since it suggests that, above and beyond the specific, directly functional object of a particular activity (the realisation of specific workplace projects), the 'meta-object' of a workplace activity system is the expansion of labour-power potential (Warmington, 2005). The development of Vygotsky's activity theory in the subsequent work of Leontiev and Engeström is rooted in a concern with the *collective* aspect of labour-power. Engeström's notion of expansive learning (in work settings) and his analytic focus on the second and third generations of activity theory implies the meta-object of working on the quality of labour-power: in particular, the quality of co-operation between labour-powers within activity systems ('second generation') and between related activity systems ('third generation').

Object-oriented activity is rendered contradictory because it constitutes both directly functional work and the social production of labour-power, which is always riven by contradictions. These contradictions are experienced by the subject (with its inhabiting labour-power), as the subject negotiates objects, rules, tools, communities and divisions of labour that are themselves contradictory (because they are elements of this double activity and expressions of labour in capitalism). Contradictions are generated because, within the labour process, the human is simultaneously marginal and central within the activity system: simultaneously actor and labour-power resource (cf. Roth et al., 2005, p. 7).

Research interventions that apply activity theory in workplace-learning studies are immersed in the contradictory double form of object-oriented activity systems: (1) the object of directly functional work and (2) the goal that is the social production of labour-power. Given this, it is unsurprising that Engeström (2001a, p. 134) speaks of object-oriented actions as 'always, explicitly or implicitly, characterized by ambiguity, surprise, interpretation, sense making, and potential for change' and urges us to abandon the presupposition that knowledge and skills acquired in the workplace are 'stable and reasonably well defined' (Engeström, 2001a, p. 137). For, insofar as the meta-object of an activity system is the social production of labour-power, it must be contradictory and, in potential, 'infinitely' expansive. These instabilities pervade the contemporary sphere of 'service industries', the 'knowledge economy', 'reflexivity' and 'learning organizations', wherein workplace activities are as much about the social production of the unstable and unfinished commodity of labour-power as they are about marshalling concrete labour to produce general commodities.

Developmental work research

Much of Engeström's work involves developmental intervention-based research. He argues that research has a dialectical, dialogic relationship with activity and he focuses on contradictions as causative and disturbances as indicators of potential. He sees interventions as enabling the construction of new instrumentalities and as bringing about, through externalisation, the 'transformative construction of new instruments and forms of activity at collective and individual levels' (Engeström, 1999, p. 376). His approach to interventionist research is derived from activity theory and has its roots in the Vygotskian method of dual or double stimulation (or 'experimental-genetic method', 'instrumental method', 'historical-genetic method') as discussed in Chapter 2. This method was the outcome of Vygotsky's struggle to find a way of studying human functioning as it developed, rather than considering functions that had developed. The essence of this approach is that subjects are placed in a situation in which a problem is identified and they are also provided with tools with which to solve the problem or means by which they can construct tools to solve the problem. This follows directly from Vygotsky's own descriptions:

> By using this approach, we do not limit ourselves to the usual method of offering the subject simple stimuli to which we expect a direct response. Rather, we simultaneously offer a *second series of stimuli* that have a special function. In this way, we are able to study the *process of accomplishing a task by the aid of specific auxiliary means;* thus we are also able to discover the inner structure and development of higher psychological processes. The method of dual stimulation elicits manifestations of the crucial processes in the behaviour of people of all ages. Tying a knot as a reminder, in both children and adults, is but one example of a pervasive regulatory principle of human behaviour, that of *signification*, wherein people create temporary links and give significance to previously neutral stimuli in the context of their problem-solving efforts. We regard our method as important because it helps to *objectify* inner psychological processes.
>
> (Vygotsky, 1978, pp. 74–5)

Engeström (2007) draws attention to the root of this approach in Vygotsky's thoughts on intentional action:

> The person, using the power of things or stimuli, controls his own behavior through them, grouping them, putting them together, sorting them. In other words, the great uniqueness of the will consists of man having no power over his own behavior other than the power that things have over his behavior. But man subjects to himself the power of things over behavior, makes them serve his own purposes and controls that power as he wants. He changes the environment with the external activity and in this way affects his own behavior, subjecting it to his own authority.
>
> (Vygotsky, 1997a, p. 212)

This affirmation of the centrality of the use of cultural tools in the establishment of control over behaviour is the key to a research endeavour which seeks to prompt or provoke expansive learning. It is through the use of these tools that subjects seek a way to engage with the contradictions that are embedded in everyday experience. The cultural artefact or tool that is presented is the third generation activity theory model. This 'scientific concept' is brought into relations with the everyday concepts that are developed by participants in the workplace. This provides a way for participants to learn and develop new tools for bringing their everyday situations under their own analytical and practical control. Engeström *et al.* (1999) view the 'reflective appropriation of advanced models and tools' as 'ways out of internal contradictions' that result in new activity systems.

An application of developmental work research

In Daniels, Leadbetter, Warmington *et al.* (2007), we outline the use of a series of 'Change Laboratory' intervention sessions, as developed by Engeström and his

Activity theory and interventionist research 133

colleagues in Helsinki (Engeström, 2007). This research intervention is based on the expansive learning cycle which consists of the following steps, often referred to as Developmental Work Research (DWR):

1. Drawing on ethnographic evidence to question existing practices (i.e. learning in and for interagency working).
2. Analysing the historical origins of existing practices and bringing these analyses to bear in analysing current dynamics within and across services.
3. Modelling an alternative way of working (i.e. a new model of learning).
4. Examining the model to understand its dynamics, strengths and pitfalls.
5. Implementing the model and monitoring the processes and impact of implementation in the dispositions and actions of professionals.
6. Drawing on these data to reflect on the processes and outcomes.

Change Laboratory sessions lie at the core of DWR. Each of these sessions lasts about two hours. The central tool of the Change Laboratory is a 3{multi}3 set of surfaces for representing the work activity (Figure 6.4). Practitioners participating in the Change Laboratory process face the surfaces and also each other. One or more researcher-interventionists are present to guide the process. A video projector is important since videotaped work situations are typically used as material in the laboratory sessions. Each session is also videotaped for research and to facilitate the reviewing of critical laboratory events in subsequent sessions. In these sessions, current working practices of team members are discussed, tensions and dilemmas are highlighted and alternative ways of working proposed.

The *mirror* surface (see Figure 6.4) is used to represent and examine experiences

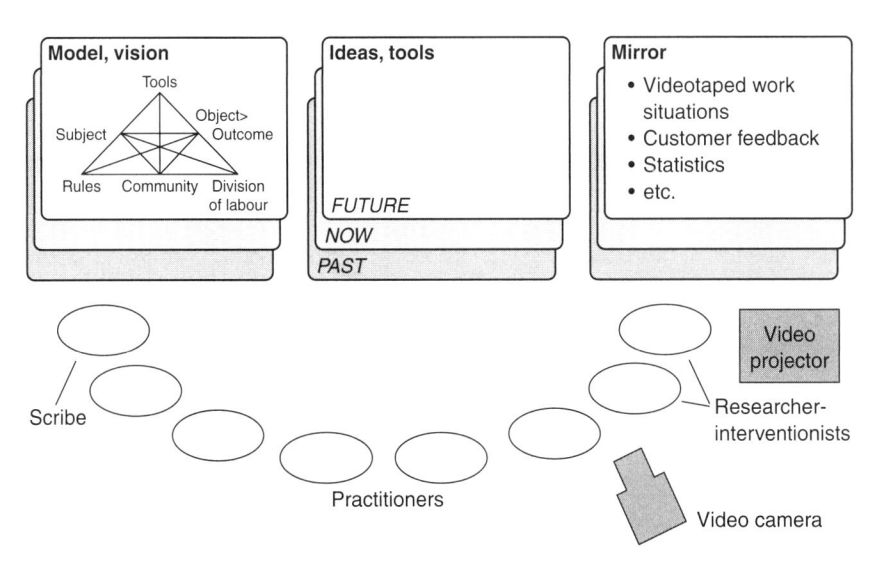

Figure 6.4 Typical DWR workshop layout.

from work practice, particularly problem situations and disturbances, but also novel innovative solutions. Videotaped work episodes as well as photographs, stories, interviews, quotations and narrative accounts can be used as mirror data. These focus upon:

- Present practice: identifying structural tensions (or 'contradictions') in current working practices.
- Past practice: encouraging professionals to consider the historical development of their working practices from their different perspectives/agencies.
- Future practice: working with professionals to suggest new forms of practice that might effect innovations in multiagency working to support effective work with clients.

Engeström (2007) describes the essence of the process of dual stimulation in the laboratories:

> the *model/vision* surface is reserved for theoretical tools and conceptual analysis. The complex triangular model of an activity system (Engeström, 1987, p. 78), displayed schematically in (Figure 6.3), is used to analyze the development and interconnections of the work activity under scrutiny. Systemic roots of specific but recurring problems and disturbances are traced and conceptualized as inner contradictions of the activity system. In addition to the general model of activity system, more specific conceptual models are often used. The third surface in the middle is reserved for *ideas and tools*.
> (Engeström, 2007, p. 10)

The triangular model is used to analyse the systemic quality and interconnections of work activity. Systemic roots of specific but recurring problems and disturbances are traced and conceptualised as inner contradictions of the activity system (after Virkkunen *et al.*, 1997).

Work in the Change Laboratory typically starts with the examples gained from the interviews and data collection, designed to mirror present problems. Discussion then moves to trace the roots of current difficulties by eliciting experiences from the past and by modelling the past activity systems. This analysis is used to prompt the progressive modelling of past, present and future activity. In later laboratory sessions, the participants are supported as they envision and draft proposals for concrete changes to be embarked upon. In this way, critical incidents and examples from the ethnographic material are brought into Change Laboratory sessions to stimulate analysis and negotiation between the participants.

The purpose of the workshops is to address the challenges of new forms of learning by:

- encouraging the *recognition* of areas in which there is a need for change in working practices;

- suggesting possibilities for change through *re-conceptualising* the 'objects' that professionals are working on, the 'tools' that professionals use in their multi-agency work and the 'rules' in which professional practices are embedded.

Daniels, Leadbetter, Soares *et al.* (2007) studied professional learning in a partnership that involved one special school, four secondary schools and several creative and artistic groups and institutions (a gallery, a dance group, the local museum, etc.) in a deprived area of a large conurbation in central England. These partnerships were formed in order to promote creativity across the entire curriculum in the schools. This intervention study was concerned with the cultures and practices of learning within and across these schools and the creative organisations with which they were linked.

In his vision for the future of schooling, Brighouse (2002), the then Director of Education for the area, outlines a model of 'collegiate academies' in which the added value of carefully developed interdependence between schools is recognised. This visionary appeal brings with it many challenges for schools and teachers. This design for the future was being implemented at a time when the dominant educational paradigm focused on what students know, rather than how they use that knowledge or create new knowledge.

Within this project, we examined how different participants discursively (and non-discursively) moved beyond their institutional and local knowledge to create new meanings and possibilities. Following a period of detailed historical and ethnographic analysis of the approaches to creativity in the schools, a research briefing was provided for schools and their creative partners. The three Change Laboratory sessions took place over five months and between each session data were collected from a range of relevant sources and in different ways.

The Change Laboratory sessions focused on concrete cases that represented significant objects of work undergoing transformation. The sessions used shared conceptual tools of activity theory to analyse the historical evolution of the work practices, as well as current contradictions, disturbances and change potentials. Thus, the laboratory sessions represented a blend of elements familiar from existing practices and new elements brought in by the researchers. The laboratory sessions were videotaped for analysis. The work then proceeded to model the current activity and its inner contradictions, which enabled the participants to focus their transformation efforts on essential sources of work-based difficulties and tensions.

Our methodological approach differed from that which is conventionally deployed, in that we developed a progressive widening of the focus for data gathering. Our initial point of entry was with the so-called creativity co-ordinators from the schools in an informal group meeting. We then moved to gather data from the Heads of the schools for the first Change Laboratory, the individual co-ordinators for the second and other teachers in the school for the third. The move was thus to gather initial data from the strategic managers, then the operational managers and finally peripheral participants in the activity. This is shown diagrammatically in Figure 6.5.

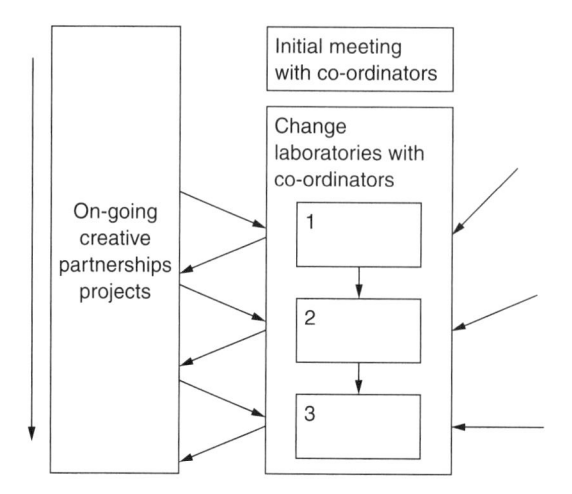

Figure 6.5 Stages of data gathering for series of workshops.

There is a clear line of development that can be traced throughout the research team's involvement with this consortium. Comparison of the data from the first group interview and that gathered in the final Change Laboratory session showed significant change in the formulation of the object of the work of the consortium and the tools that were developed and deployed.

The staged development of the activity took place as contradictions were surfaced. Over the period of the Change Laboratory sessions, the development and expansion of the object and the development of new tools, rules and division of labour was witnessed.

Expansion of the object

The object of activity expanded and was enriched through several stages from the first group interview to the last Change Laboratory session. Our analysis suggests the following changes in terms of the focus of the work of the group:

1 Multiple diffuse objects in play (e.g. visitor numbers, linking with others, motivation);
2 Forming a consortium;
3 The Projects;
4 Professional identity;
5 Transformation of cultures of learning.

Stage 1: multiple objects

Initially, articulating an answer to the question of what the co-ordinators were working on was a challenge for all concerned. The group admitted that they had not discussed this question before, and for this reason found it hard to say what it was they were working on, apart from generic projects. This finding is not confined to this project. We have found that asking practitioners about the object of their activity (albeit not using the term object in the questions) has proved to be a very powerful first step in the identification of systemic contradictions. When confronted with the question, practitioners were somewhat shocked to realise that they had not considered what it was they were 'working on' or trying to shift and change; rather, their thoughts had been directed to what they could do irrespective of the object. As time progressed, the accounts of the object changed and developed. Two examples of what co-ordinators stated they were working on are given below.

The following quotation, taken from the group interview, was an answer to the question 'what are you working on?' regarding their work: 'One thing from [the gallery's] point of view, not necessarily mine, is visitor figures ... not from my point of view, but certainly from a marketing point of view' (A). Boosting visitor figures was mentioned by the gallery co-ordinator as an initial reason for collaborating with the project. However, once pressed, the gallery co-ordinator offered a number of objects he was working on, in order that this outcome would result from the work. He cited accessibility of artists to younger people and overcoming barriers for pupils who may never have been to a gallery before.

Another of the many objects that were in circulation at the point of research engagement was that of workload:

> Before I talk to anyone who might be interested in the project, making sure that things are photocopied for them, to have the kids ready. To let them know how it's going to be in order for them ... [For one member of staff] it was pretty much holding this man's hand, so to speak, until he felt comfortable enough to go off and speak to someone else ... The idea [for staff is] 'what will I have to do to make this project work, how much extra time for me' and so I found that people are much more willing to go for it if it's pretty much handed to them on a plate, without them having to think and take risks.
>
> (C)

Here, the object of the co-ordinators' work was the workload of colleagues. The suggestion was made that unless the workload could be reduced then participation would have been denied.

Another co-ordinator was working on her own professional identity in her school, in order that she could progress the work of the consortium. She used the headteacher as a 'defence' against professional jealousy: 'Some of the paperwork I

138 Activity theory and interventionist research

pass to [the head], my name doesn't go on it. The headteacher's name goes on it ... to protect me'. Another co-ordinator sought to share the success of project work with other members of staff during morning briefing sessions or other opportune moments in the school day. In this way, she was working on communication within the school:

> What I like to do is share the success with members of staff after an event has taken place ... and I think that does involve more staff because initially, CP in our school, they just saw it as the creative subjects and had staff saying 'well how are we going to benefit?' ... It's just very brief just to share the results and we've found that's had a huge impact.
>
> (CAS)

Stage 2: forming the consortium

Creating an alliance of schools in partnership with external agencies was a specific priority for the work: 'I am absolutely adamant that we are included in initiatives and in the local community. That means for me working in collaboration with as many schools as possible and not being isolated' (Headteacher B). '[The school was] traditionally an island ... Absolutely no collaboration ... there's a lot of strength in the North-West partnership. [The school] would not have survived much longer had they not embraced that' (Headteacher C). The importance of combating isolation through the formation of groupings or consortia of local schools and the community was seen as an essential element for the success of the individual schools. Headteachers could see that their school would be assisted through the strengthening of local initiatives.

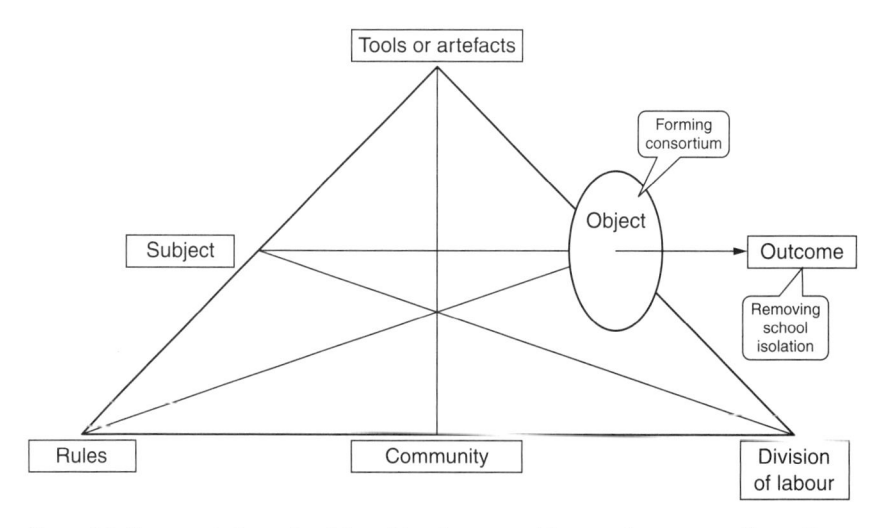

Figure 6.6 Representation of activity with a focus on objects and outcomes (Stage 2).

Stage 3: a focus on the projects

As the research intervention progressed, the object appeared to change. Working on the projects was seen as an object of activity by the co-ordinators. The projects offered an opportunity for pupils to develop creativity in learning. However, working on the projects was discussed in narrow terms of doing and completing the task. Whilst working on projects was important, the opportunity that the projects gave to co-ordinators was wider than first realised by the group, and the way in which the object was discussed in later Change Laboratory sessions highlights the co-ordinator's ability to see beyond the level of directly functional project work.

Stage 4: a focus on professional identity

Interviews and subsequent discussions during the sessions emphasised underlying tensions that, if not acknowledged, could undermine the efforts of CP. The core concern was the notion of professional or subject identity. It was noted that, for some teachers, the prospect of getting involved in work which required flexibility and was, to some extent, unpredictable and diverse in its nature, was daunting. Some staff questioned the relevance and usefulness of creativity in their own subject area. Arguably, much of secondary schooling is focused on certain instrumental outcomes. In such a setting, creativity may be viewed as an additional burden to the processes and outcomes that schools are required to focus on. The important message for the funders of the work was to recognise that professional fear/insecurity could inhibit the progression of the work. The data suggest that many teachers were seen to have professional identities which were threatened by

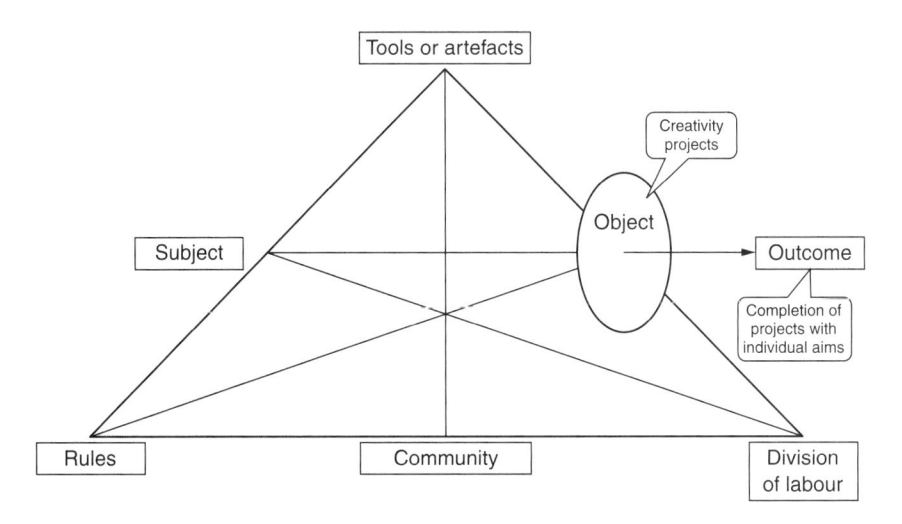

Figure 6.7 Representation of activity with a focus on objects and outcomes (Stage 3).

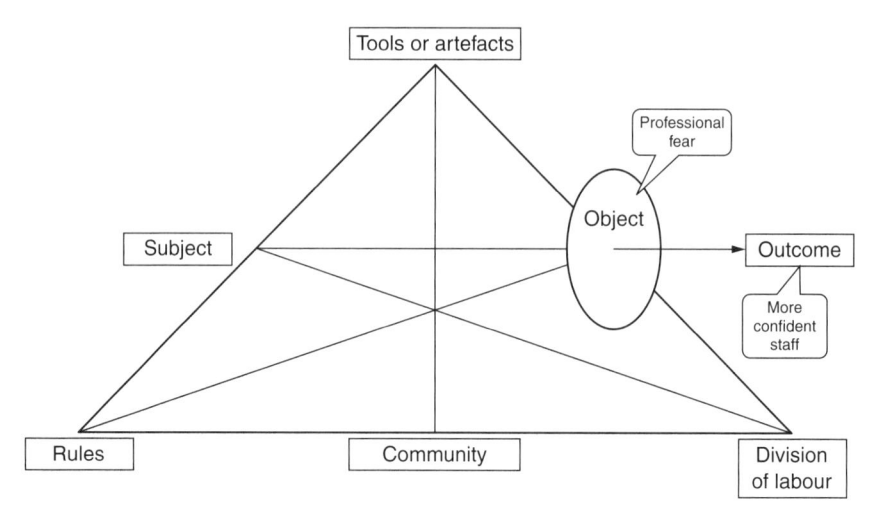

140 Activity theory and interventionist research

Figure 6.8 Representation of activity with a focus on objects and outcomes (Stage 4).

the forms of risk-taking and exploratory work that was being promoted. At this stage in the research, the co-ordinators talked about professional identity as an emergent object of their work.

Stage 5: transformation of cultures of learning

In the final laboratory, it was recognised that there was a need to reflect on staff learning and arrangements to support learning. Co-ordinators felt that it was particularly important to encourage headteachers to adopt the notion of 'teachers as learners'. It was argued that headteachers and senior management need to get involved in the 'middle' of project work. That is, they need to be aware of and allow for the learning and development that occurs between the start and end of the projects. It was argued that the processes of learning that happen 'in between' needs to be recognised, understood and supported by headteachers and senior management teams. The proposal was made that the development of the work requires a professional learning environment that stretches across the whole school. The notion of the project work as a tool for professional learning emerged from final conversations. Such an understanding gives rise to a reconsideration of the forms of planning and intervention that are required in order to facilitate the forms of staff development that would allow the project work to function as a vector for general pedagogic change in schools.

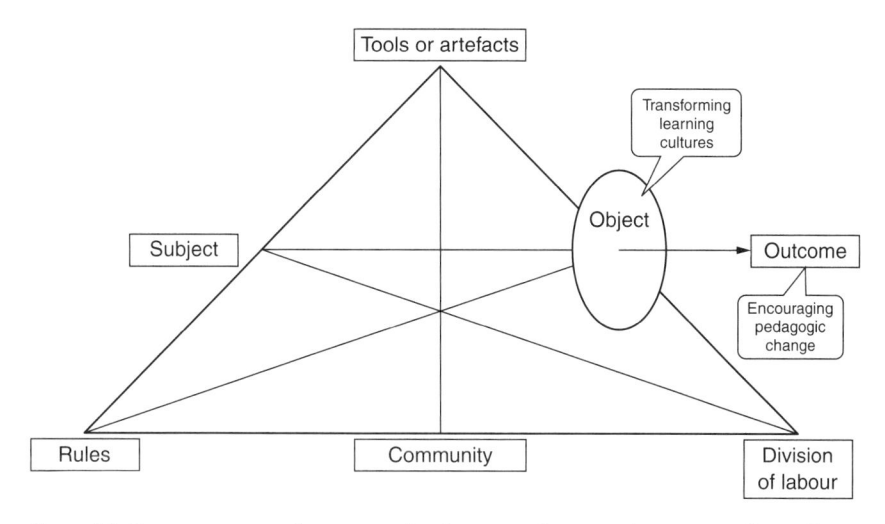

Figure 6.9 Representation of activity with a focus on objects and outcomes (Stage 5).

Tool development

The nature of the tools used by the co-ordinators has also undergone substantial change and these acted to promote expanded learning in practice.

Stage 1: tool development for communication

The group recognised that an important piece of learning in relation to tool development had happened with the introduction of an agreement on a suitable time to contact one another. Although timing of phone-calls seems obvious, reaching an accord on a suitable time to contact each other facilitated the management and organisation of the projects:

> I think the main thing was communication and having to get through to the correct person ... now it's a lot easier because I know the teachers and they know me ... I don't start till ten; teachers are there from eight o'clock. So I guess it's a balance really.
>
> (A)

At the outset, communication was not always easy within and between the consortium we studied. This sometimes led to confusion and a sense of isolation. The development of tools for communication was an important feature of the early developmental work.

Engeström *et al.* (1997) emphasise the special importance of 'future-orientated tools': practices and instruments that do not merely address immediate working

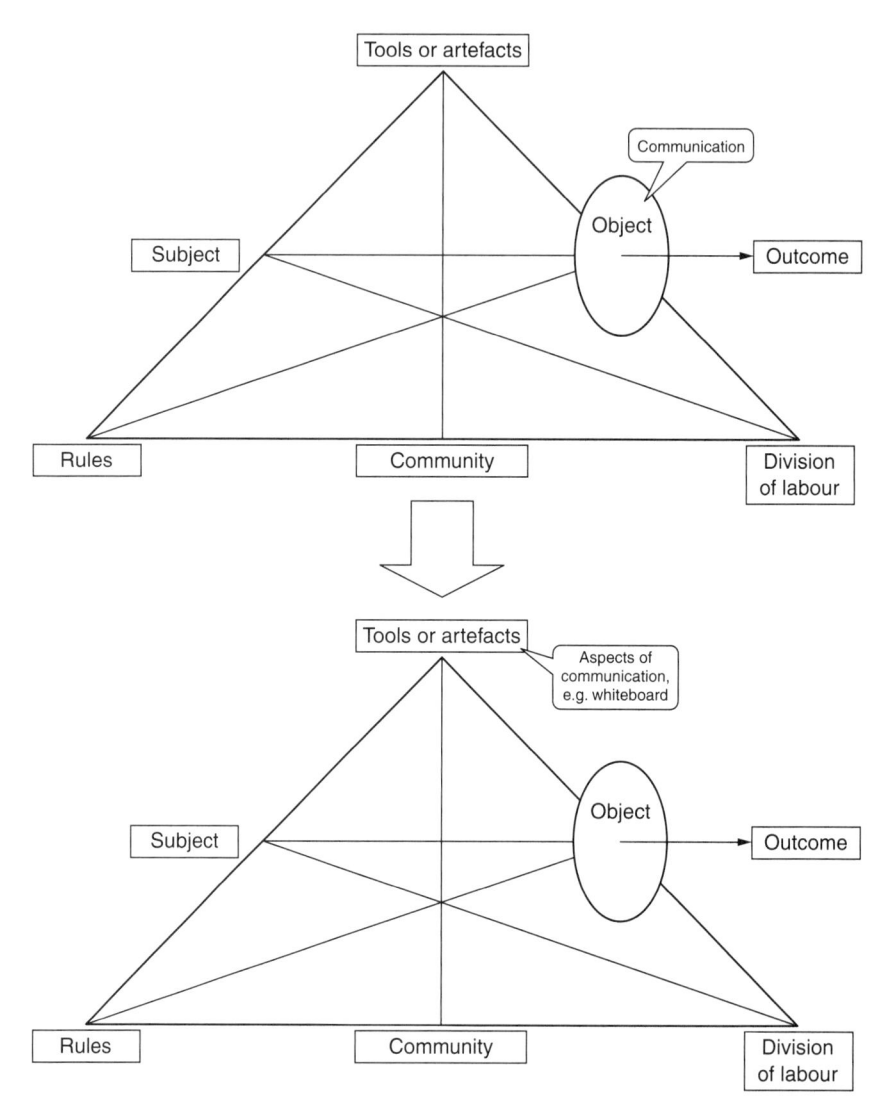

142 Activity theory and interventionist research

Figure 6.10 Representation of activity with a focus on objects and subsequent tool development.

needs but that suggest means by which to expand learning and practice, so as to encourage continual innovation. By the end of the last session, co-ordinators were concerned with how they could convey information more effectively within and between schools. Several suggestions were proposed: constructing a cohesive, coherent communication plan before embarking on any future cluster formation; employing a whiteboard; employing mentors for new co-ordinators; utilising a web forum and attending training events.

Stage 2: tool development for working on the object of professional fear

Participants argued that seminars, conferences or training days may lead to networking and offer the opportunity for staff to talk about the difficulties and successes they have experienced. It was also felt that such events could provide the opportunity to discover and develop new knowledge with which to enhance the work. Participants recognised the need for schools to work together on this issue and for staff to develop the professional disposition to consult colleagues for support.

It was further suggested that for the success of the study cluster and that of others to be sustained and expanded, it will be necessary to involve headteachers and senior management in the learning that staff experience.

Stage 3: tool development for managing conflict

The data suggest that the development of the consortium had witnessed a number of disagreements. At one time, the co-ordinators learned to manage disagreement by going outside the group for help in order to obtain authority to repair or sustain the functioning of the group. The positive group dynamics that were witnessed in the research were protected by the co-ordinators who sought out 'honest brokers' from outside if they sensed conflict. The group were aware that unmanaged conflicts could damage relationships and thus deployed the services of a third party to resolve any difficulties. However, it was recognised that this deployment of external agents serves a short-term purpose. The group recognised the need to develop their own tools for managing disagreement in future. It was suggested that these new ways of working would evolve as the consortium became more established.

An activity theory analysis of learning in and for inter-school work

Figure 6.11 is a visual depiction of the change that has occurred with this group since the research team's involvement. The first three activities (including the intermediary activity) had occurred before the research intervention took place.

Although the process was not smooth, the transformations and the learning involved could be traced back to events that took place before the start of the research intervention. At the start of the research project, there was an uncertainty about the nature of the object. A series of objects were identified by individuals within the group. An intermediary activity involved the co-ordinators in the development of tools for communication. These tools enabled them to work on the formation of consortia. Once the co-ordinators had established appropriate

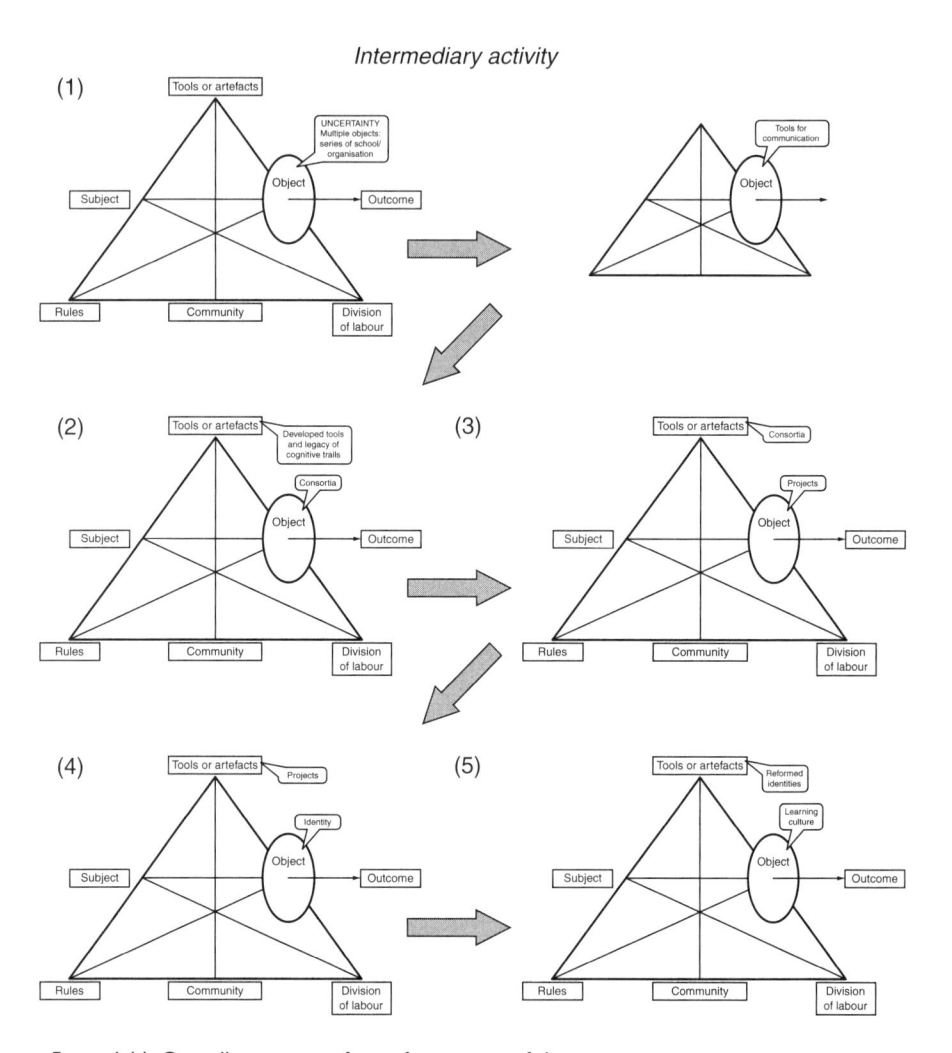

144 Activity theory and interventionist research

Figure 6.11 Overall sequence of transformations of the activity.

practices of communication within the consortium, they were in a position to work on joint projects. The legacy of cognitive trails (as in Cussins, 1992) formed in previous professional encounters helped the co-ordinators build upon their past working relationships. The co-ordinators were able to follow familiar paths through their experience of previous working environments. The co-ordinators acknowledged that the projects allowed them to work on aspects of their identity and elements of other subject teachers' dispositions, attitudes and beliefs. In this stage of the activity, the outcome was the formation of new professional identities for themselves and the shaping of the subject identities of others. With these newly formed identities, the co-ordinators were and will be able to work on transforming learning cultures in their schools.

We suggest that there are at least two dimensions to the learning we studied:

- a *horizontal dimension* where learning takes place across boundaries – between departments within schools, between schools, between schools and partners; and
- a *vertical dimension* in which learning takes place across boundaries between strategic and operational staff within schools.

Through the projects, learning opportunities are available not just for pupils involved in the work, but also staff. The project funders' and senior school management's ability to help effect change in teaching style and learning cultures were seen as major priorities for the future. Expansive learning processes in inter-agency settings are predicated upon horizontal movements, wherein mutual learning takes place through the shifts and tensions that occur when professionals from different backgrounds collaborate. Vertical expertise (learning across the hierarchy within an organisation) is not sufficient to meet the increase in demands on dialogical problem-solving in contemporary pedagogic environments undergoing change. Engeström (2004b, p. 4) notes that expansive learning is 'intertwined with horizontal or sideways movement across competing or complementary domains and activity systems'.

Engeström (1995) argues that while the vertical dimension remains important, a horizontal dimension is central for the understanding and acquisition of expertise. Standard notions of professional expertise imply a vertical model in which practitioners develop in competence over time as they acquire new levels of professional knowledge 'from above'. By contrast, boundary-crossing suggests that expertise is also developed when practitioners collaborate *horizontally* across sectors. With the introduction of the projects, horizontal learning evolved in this cluster. The research team observed both horizontal and vertical learning in the following situations:

Horizontal
School ↔ School
Mainstream school ↔ Special school
School ↔ Creative agency

Several boundaries have been crossed. Learning has taken place between schools and, at a more micro level, between mainstream schools and a special school. Interaction, boundary-crossing and learning have also occurred between the schools involved in this cluster and different creative agencies, including the art gallery and theatre groups. The diagram below highlights the vertical boundary-crossing that has occurred, with learning taking place between the projects and the co-ordinators, school management and co-ordinators and co-ordinators and other staff members.

Vertical
Creative (projects) ↔ Co-ordinators partnerships
School management ↔ Co-ordinators
Co-ordinators ↔ Other teachers

The intervention by the research team comprised a new type of professional practice in and of itself. It will take time to embed this learning in and across the professional bodies involved with such projects. It will also require sensitive assistance from all involved in interagency work (cross-school work). New consortia can follow the positive example by this consortium. The stages of learning this group went through are stages we believe other groups would have to follow to resolve some of the problems inherent in developing new forms of pedagogic work.

One way of summarising the social processes we studied is captured by Hakkarainen *et al.* (2004):

> Expertise in a certain domain may also be represented in a hybrid expert who is able to translate one expert culture's knowledge into form that participants of another expert culture can understand ... [I]nnovations do not emerge linearly from ideas to their technical implementations and practical applications because the meaning of an idea or discovery becomes transformed when novel and unanticipated uses are found for technical artifacts; this transformation may open up novel spaces of innovative activity that were completely beyond the participants' epistemic horizon before trying ideas out in practice. Ultimately only transformation of social practices determines the meaning of innovations. Consequently, the participants' socially distributed collaborative activities have crucial role in networked intelligence.
>
> (Hakkarainen *et al.*, 2004, p. 6)

We argued that the creation of creative activity in the workplace requires, as Vygotsky (2004) suggested, close attention to the creation and adoption of tools for creativity and contexts that support its enactment. This involves a social process of learning and transformation. The goal of promoting creativity in schools will not be achieved if the construct of creativity remains that of an individualistic capability.

There is often considerable resistance to change that arises when participants in our workshops understand that they should make changes but cannot engage with the processes of making those changes. Engeström (2005a) has referred to the 'agony' that confrontation with changes in professional practice and identity may entail. Another potential way of conceptualising this 'agony' is that it is the lived experience of contradictions between the efforts of organisations to manage and innovate co-operation between labour-powers, the demands that this places upon subjects in terms of how they are required to activate their labour-power potential within the labour process, and subjects' own, wilful control over activating their 'actual' labour within the labour process. The Russian writer Vasilyuk (1991) discussed the particular internal work by means of which 'a person overcomes and conquers a crisis, restores lost spiritual equilibrium and resurrects the lost meaning of existence' (Vasilyuk, 1991, p. 10).

In Engeström's (2007) latest interventionist research, he has noted that whilst individual practitioners were happy to construct new models and tools for changing their work, they sometimes appeared reluctant to proceed with implementation. This resistance to the construction of new professional identities presents a challenge to the overly cognitive orientation of much activity-theory-based research. In the last year of his life, Vygotsky turned his attention to a new unit of analysis, namely *perezhivanie*, as discussed in Chapter 2.

This idea has been largely ignored in the development of activity theory. It was refined in the writing of Vasilyuk (1991), when he introduced the notion of experiencing defined as a particular form of activity directed towards the restoration of meaning in life. He contrasted his activity-theory-based understanding with that of a reflection of a state in the subject's consciousness and with forms of contemplation. The general working hypothesis of learning itself requires expansion to include notions of experiencing and identity formation within an account that includes a systematic and coherent analysis of the wider social structuring of society as an inseparable part of the analysis.

Chapter 7

Institutions and beyond

In this final chapter I will explore *some* of the directions in which post-Vygotskian theory and research is striving to develop and extend its range. I will argue that there is a need to extend the scope of the understanding of the 'social' and to develop research tools that enable us to see talk in context and context in talk (Makitalo and Säljö, 2002) and the implications of the ways in which individuals take up positions and are positioned in practices.

The production of artefacts and the institutional level of analysis

In what Minick (1987) refers to as the second phase to be found in parts of *Thinking and Speech*, Vygotsky discusses the process of development in terms of changes in the functional relationship between speaking and thinking. He asserts that 'change in the functional structure of consciousness is the main and central content of the entire process of mental development' (Vygotsky, 1987c, p. 188). He illustrates the movement from a social plane of functioning to an individual plane of functioning. From his point of view, the 'internalisation of socially rooted and historically developed activities is the distinguishing feature of human psychology' (Vygotsky, 1978, p. 57). I do not wish to embroil myself in the 'internalisation–appropriation' debate at this juncture. Instead, I wish to start from his assertion that interpersonal processes are transformed into intrapersonal processes as development progresses and move to question the way in which interpersonal processes are theorised and described. Vygotsky provides a theoretical framework which rests on the concept of mediation by what have been referred to as psychological tools or cultural artefacts. This has found expression in the study of the mediating role of specific cultural tools and their impact on development, as well the mediational function of the social interaction that gives access to specific tools. From this point in the development of his work, the challenges that confront us are at least twofold: first, have we developed an account of mediation that is both necessary and sufficient for a satisfactory account of the social, cultural and historical formation of mind; and, second, have we developed a sufficiently robust understanding of the ways in which mediational means are produced? In respect of the first challenge, as I noted in Chapter 2, Wertsch (2007) is developing an account of implicit mediation which echoes some of Bernstein's (2000) work on invisible mediation which can also be thought of as tacit mediation. It would seem that a similar challenge has also been noted by Abreu and Elbers (2005):

> ...the impact of broader social and institutional structures on people's psychological understanding of cultural tools. We argue that in order to understand social mediation it is necessary to take into account ways in which the practices of a community, such as school and the family, are structured by their institutional context. Cultural tools and the practices they are associated with, have their existence in communities, which in turn occupy positions in the broader social structure. These wider social structures impact on the interactions between the participants and the cultural tools.
> (Abreu and Elbers, 2005, p. 4)

Or, in the case of Lemke (1995), who points to the same aspect of mediation when he suggests that:

> Our meanings shape and are shaped by our social relationships, both as individuals and as members of social groups. These social relationships bind us into communities, cultures and subcultures. The meanings we make define not only our selves, they also define our communities ... [and] the relationships between communities ... all of which are quintessentially political relationships.
> (Lemke, 1995, p. 1)

The search for methodological and theoretical coherence must also be matched by the creative development of methods that, by their very nature, do not deny access to the data that are central to the epistemological and ontological orientations of research.

In respect of the second challenge, again as I outlined in Chapter 2, Wertsch (1998) has advanced the case for the use of mediated action as a unit of analysis in social-cultural research because, in his view, it provides a kind of natural link between action, including mental action, and the cultural, institutional and historical context in which such action occurs. This is so because the mediational means, or cultural tools, are inherently situated culturally, institutionally and historically. However, as he had recognised earlier, the relationship between cultural tools and power and authority is still under-theorised and in need of empirical study (Wertsch and Rupert, 1993). This recognition is an important step forward from the original Vygotskian thesis which, as Ratner (1997) notes, did not consider the ways in which concrete social systems bear on psychological functions. He discussed the general importance of language and schooling for psychological functioning; however, he failed to examine the real social systems in which these activities occur. The social analysis is thus reduced to a semiotic analysis which overlooks the real world of social praxis (Ratner, 1997). Nonetheless, some notable writers in the field have recognised the need for such a form of theoretical engagement (e.g. Hedegaard, 2001; Makitalo and Säljö, 2002).

Categories and the regulation of institutional activities

Makitalo and Säljö enter into the challenge of accounting for the breadth of social, cultural and historical influences through the study of categories, arguing that an important window on the creation of social orders may be gleaned from the study of processes of categorisation. They suggest that, once produced, categories become an important feature of the regulation of institutional activities:

> we have argued that language categories are produced within collective practices to serve as mediational means (Wertsch, 1991). They are also used by people as constitutive resources in such practices. Through the sedimentation of traditions of argumentation, categories have been produced to form collective ways of understanding people, actions, events, and social practices. Institutionalization implies that categories serve as tools in the process of accounting for the relation between the collective and the individual. Categories are manifested in the concrete infrastructure of organizations – in documents, administrative routines, databases, and other tools. In this sense, they are embedded in political, economic, social and material circumstances.
> (Makitalo and Säljö, 2002, p. 64)

At the individual level, these processes may well operate at a tacit or relatively unobservable or unseen level, as described by Bernstein (2000) and Wertsch (2007). Hjörne and Säljö (2004) argue that categorisation is a form of work that people often do in order to cope with the demands of their job. Their emphasis is also on the study of categories as they are deployed and function in institutions. In addition, they are concerned with the material consequences of these categories, whatever their ontological status, in institutions such as schools. They see the category as a form of institutional argumentation, irrespective of the validity of the claims that are made about its knowledge base or status. This form of argumentation is seen as a resource that is actively used for dealing with problems within the sociocultural processes of schooling. At the same time, the category and the categorisation process carries consequences for the use of resources and, worryingly, for the processes of identity formation of young people (Hjörne and Säljö, 2004, 2005).

They also studied institutional reasoning and how events and people are categorised. They considered categories as historically emerging tools for co-ordinating social action and for mediating between collectives and individuals, and examined argumentation in institutional settings. This was undertaken as a longitudinal case study of the Swedish system of pupil welfare conferences. They found high levels of ambiguity and competing ways of representing the child's problems, in that participants in these meetings were forced to be quite flexible when connecting the broad range of contradictory behaviours and attitudes to categories. One of Hjörne and Säljö's (2004) conclusions was that the classification carries with it significant consequences for children and their participation in schooling. This research provides a way of thinking about interpersonal processes as they are enacted in institutions. The question remains as to whether the way in which institutions are structured requires more analysis both at specific points in time and as they change through activity with time.

The structure of institutions

Makitalo and Säljö (2002) argue that, as we talk, we enter the flow of communication in a stream of both history and the future (p. 63) and that researchers need to have some definition of the situation or activity at hand (p. 66). Ludvigsen (in press) acknowledges this and alludes to a process whereby categories are constructed in institutions:

> By sorting things out we are able to cope with complexity and maintain a measure of social order in our private and professional lives (Bowker and Star, 1999). This is a historical process initiated by individuals in specific activities (e.g. personal concerns), but when generalized, the resulting categories may serve as governing parts of institutional activities (e.g. laws).

At a very general level, the challenge has been set within modern interpretations of Marxist theory by Calhoun *et al.* (1993), who argued that 'social life ... must be understood in terms that do justice both to objective material, social, and cultural structures and to the constituting practices and experiences of individuals and groups' (Calhoun *et al.*, 1993, p. 3). There is a long-running debate as to whether Vygotsky was a Marxist who wished to create a Marxist psychology. There is no doubt that he drew on theoretical Marxism. It has been argued, for example, by Bernstein, that this, in itself, presented him with a particular theoretical challenge.

> A crucial problem of theoretical Marxism is the inability of the theory to provide descriptions of micro level processes, except by projecting macro level concepts on to the micro level unmediated by intervening concepts though which the micro can be both uniquely described and related to the macro level. Marxist theory can provide the orientation and the conditions the micro language must satisfy if it is to be 'legitimate'. Thus such a language must be materialist, not idealist, dialectic in method and its principles of development and change must resonate with Marxist principles.
>
> (Bernstein, 1993, p. xv)

In addition, Engeström and Miettinen also note limitations in their discussion of a Marxian interpretation of Hegel's conception of self-creation though labour:

> Human nature is not found within the human individual but in the movement between the inside and the outside, in the worlds of artefact use and artefact creation ... the creative and dynamic potential of concrete work process and technologies remains underdeveloped in his (Marx's) work.
>
> (Engeström and Miettinen, 1999, p. 5)

Describing discourse as a cultural historical product

If activities are to be thought of as 'socially rooted and historically developed', how do we describe them in relation to their social, cultural and historical contexts of production? If Vygotsky was arguing that formation of mind is a socially mediated process, then what theoretical and operational understandings of the social, cultural and historical production of 'tools' or artefacts do we need to develop in order to empirically investigate the processes of development? Bernstein has suggested that the metaphor of the 'tool' itself serves to distract attention away from the relation between its structure and the context of its production:

> The metaphor of 'tool' draws attention to a device, an empowering device, but there are some reasons to consider that the tool, its internal specialised structure is abstracted from its social construction. Symbolic 'tools' are never neutral; intrinsic to their construction are social classifications, stratifications, distributions and modes of recontextualizing.
>
> (Bernstein, 1993, p. xvii)

These questions concerning the production of artefacts or tools would appear to be a matter of some priority for the development of the field, as so much of the empirical work that has been undertaken struggles to connect the analysis of the formative effect of mediated activity or tool use with the analysis of tool or artefact production. I intend to try to invoke an account of the production of psychological tools or artefacts, such as discourse, that will allow for exploration of the formative effects of the social context of production at the psychological level. This will also involve a consideration of the possibilities afforded to different social actors as they take up positions and are positioned in social products such as discourse. This discussion of production will thus open up the possibility of analysing the possible positions that an individual may take up in a field of social practice. I will use the following statement as a device with which to open a debate about the relationship between principles of social production, regulation and individual functioning:

> The substantive issue of the theory is to explicate the processes whereby a given distribution of power and principles of control are translated into spe-

cialised principles of communication differentially, and often unequally, distributed to social groups/classes. And how such an unequal distribution of forms of communication, initially (but not necessarily terminally) shapes the formation of consciousness of members of these groups/classes in such a way as to relay both opposition and change. The critical issue is *the translation of power and control into principles of communication which become (successful or otherwise) their carriers or relays.*

(Bernstein, 2000, p. 91)

I wish to suggest that, particularly when the cultural artefact takes the form of a pedagogic discourse, we should also analyse its structure in the context of its production. As a rider to this statement, I must add that when I invoke the term 'pedagogic' I do not mean just those discourses which are enacted in educational institutions. Instead, I am referring to a much broader conception of pedagogy in human interaction, a definition such as that to be found Bernstein (1999), in which pedagogy is thought of a sustained process whereby

somebody(s) acquires new forms or develops existing forms of conduct, knowledge, practice and criteria, from somebody(s) or something deemed to be an appropriate provider and evaluator. Appropriate either from the point of view of the acquirer or by some other body(s) or both.

(Bernstein, 1999, p. 259).

This definition emphasises that conduct, knowledge, practice and criteria may all be developed. This sets it apart from definitions that attend only to matters of skills and knowledge. It suggests that a complete analysis of processes of development and learning within pedagogic practice must consider cognitive and affective matters. It also suggests that pedagogic practice may be thought of in terms of material things as well as persons. Defined in this way, the general practitioner, the policy maker, the therapist, the broadcaster and the journalist are all involved in a form of pedagogic practice. From this point of view then (and given that human beings have the capacity to influence their own development through their use of the artefacts, including discourses, which they and others create or have created), we need a language of description that allows us to identify and investigate:

- the circumstances in which particular discourses are produced;
- the modalities of such forms of cultural production;
- the implications of the availability of specific forms of such production for the shaping of learning and development.

As Bernstein (1993) argued, the development of Vygotskian theory calls for the development of languages of description which will facilitate a *multi-level* understanding of pedagogic discourse, the varieties of its practice and contexts of its realisation and production. There is a need to connect the theory of social formation of mind with the descriptions that are used in the activity of research. This should provide a means of relating the social-cultural-historical context to the form of the artefact. If processes of social formation are posited, then research requires a theoretical description of the possibilities for social products in terms of the principles that regulate the social relations in which they are produced. We need to understand the principles of communication in terms derived from a study of principles of social regulation.

Lemke (1995) argues that, as communication plays a critical role in social dynamics, then social theories about discourse should point the way to a dynamic, critical, unitary social theory. He suggests that whilst linguistics furnishes theories of description and psychology provides theories of mind, both tend to ignore the social functions of language and the social origins of human behaviour. He laments the lack of progress in advancing this agenda:

> Unfortunately, most theories of discourse are not social theories. Indeed most theories of discourse are mainly linguistic and psychological, paying relatively little attention to the question of who says what when, why, and with what effects. The social context of discourse, and issues of discourse as social action are largely ignored. Instead discourse is mostly seen as the product of autonomous mental processes, or it is simply described as having particular linguistic features.
>
> (Lemke, 1995, p. 56)

The concepts of both 'habitus' and 'genre' have been proposed as theoretical devices for 'bridging' the gap. Bernstein is critical of habitus for its weaknesses when it comes to operational description and thus comparative analysis. Although Wertsch (1998) has turned to Bakhtin's theory of speech genres for such a theory, Hasan has argued that, whilst Bakhtin's views concerning speech genres are

> rhetorically attractive and impressive, the approach lacks ... both a developed conceptual syntax and an adequate language of description. Terms and units at both these levels in Bakhtin's writings require clarification; further, the principles that underlie the calibration of the elements of context with the generic shape of the text are underdeveloped, as is the general schema for the description of contexts for interaction.
>
> (Hasan, 2005, p. 143)

Hasan is also concerned with the bias within activity theory towards the experiential function of language. She equates this with the 'field of discourse' within systemic functional linguistics. Her concern is with the absence of analysis of what she refers to as the 'tenor of discourse', by which she means the social relations and the positioning of the interactants and the 'mode of discourse', the nature of semiotic and material contact between the discursive participants. Bernstein provides the basis for a language of description which may be applied at the level of principles of power and control, which may then be translated into principles of communication. Bernstein also seeks to show how these principles of communication differentially regulate forms of consciousness.

As he noted in a discussion of sociolinguistics:

> Very complex questions are raised by the relation of the socio to the linguistic. What linguistic theories of description are available for what socio issues? And how do the former limit the latter? What determines the dynamics of the linguistic theory, and how do these dynamics relate, if at all, to the dynamics of change in those disciplines which do and could contribute to the socio. If 'socio' and linguistics are to illuminate language as a truly social construct, then there must be mutually translatable principles of descriptions which enable the dynamics of the social to enter those translatable principles.
> (Bernstein, 1996, pp. 151–2)

Different social structures give rise to different modalities of language that have specialised mediational properties. They have arisen, have been shaped by, the social, cultural and historical circumstances in which interpersonal exchanges arise and they in turn shape the thoughts and feelings, the identities and aspirations for action of those engaged in interpersonal exchange in those contexts. Hence, the relations of power and control that regulate social interchange give rise to specialised principles of communication. These mediate social relations.

In Engeström's (1996a) work within activity theory, the production of the outcome is discussed but not the production and structure of the tool itself. The rules, community and division of labour are analysed in terms of the contradictions and dilemmas which arise within the activity system specifically with respect to the production of the object. The production of the cultural artefact, the discourse, is not analysed in terms of the context of its production, that is the rules, community and division of labour that regulate the activity in which subjects are positioned.

Tentative application of a Bernsteinian approach within CHAT

The language that Bernstein has developed, uniquely, allows researchers to take measures of institutional modality. That is, to describe and position the discursive, organisational and interactional practice of the institution. Through the concepts of classification and framing, Bernstein provides the language of description for moving from those issues that activity theory handles as rules, community and division of labour to the discursive tools or artefacts that are produced and deployed within an activity. Research may then seek to investigate the connections between the rules the children use to make sense of their pedagogic world and the modality of that world. For example, in a school, the curriculum may then be analysed in terms of a social division of labour and pedagogic practice as its constituent social relations, through which the specialisation of that social division (subjects, units of the curriculum) are transmitted and expected to be acquired. Power is spoken of in terms of classification which is manifested in category relations that themselves generate recognition rules (possession of which allows the acquirer to recognise difference that is marked by a category). Control is spoken of in terms of framing, which is manifested in pedagogic communication governed by realisation rules (possession of which allows the acquirer to perform — in this case talk — in a way that is seen as competent and realise difference that is marked by a category). The distribution of power and principles of control differently specialise structural features and their pedagogic communicative relays.

Bernstein (2000) provides an outline of a key feature of the structure of pedagogic discourse with the distinction between instructional and regulative discourse. The former refers to the transmission of skills and their relation to each other, and the latter refers to the principles of social order, relation and identity. Regulative discourse communicates the school's (or any institution's) public moral practice, values, beliefs and attitudes, and principles of conduct, character and manner. It also transmits features of the school's local history, local tradition and community relations.

Different institutional modalities may be described in terms of the relationship between the relations of power and control which gives rise to distinctive discursive artefacts. For example, with respect to schooling, where the theory of instruction gives rise to a strong classification and strong framing of the pedagogic practice, it is expected that there will be a separation of discourses (school subjects), an emphasis upon acquisition of specialised skills, the teacher will be dominant in the formulation of intended learning and the pupils are constrained by the teacher's practice. The relatively strong control on the pupils' learning itself acts as a means of maintaining order in the context in which the learning takes place. This form of the instructional discourse contains regulative functions. With strong classification and framing, the social relations between teachers and pupils will be more asymmetrical, that is, more clearly hierarchical. In this instance, the regulative discourse and its practice is more explicit and distinguishable from the instructional discourse. Where the theory of instruction gives rise to a weak classification and weak framing of the practice, then children will be encouraged to be active in the classroom, to undertake enquiries and perhaps to work in groups at their own pace. Here, the relations between teacher and pupils will have the appearance of being more symmetrical. In these circumstances, it is difficult to separate instructional discourse from regulative discourse as these are mutually embedded. The formulation of pedagogic discourse as an embedded discourse comprising instructional and regulative components allows for the analysis of the production of such embedded discourses in activities structured through specifiable relations of power and control within institutions.

Albeit somewhat crude, an attempt was made to apply these understandings in a study of subject-specific speech in special schools (Daniels, 2006). The first step in the study was to construct a model of description that could be applied to the sample of four schools. This is shown in Figure 7.1

The point of departure was the theory of instruction. As Bernstein (2000) states:

> The theory of instruction is a crucial recontextualized discourse as it regulates the orderings of pedagogic practice, constructs the model of the pedagogic subject (the acquirer), the model of the transmitter, the model of the pedagogic context *and* the model of communicative pedagogic competence.
> (Bernstein, 2000, p. 14)

The second step was to develop a coding frame for the model. The schools were referred to as Temple Centre (TC), Abbey (A), Wolf House (WH), and Chapel Hill (CH). The coding of each school in terms of specific classification (strength of category relation) and framing (social relation) values was based upon observation and interview data, together with the agreed statements from which each school's theory of instruction could be reliably inferred. Codings and descriptions were subsequently discussed and ratified with members of staff in the schools.

The coding of information was performed using a four-level scale where ++ represents strongest and − represents weakest. This was applied to values of Classification (C) and Framing (F). Examples of such coding are shown in Table 7.1.

In this way, different modalities of schooling were described in terms of the relationship between the relations of power and control which give rise to distinctive discursive artefacts.

In terms of general values of classification and framing of teachers and subjects, there was a cline of schools from Temple Centre (weaker) to Wolf House

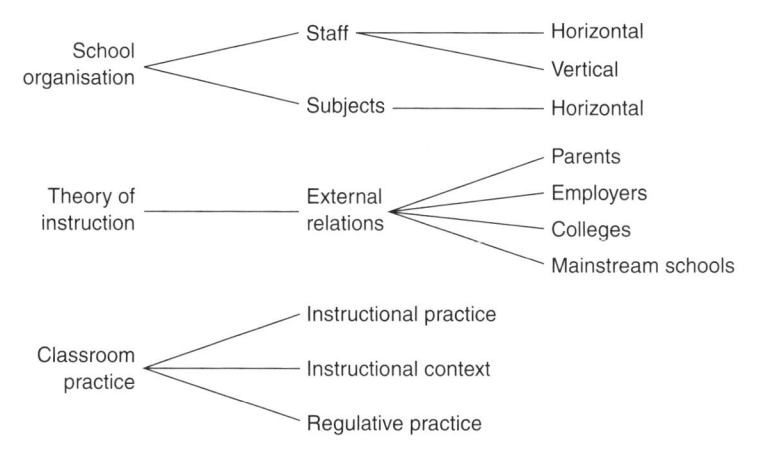

Figure 7.1 Overall model of description.

158 Institutions and beyond

Table 7.1 Extract from the coding frame for describing the classification and framing at the classroom level

Strength of classification	Descriptor
C– (very weak)	Children working in groups or as individuals pursuing different tasks
C–	As above but similar tasks
C+	Classwork as individuals but on different tasks
C++ (very strong)	Classwork as individuals but on same tasks
Strength of framing	Descriptor
F– (very weak)	Children control selection sequencing and pacing of instruction
F–	Teachers provide broad indications of areas in which children should be working
F+	Children have some influence on selection, criteria sequencing and pacing of instruction. Control largely in hands of teacher
F++ (very strong)	Teachers control selection, criteria sequencing and pacing of instruction

Table 7.2 Coding of classroom practice in the four schools

	Instructional	Regulative
Temple Centre	C– F–	F–
Abbey	C– F–	F–
Chapel Hill	C++ F++	F+
Wolf House	C++ F++	F+

(stronger). The very general overall codings were written in Instructional/Regulative (I/R) format as shown in Table 7.2.

It was theoretically expected that the move from the values of classification and framing of the school and classroom to the pupils' practice is mediated through recognition and realisation rules of the instructional practice. These rules are hypothesised functions of the values of classification and framing. Concretely, it was expected that children would produce different texts under different conditions of classification and framing.

Figure 7.2 provides a display of the percentage of correct discriminations between categories of subject-specific talk as agreed by two teachers (full details are to be found in Daniels (2006), which shows that these differences are statistically significant).

Where the values of classification and framing of the culture of subjects were strong, the children realised the criteria of communicative competence held by their teachers with respect to discrimination between subjects to a greater extent than when, in a school such as Temple Centre, values of classification and

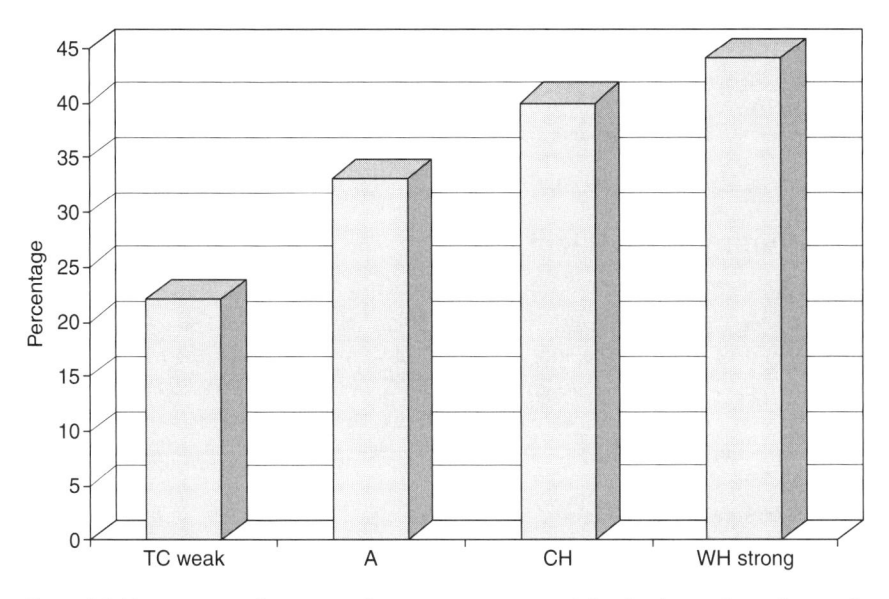

Figure 7.2 Percentage of correct discriminations agreed by both teachers for each school.

framing were weak. The individual measures of expressive language ability would suggest that the school differences revealed in the study are not attributable to individual differences. A high level of agreement of teacher evaluation is suggestive of a common basis of understanding as to the language of school subjects. The implication being that it is neither the ability of the pupils nor teacher capacity/understanding that conditions the variations in school responses, rather the responses are modulated by the schools themselves. The study confirmed a relation between organisational form and the possession of realisation rules.

Although tentative, the data provide some grounds for increased acceptance of an extended Vygotskian model of analysis. This research sought to establish the relationship between modalities of pedagogic practice (in terms of their classification and framing values) and the distribution of recognition and realisation rules for the construction of an appropriate text. At the institutional level there is some evidence of the relation between the pedagogic code and acquisition of the rules that underly specific forms of communicative competence.

Further development and research may yield an important framework for developing a greater understanding of institutional modalities and the ways in which they affect participants' construction of reality. Bernstein (2000) paid very close attention to how the everyday discourse mediates mental dispositions, tendencies to respond to situations in certain ways and how it puts in place beliefs about the world one lives in, including about phenomena that are both supposedly in nature and those that are said to be in our culture. In order to understand

and investigate these processes, there is an urgent need to refine a language of description which allows us to 'see' institutions as they do their psychological work through the discursive practices which they shape and other, more invisible, means of mediation. My argument is that this approach is suggestive of benefits that may be accrued from bringing a Bernsteinian perspective to bear on CHAT.

Positioning the subject

Hasan brings Bernstein's concept of social positioning to the fore in her discussion of social identity. Bernstein (1990, p. 13) used this concept to refer to the establishing of a specific relation to other subjects and to the creating of specific relationships within subjects. As Hasan (2005) notes, social positioning through meanings are inseparable from power relations. Bernstein provided an elaboration of his early general argument:

> More specifically, class-regulated codes position subjects with respect to dominant and dominated forms of communication and to the relationships between them. Ideology is constituted through and in such positioning. From this perspective, ideology inheres in and regulates modes of relation. Ideology is not so much a content as a mode of relation for the realizing of content. Social, cultural, political and economic relations are intrinsic to pedagogic discourse.
>
> (Bernstein, 1990, pp. 13–14)

Here the linkage is forged between social positioning and psychological attributes. This is the process through which Bernstein talks of the shaping of the possibilities for consciousness. The dialectical relation between discourse and subject makes it possible to think of pedagogic discourse as a semiotic means that regulates or traces the generation of subjects' positions in discourse. We can understand the potency of pedagogic discourse in selectively producing subjects and their identities in a temporal and spatial dimension (Diaz, 2001, pp. 106–8). As Hasan (2005) argues, within the Bernsteinian thesis there exists an ineluctable relation between one's social positioning, one's mental dispositions and one's relation to the distribution of labour in society. Here the emphasis on discourse is theorised not only in terms of 'the shaping of cognitive functions but also, as it were invisibly, in its influence on dispositions, identities and practices' (Bernstein, 1990, p. 33).

Within Engeström's approach to CHAT, the subject is often discussed in terms of individuals, groups or perspectives/views. I would argue that the way in which subjects are positioned with respect to one another within an activity carries with it implications for engagement with tools and objects. It may also carry implications for the ways in which rules, community and the division of labour regulate the actions of individuals and groups.

Holland *et al.* (1998) have studied the development of identities and agency specific to historically situated, socially enacted, culturally constructed worlds. They draw on Bakhtin (1978, 1986) and Vygotsky to develop a theory of identity as constantly forming and person as a composite of many, often contradictory, self-understandings and identities that are distributed across the material and social environment and rarely durable (p. 8). They draw on Leontiev in the development of the concept of socially organised and reproduced *figured worlds* which shape and are shaped by participants and in which social position establishes possibilities for engagement. They also argue that figured worlds:

> distribute 'us' not only by relating actors to landscapes of action (as personae) and spreading our senses of self across many different fields of activity, but also by giving the landscape human voice and tone. – Cultural worlds are populated by familiar social types and even identifiable persons, not simply differentiated by some abstract division of labour. The identities we gain within figured worlds are thus specifically historical developments, grown through *continued participation in the positions defined by the social organization of those world's activity.*
>
> (Holland *et al.*, 1998, p. 41; italics added)

This approach to a theory of identity in practice is grounded in the notion of a figured world in which positions are taken up, constructed and resisted. The Bakhtinian concept of the 'space of authoring' is deployed to capture an understanding of the mutual shaping of figured worlds *and* identities in social practice. Holland *et al.* (1998) refer to Bourdieu (cf. 1977) in their attempt to show how social position becomes disposition. They argue for the development of social position into a positional identity into disposition and the formation of what Bourdieu refers to as 'habitus'. It is here that I feel that this argument could be strengthened through reference to a theoretical account which provides greater descriptive and analytical purchase on the principles of regulation of the social figured world, the possibilities for social position and the voice of participants.

Engeström (1999b), who has tended to concentrate on the structural aspects of CHAT, offers the suggestion that the division of labour in an activity creates different positions for the participants and that the participants carry their own diverse histories with them into the activity. This echoes the earlier assertion from Leontiev:

> Activity is the minimal meaningful context for understanding individual actions.... In all its varied forms, the activity of the human individual is a system set within a system of social relations.... The activity of individual people thus *depends on their social position*, the conditions that fall to their lot, and an accumulation of idiosyncratic, individual factors. Human activity is not a relation between a person and a society that confronts him ... in a society a person does not simply find external conditions to which he must

adapt his activity, but, rather, these very social conditions bear within themselves the motives and goals of his activity, its means and modes.

(Leontiev, 1978, p. 10; italics added)

In activity, the possibilities for the use of artefacts depend on the social position occupied by an individual. Sociologists and sociolinguists have produced empirical verification of this suggestion (e.g. Bernstein, 2000; Hasan, 2001; Hasan and Cloran, 1990). My suggestion is that the notion of 'subject' within activity theory requires expansion and clarification. In many studies the term 'subject perspective' is used, which arguably infers subject position but does little to illuminate the formative processes that gave rise to this perspective.

Holland *et al.* also argue that multiple identities are developed within figured worlds and that these are 'historical developments, grown through continued participation in the positions defined by the social organization of those worlds' activity' (Holland *et al.*, 1998, p. 41). This body of work represents a significant development in our understanding of the concept of the 'subject' in activity theory. As Roth (2007a) notes:

> Goals and actions are free-floating, generally intelligible, cultural-historically contingent possibilities. Because concrete embodied actions articulate between society and the self, a person's identity does not constitute a singularity but is itself inherently intelligible within the cultural unit. It is because of what they see each other doing that two (or more) persons come to 'recognize themselves as mutually recognizing one another' (Hegel, 1806/1977, p. 112). Publicly visible actions serve as the ground of recognizing in the other another self that recognizes in me its corresponding other. It is this linkage between self and other through patterned embodied actions that have led some to theorize identity in terms of agency and culture in which a person participates (e.g., Holland *et al.*, 1998).
>
> (Roth, 2007a, p. 146)

For my point of view, there remains a need to develop the notion of 'figured world' in such a way that we can theories, analyse and describe the processes by which that world is 'figured'. Bernstein's (1990, p. 13) concept of social positioning seems to me to concur with the analysis outlined by Holland *et al.* (1998). He relates social positioning to the formation of mental dispositions in terms of the identity's relation to the distribution of labour in society. It is through the deployment of his concepts of voice and message that Bernstein forges the link between division of labour, social position and discourse and opens up the possibilities for a language of description that will serve empirical as well analytical purposes. The distinction between what can be recognised as belonging to a voice and a particular message is formulated in terms of distinction between relations of power and relations of control. Bernstein (1990) adapted the concept of voice from his reading of *The Material Word* by Silverman and Torode (1980):

> From this perspective classificatory (boundary) relations establish 'voice'. 'Voice' is regarded somewhat like a cultural larynx which sets the limits on what can be legitimately put together (communicated). Framing (control) relations regulate the acquisition of this voice and create the 'message' (what is made manifest, what can be realized).
>
> (Bernstein, 1990, p. 260)

In his last book he continues:

> Voice refers to the limits on what could be realized if the identity was to be recognized as legitimate. The classificatory (boundary) relation established the voice. In this way power relations, through the classificatory relation, regulated voice. However voice, although a necessary condition for establishing what could and could not be said and its context, could not determine what was said and the form of its contextual realization; the message. The message was a function of framing (control). The stronger the framing the smaller the space accorded for potential variation in the message.
>
> (Bernstein, 2000, p. 204)

Thus, social categories constitute voices and control over practices constitutes message. Identity becomes the outcome of the voice – message relation. Production and reproduction have their social basis in categories and practices; that categories are constituted by the social division of labour and that practices are constituted by social relations within production/reproduction; that categories constitute 'voices' and that practices constitute their 'messages'; message is dependent upon 'voice', and the subject is a dialectical relation between 'voice' and message (Bernstein, 1990, p. 27).

Hasan (2001, p. 8) suggests that Bernstein's analysis of how subjects are positioned and how they position themselves in relation to the social context of their discourse, offers an explanation of discursive practice, in terms of the relations of power and control that regulate speaking subjects. However, the theoretical move which Bernstein makes in relating positioning to the distribution of power and principles of control opens up the possibility of grounding the analysis of social positioning and mental dispositions in relation to the distribution of labour in an activity. Through the notions of 'voice' and 'message', he brings the division of labour and principles of control (rules) into relation with social position in practice. This theoretical stance suggests that activity theory could also develop a language of description which allows for the parameters of power and control to be considered at structural and interactional levels of analysis. A systematic approach to the analysis and description of the formation of categories through the maintenance and shifting of boundaries and principles of control as exercised within categories would bring a powerful tool to the undoubted strengths of activity theory. This would then allow the analysis to move from one level to another in the same terms, rather than treat division of labour and discourse as analytically independent items. Bernstein argues that positioning is in a systematic relation to the distribution of power and principles of control. I suggest that this approach to understanding the notion of social positioning as the underlying, invisible component which 'figures' (as in Holland) practices of communication and gives rise to the shaping of identity provides an important potential development from the current status of third generation activity theory. This possibility has yet to be fully explored within a CHAT perspective.

Subject–subject and within-subject relations are under-theorised in CHAT. It requires a theoretical account of social relations and positioning. The theoretical move which Bernstein makes in relating positioning to the distribution of power and principles of control opens up the possibility of grounding the analysis of social positioning and mental dispositions in relation to the distribution of labour in an activity. Through the notions of 'voice' and 'message', he brings the division of labour and principles of control (rules) into relation with social position in practice. The implication is that 'subject' in an activity-theory-driven depiction should be represented by a space of possibility (voice) in which a particular position (message) is taken up. Thus, subject would be represented by a socially structured zone of possibility rather than a singular point. This representation would signify a move to attempt to theorise the subject as emerging in a world that was 'figured' by relations of power and control.

Change

The focus of activity theory is on instability (internal tensions) and contradiction as the 'motive force of change and development' (Engeström, 1999, p. 9) and the transitions and reorganisations within and between activity systems as part of evolution. It is not only the subject, but also the environment, that is modified through mediated activity. Rules, community and division of labour are analysed in terms of the contradictions and dilemmas that arise within the activity system specifically with respect to the production of the object. Activity systems do not exist in isolation; they are embedded in networks that witness constant fluctuation and change. Activity theory needs to develop tools for analysing and transforming networks of culturally heterogeneous activities through dialogue and debate (Engeström and Miettinen, 1999, p. 7). Bernstein's work has not placed particular emphasis on the study of change (see Bernstein, 2000). The introduction of the third generation of activity theory initiated the development of conceptual tools to understand dialogues and multiple perspectives on change within networks of interacting activity systems; all of which are underdeveloped in Bernstein. The idea of networks of activity within which contradictions and struggles take place in the definition of the motives and object of the activity calls for an analysis of power and control within and between developing activity systems. The latter is the point at which Bernstein's emphasis on different layers and dimensions of power and control becomes key to the development of the theory.

Lemke (1997) suggests that it is not only the context of the situation that is relevant but also the context of culture when an analysis of meaning is undertaken. He suggests that 'we interpret a text, or a situation, in part by connecting it to other texts and situations which our community, or our individual history, has made us see as relevant to the meaning of the present one' (Lemke, 1997, p. 50). This use of notions of intertextuality, of networked activities, or network of connections provides Lemke with tools for the creation of an account of ecosocial systems that transcend immediate contexts. Engeström and Miettinen recognise the strengths and limitations of this position. They imply a need for an analysis of the way in which networks of activities are structured – ultimately for an analysis of power and control.

> Various microsociologies have produced eye-opening works that uncover the local, idiosyncratic, and contingent nature of action, interaction, and knowledge. Empirical studies of concrete, situated practices can uncover the local pattern of activity and the cultural specificity of thought, speech and discourse. Yet these microstudies tend to have little connection to macrotheories of social institutions and the structure of society. Various approaches to analysis of social networks may be seen as attempts to bridge the gap. However, a single network, though interconnected with a number of other networks, typically still in no way represents any general or lawful development in society.
>
> (Engeström and Miettinen, 1999, p. 8)

Leontiev (1981a) explored this issue from the perspective of development through time. He suggested that in the study of human ontogeny, one must take account of the ordering of categories of activity that corresponds to broad stages of mental development. According to Leontiev:

> In studying the development of the child's psyche, we must therefore start by analyzing the child's activity, as this activity is built up in the concrete conditions of its life ... Life or activity as a whole is not built up mechanically, however, from separate types of activity. Some types of activity are the leading ones at a given stage and are of greatest significance for the individual's subsequent development, and others are less important. We can say accordingly, that each stage of psychic development is characterized by a definite relation of the child to reality that is the leading one at that stage and by a definite, leading type of activity.
>
> (Leontiev, 1981a, p. 395)

This analysis of development in terms of stages characterised in terms of particular dominant activities is often associated with the work of Elkonin. In the terms of contemporary activity theory, this account is one of progressive transformation of the object through time. This could be termed a horizontal analysis.

[W]hen we speak of the dominant activity and its significance for a child's development in this or that period, this is by no means meant to imply that the child might not be simultaneously developing in other directions as well. In each period, a child's life is many-sided, the activities of which his life is composed are varied. New sorts of activity appear; the child forms new relations with his surroundings. When a new activity becomes dominant, it does not cancel all previously existing activities: it merely alters their status within the overall system of relations between the child and his surroundings, which thereby become increasingly richer.

(Elkonin, 1972, p. 247)

Griffin and Cole (1984) noted that in the course of a single session of an after-school activity designed for 7–11-year-olds, there could be fluctuations in which activity seemed to be 'leading'. This could be termed a situated analysis. In Figure 7.4, an analysis of a particular moment in time (A or B or C) would consider the network of activity systems in which subjects were located and seek to discern the shifts in dominance that take place in short periods of real time in a particular context. For example, at time A activity 1A assumes dominance, whereas at time B, activity 2B is represented as dominant or leading. This analysis could be pursued through the application of Bernstein's model to several activities and systems (rather than the one which is usually referenced) and also seek to apply his analysis of power and control to the emergence of dominance (1A vs 2A vs 3A). This situated analysis would combine the strengths of activity theory, with its emphasis on networks of activity and the formation of objects of activity, with the analytical power and descriptive elegance of Bernstein's work. The implications of different social positions would have to be taken into account, as would the recognition that activity systems may be invoked in the absence of the physical presence of all the actors involved (Vygotsky, 1978). The analysis is thus one in which the relational interdependence of individual and social agencies is recognised. The historical analysis would focus on the transformation of dominance through time.

The historical background of much of what is now termed 'activity theory' posits 'networks' of activity systems in which dominance arises at particular moments in both long- and short-term periods. I have placed inverted commas around the word network because I wish to signify a resistance to the notion of network as a connected system, within which component parts share some function. Here I am concerned with the existence of multiple activity systems that may supplant each other and may be mutually transformed. By way of illustration, I offer this rather crude example: suppose a person is both a care-giver to their own child as well as a professional teacher. If that teacher has a need to collect their child from a nursery at the end of the school day then the way that teacher might respond to class disruption close to the final bell of the day may be very different to the way in which they might respond earlier in the day. Here, two activity systems assume a different relationship to one another at particular

Institutions and beyond 167

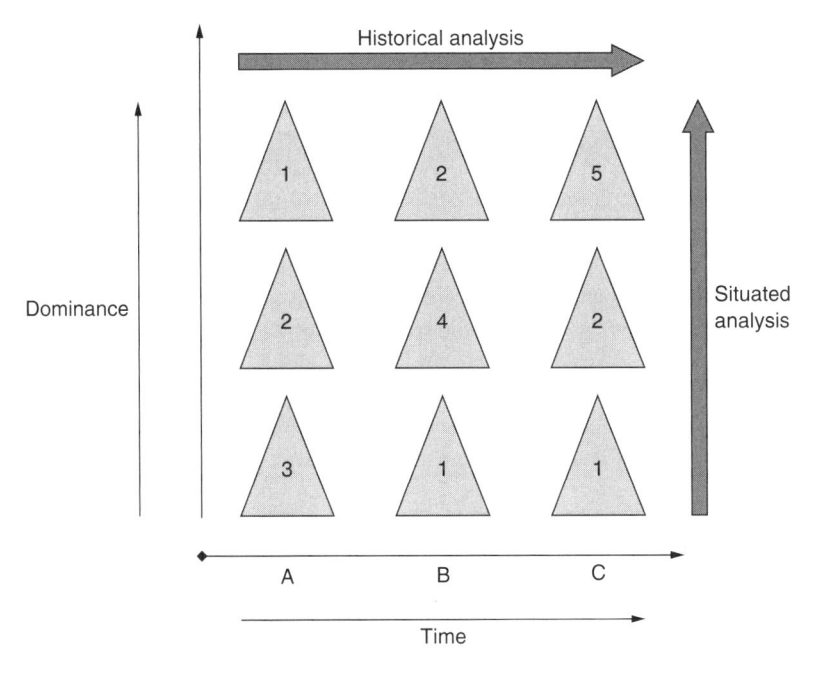

Figure 7.3 Dominance in networks of activity systems through time.

times of the day. These pulsations in dominance are rarely subjected to rigorous empirical scrutiny. Some of the empirical work which proclaims a CHAT orientation seems to constrain its analysis to one activity system, let alone a network of activity systems, and rarely strays into the analysis of shifts in dominance. Taken together, the implications of the work of Griffin and Cole, Lemke, Leontiev and Elkonin suggests that such an analysis should be deployed both at the levels of long-term ontogenesis as well short-term or even micro-analysis. Makitalo and Säljö (2002) argue that it is through the analysis of categories that 'people draw on the past to make their talk relevant to the accomplishment of interaction within specific traditions of argumentation' (p. 75). They note, along with Sacks (1992), that categories are activity-bound and that their use is inextricably bound up with a particular interactional and moral order (Jayyusi, 1984, p. 2). Such analyses would share the concern to explore the way in which subjects are shaped by fluctuating patterns of dominance from the perspective of those actors. However, the emergence of categories is not explored in relation to the principles of regulation of the social setting in which they emerge. I want to suggest that there may be some benefit in pursuing the Bernsteinian perspective in the context of the analysis of fluctuating patterns of dominance within networks of activity systems within this framework, but from the point of view of the pathway of the object through networks of activity.

Institutions as historical products

I now wish to move to the development of an account of institutional structures as cultural-historical products (artefacts) that play a part in implicit (Wertsch, 2007) or invisible (Bernstein, 2000) mediation. Earlier in this chapter I cited Abreu and Elbers, who argue that it is necessary to take into account ways in which the practices of a community, such as school and the family, are structured by their institutional context and that social structures impact on the interactions between the participants and the cultural tools (Abreu and Elbers, 2005, p. 4). In a footnote to the introduction of a recent volume of the journal *Mind, Culture, and Activity*, Roth sees what might be the root of a problem in translation:

> English translations of Marx and Leont'ev use the adjective *social* (sozial, [sozial'no]) where the German/Russian versions use *societal* (gesellschaftlich, [obshchestvenno]). The two English adjectives have very different implications in that the latter concept immediately introduces society as a major mediating moment into the kinds of relations that people entertain and realize.
>
> (Roth, 2007a, p. 143)

The point of departure I wish to mark is that it is not just a matter of the structuring of interactions between the participants and other cultural tools, rather it is that the institutional structures themselves are cultural products that serve as mediators in their own right. In this sense they are the 'message', that is, a fundamental factor of education as discussed by Ivic (1989), because, as an institution and quite apart from the content of its teaching, it implies a certain structuring of time and space and is based on a system of social relations (between pupils and teacher; between the pupils themselves; between the school and it surroundings; and so on) (Ivic, 1989, p. 429). When we talk, as Makitalo and Säljö (2002) argue, we enter the flow of communication in a stream of both history and the future (Makitalo and Säljö p. 63). When we talk in institutions, history enters the flow of communication through the invisible or implicit mediation of the institutional structures. My suggestion is that there is a need to analyse and codify the mediational structures as they deflect and direct attention of participants and as they are shaped through interactions that they also shape. In this sense, I am advocating the development of cultural-historical analysis of the invisible or implicit mediational properties of institutional structures that themselves are transformed through the actions of those whose interactions are influenced by them. This move would serve to both expand the gaze of CHAT and at the same time bring sociologies of cultural transmission, such as that developed by Bernstein (2000), into a framework in which institutional structures are analysed as historical products that themselves are subject to dynamic transformation and change.

I will now refer to a project which serves to illustrate an attempt to move towards this aspiration. The Learning in and for Interagency Working project (LIW)[1] was concerned with the learning of professionals in the creation of new forms of practice that require joined-up solutions to meet complex and diverse client needs. We studied professional learning in children's services that aim to promote social inclusion through interagency working. Working with other professionals involves engaging with many configurations of diverse social practices. It also requires the development of new forms of hybrid practice. It calls for 'joined-up' responses from professionals and stresses the need for new, qualitatively different forms of multiagency practice, in which providers operate across traditional service and team boundaries. In this context, the LIW Project is concerned with examining and supporting the learning of professionals who are engaged in the creation of new forms of multiagency practice.

We worked in three multiagency settings: (a) Liberton, a school whose remit has been extended to act as base for other agencies; (b) Wildside, a children in public care team; and (c) Seaside, a multi-professional team that originally comprised education professionals but expanded to incorporate social care and health practitioners. We organised six DWR workshops at each site (as discussed in Chapter 6). Prior to the workshops, interview and observational data were used as a base from which to select mirror data that embodied tensions, dilemmas and structural contradictions in the practices of each site. The aim was to build upon professionals' 'everyday' understandings of multiagency working, juxtaposing these with reflective, systemic analyses of the ways in which current working practices either enable or constrain the development of innovative multiagency working. The stated aim of the workshops was to address the challenges of multiagency professional learning by:

- encouraging the *recognition* of areas in which there is a need for change in working practices;
- suggesting possibilities for change through *re-conceptualising* the 'objects' that professionals are working on, the 'tools' that professionals use in their multiagency work and the 'rules' in which professional practices are embedded.

One of the defining features of the settings in which we have worked is distributed expertise. Joined-up service provision means that the case of an 'at risk' child will rarely be the province of one 'team' but will entail diverse professionals from education, social care, health and other agencies coalescing around the child's case. Therefore, issues of how expertise and specialist knowledge are claimed, owned and shared are extremely important and can be problematic. Clearly, it is not only how expertise is distributed between professionals that is key in multiagency functioning; there must also be examination of philosophies and beliefs about being a professional and about working with other professionals whose values, priorities, targets and systems may be different (see Engeström, 1992). A model of description of the sites was developed with this understanding in mind.

A model of the setting in which the development of such multiagency functioning progresses must refer to the group of professionals who were involved in the workshops, the wider local authority and the clients who were to be served by emergent multiagency practices. The basic elements of the model were thus:

- DWR group;
- Local Authority;
- Clients.

Bernstein's (2000) concepts of boundary strength (classification) and control (framing) can be applied to many aspects of such a model. Here I will use the terms 'instrumental' or 'instructional' practice to refer to the pragmatic actions within practice. Within the workshop group, the strength of classification (horizontal division of labour) in the practices of professional agencies and control (framing) over the membership of these groups was examined. The strength of distinctions in the vertical division of labour, the strength of the marking of hierarchy and the associated relations of control within this hierarchy was also seen to be a central facet of the structuring of the workshop groups. The strength of control over the regulative practice (matters of order, identity and relation) was also noted. In many respects, this shows similarities with Engeström's (1992) discussion of the 'why and where to' aspects of activity in that the reference is to the values and beliefs which underpin practice. The features of the practices within the DWR group were modelled as follows:

Instrumental or instructional practice
   Horizontal   Classification and framing
   Vertical   Classification and framing
Regulative Practice   Framing

In the local authority, the vertical division of labour between members of the workshop and their colleagues in the wider authority was also taken as a key feature of the research sites, as was the extent to which boundaries were maintained between the professions in the local authority. The control over the boundary relations between the workshop groups and the local authority was modelled, somewhat awkwardly, as the framing of those relations where strong framing was taken as a boundary maintained by the authority, weak framing as a boundary relation in which the workshop group maintained control and an intermediary position in which a relatively fluid two-way flow of communication was maintained. The features of the practices within the local authority were modelled as follows:

Instrumental or instructional practice
   Horizontal   Classification
   Vertical   Classification and framing
   Control over boundary   Framing

Institutions and beyond 171

The extent to which clients were classified as belonging to a particular category of need (strong classification) or as the 'whole child' (weak classification) was also noted. This was taken as the division of labour within the client community.

The overall model became:

DWR group
Instrumental or instructional practice
   Horizontal   Classification and framing
   Vertical   Classification and framing
Regulative Practice   Framing

Local authority
Instrumental or instructional practice
   Horizontal   Classification and framing
   Vertical   Classification and framing
   Control over boundary   Framing

Clients
Instrumental or instructional practice
   Horizontal   Classification

Each aspect of this model was described for each site through data gathered through extensive observations and interviews. A coding grid was developed for each aspect (see Figure 7.4 for examples). The codings were independently validated by two researchers.

The codings for the full model for each site were as shown in Table 7.3.

We also noted the means by which attempts were made to co-ordinate services in the wider local authority as well the form of any recent disruption in the order of the local authority. These features are given in Table 7.4.

Model Feature – Division of labour (vertical)
Exemplar interview question – How hierarchical is the management in your work?

	1 C– –	2 C–	3 C+/–	4 C+	5 C++
Seaside	X				
Wildside	X				
Liberton				X	

Coding
1. C– – = All members of a 'flat' team
2. C++ = Strong hierarchy (director, deputy director, principal, senior, junior)

Figure 7.4 Example of coding grids applied to model of description.

172 Institutions and beyond

Table 7.3 The codings for each site

	Wildside	Seaside	Liberton
DWR group			
Horizontal	C– F–	C+/– F+/–	C++ F++
Vertical	C– – F–	C– – F+/–	C+ F++
Regulative practice	F+/–	F++	F– –
Local authority			
Horizontal	C+ F+	C+ F+	C+ F+
Vertical	C– F–	C++ F+/–	C++ F++
Control over DWR	F+/–	F++	F– –
group boundary	Free flow	Control with LA	Control with DWR
Clients			
Horizontal	C–	C– –	C++

Table 7.4 Features of the local authority

	Seaside	Wildside	Liberton
Co-ordination of agencies and agents	Perceived lack of response to operational staff views (at several levels)	Strong strategy	No stategy which impacted on case study site. Strategy developing within rest of LA
Disruptions	Several major re-organisations Radical localisation of services		Recent leadership changes and reconfigured systems

At a very general level, there are stronger values of classification and framing of the instructional practice in Liberton and progressively weaker values in Seaside and Wildside. In addition, a consideration of the nature of the regulative practice in each site suggests strong framing in Seaside, weak framing in Liberton, with Wildside occupying an intermediary position. Thus, in Liberton, the instructional practice (which is strongly classified and highly framed) predominates over the weak regulative discourse. Whereas in Seaside, the relatively weak boundaries witnessed in the weaker values of classification of the instructional practice are embedded in the regulative practice through which common values and meanings have been the object of much of the early work of the team. In Wildside, an intermediary position is witnessed in the embedding of the instruction and regulation.

A crude typification of these sites in terms of a general application of Bernstein's model of the embedded features of pedagogic practice in which instruc-

- Seaside   I/**R**   The regulative aspect of predominant
- Liberton **I**/R   The instructional/instrumental aspect predominant
- Wildside I/R   An intermediary/balance position

Figure 7.5 Representation of the structure of pedagogic practices at each study site.

tional practice (I) and regulative practice (R) are mutually embedded but in which one may predominate.

In this way, we arrived at condensed codings of what may be seen as the historical legacy presented at the moment when we sought to engage with groups of professionals at each site. In each case study, we carried out six two-hour developmental workshops over one year. Workshops were attended by the practitioners who were working together or were moving towards working together. As noted in Chapter 6, a key concept in DWR is dual stimulation. We used activity theory and cognate concepts to stimulate their reflections on the contradictions that emerged from a consideration of the ways in which the histories of their work had shaped the present and potential for future work.

In order to handle the diversity of material gathered at the empirical sites and to co-ordinate multi-centred analysis, it was necessary to develop accessible archiving of the primary data and clear protocols for maintaining the coherence of the analysis across the centres. Analytic protocols were developed to support in-depth communicative analysis of the audio- and video-tape-recorded empirical data. The aim was to provide an analytical evidence base to substantiate CHAT-based analysis. David Middleton proposed an approach to analysis which focused on the forms of social action that are accomplished in talk and text and the sorts of communicative devices that are used. Middleton suggested the use of a conceptual bridge for textual analysis across cases. The particular focus of what became known as the 'D-analysis' grew out of a concern to examine the emergence of what-it-is-to-learn in multiagency settings as an analytic object across the workshops. A minimal model of learning as the introduction of a difference was adopted and stages of learning-related talk were formulated:

> **1 Deixis** – indication, pointing
> This stage involves making a start on a subject during a conversation to draw the audience's attention towards a particular problem.
>
> **2 Delineation and definition**
> This involves a reaction to what has been said in the conversation indicating that sense has been made. When another person moves on to explain the point from their own perspective by: (a) acknowledging and qualifying that point; (b) explaining further that point by drawing on their local context; or (c) emphasising a different view (that may serve as a basis for expanding the conversation to explore what has just been seen as important).

3 Deliberation

This involves narrowing down the thinking process towards reaching an agreement. This is actioned through either giving or asking for consent in the conversation: (a) building a consensus by evoking *local situation/knowledge*; or (b) building a consensus based on *general knowledge*.

4 Departure

A departure could be seen as a shift towards a qualitatively different stage in communicative interaction. At this stage we can see progress in the group's conceptualisation of the problem.

5 Development

This involves finding a tool from within the previous conversation that enables people to discuss a solution to an identified problem and moving the conversation to a more 'action' oriented level. In this way the conversation reaches the level of 'recognition' of a particular issue (Middleton, 2007).

Sequences of communicative action were analysed in the transcripts of the workshops. Some sequences progressed to departures; others remained at other stages within the model. Each sequence was coded and described as shown in Table 7.5.

Table 7.5 Sequences of communicative action

Short description of the topic as it occurs in the discourse VERTICAL RELATIONS	Workshop	Transcript page
Understanding, recognising and accepting others' expertise is related to their power and authority (vertical division of labour)	DS1	p. 17
Rule conflict between operation, strategy and monitoring	DS1	p. 38
Professional confidence in the light of power and hierarchy (it takes a lot of confidence and experience to be a lonely voice expressing a different opinion)	DS2	pp. 40–2
Researcher intervention: How do strategists learn about problems the operation faces?	DS4 DS5	pp. 10, 12, 27 pp. 41, 43
Ideas on how to communicate with strategists	DS4 DS5 DS7	pp. 28–9, 32, 41 pp. 44, 48, 52 p. 37

Related sequences were identified and these were grouped into strands of talk that wove their way through the progress of the each series of workshops. These strands (comprising different types of sequences) witnessed the progression of learning through and with talk in the workshops. The themes that these strands addressed and the contradictions that gave rise to their emergence were analysed in activity theoretic terms. At the end of the project, participants were interviewed about what they had gained from the experience and subsequent analysis revealed the traces of each site's strands in the interviews at each site. In this way, we developed an approach to the analysis of communicative action in the workshops themselves along with a rudimentary approach to validation. The next move was to consider the relation between the communicative action that took place and the historically given structures which shaped the practices of participants.

Over the period of interventions in the workshops, many structural transformations were witnessed and by the end of the intervention it was the weaker regulative practice of Liberton which was the object of intervention from an external agent. The historical legacy of the strongly boundaried extended school site, within which professional practices were highly controlled and which remained distinct from each other, provided a setting in which a move to multiagency working and thus weakening of boundaries was most likely to be achieved through external influence on the values and beliefs within the DWR group (the regulative practice). This was confirmed through the analysis of communicative action within the workshops. An educational psychologist acted in this way.

In Seaside, the focus of communicative action was on the rules and practices of communication within the instructional practice. Participants became frustrated by the contradiction between legacy rules (maintained by the local authority) and the new emergent objects of multiagency work. They had already established a strong regulative practice before the DWR intervention was initiated. On the basis of this legacy, they sought to examine the contradictions in the instrumental aspects of their practice and began to bend (or even break) the legacy rules. The strong boundary between the workshop group and the local authority was maintained through practices of communication in which instructions (rules) were formulated and transmitted by local authority strategists, who were unresponsive to replies or ideas formulated by operational professionals within the workshop group. The d-analysis confirmed that the boundary between the workshop groups was the focus of the communicative action in the workshops.

In Wildside, the relation with clients became the predominant concern. There were no strong barriers between the group and the authority and, although the categories of professional agencies within the authority remained strong, the learning focused on ways in which multiagency work could be co-ordinated through strategic tools. These tools were the focus of much of the communicative action in the Wildside workshops. The combination of the Bernsteinian analysis of structure and the D analysis enabled us to see how the institution shaped the communicative action and also how the communicative action started to shape the institutional structures. This application of Bernstein's model permits the study of institutional transformation and the D analysis gives a view of communication at work as it transforms settings. This early day development may prove to be a useful point of departure in the development of a methodology for studying inseparability in action.

Hybridity

In order to refine an understanding of organisational, discursive and transmission practices in such situations, new theories of concept formation that emphasise the complex nature of concepts will need to be deployed. There is a need to develop current work on the predictive relationships between macro-structures and micro-processes. An important part of the challenge is to show how written and spoken hybrid discourse arises and to investigate the consequences of its deployment. In response to this challenge, an understanding of discursive hybridity (Sarangi and Roberts, 1999) may provide an important opening for the development of an understanding of changes in discursive practice as different activity systems are brought into different forms of relation with each other. Research in this field requires a unified theory that can give rise to a coherent and internally consistent methodology, rather than a collection of compartmentalised accounts of activity, discourse and social positioning that have disparate and often contradictory assumptions.

The strong boundaries around the professional categories and the strong control over professional behaviour in Liberton maintained the practices of individual specialists. At Wildside there were weak boundaries around the professional categories in which professionals were situated in the workshop. They were more in control than their peers in Liberton. However, in Wildside operational professional practice witnessed strong boundaries between services and their professional values coordinated by strategy resulted in a coordinated collec-

Table 7.6 Tentative typology of hybridities

	Weak control over professional behaviour (F– –)	Strong control over professionl behaviour (F++)
Strong categories of professional (C++)	Switching between specialisms	Collection of distinct specialists
Weak categories of professional (C– –)	Generalists 'melting pot' which may be given coherence through a strong regulative practice	Succession of generalists (people)

tion of specialists in the field. In Seaside, the weakened professional boundaries and relations of control that had been weakened through rule-breaking and bending gave rise to a collection of hybrid workers who drew on the primary strengths of their colleagues when they recognised the need for their expertise.

This approach to modelling the structural relations of power and control in institutional settings, theorised as cultural-historical artefacts that invisibly or implicitly mediate the relations of participants in practices in which communicative action may be analysed in terms of the strands of evidence of learning in and for new ways of working, gives some insight into the shaping effect of institutions as well the ways in which they are transformed through the agency of participants. It opens up the possibility of developing increasingly delicate descriptions of the rules and division of labour that obtain within and between settings. At the same time it carries with it the possibility of rethinking notions of agency and reconceptualising subject positions in terms of the relations between possibilities afforded within the division of labour and the rules that constrain possibility and direct and deflect the attention of participants. This is one approach to meeting the challenge of investigating learning as theorised by Roth and Lee (2007):

> Hence, learning is equivalent to the mutual change of object and subject in the process of activity; human beings plan and change the material world and societal life just as these settings mutually transform agents and the nature of their interactions with each other. Learning ... occurs during the expansion of the subject's action possibilities in the pursuit of meaningful objects in activity.
>
> (Roth and Lee, 2007, p. 198)

I have offered this extended example from some of our recent work not because of the specificities of the research topics themselves but because I hope that they provide some, albeit emergent, illustrations of the way in which a creative approach to the development of research methodologies can help us to pursue research objects that may be obscured through the limitations of the research gaze of other approaches.

At the beginning of this book, I referred to the notion of the sociological imagination. In the chapters of the book I have sketched some of the major traditions that have sought inspiration in the work of Vygotsky. Such 'Vygotskian imaginations' have appeared, at one moment, to be welded to a past dominated by the concerns of traditional cognitive psychology and, at another moment, to anthropology. They take a linguistic and semiotic view in some quarters and a systemic view in others. The metaphor of the city that I drew from Puzyrei (2007) at the outset of Chapter 1 holds firm. There are ghettoes and subterranean pockets of imagination at play in this theoretical domain, just as there are well-trodden boulevards and highways. Changes in climate bring about new perspectives on old artefacts. Just because these influences emanate from a long-dead

Russian does not mean that we are engaged in some bizarre form of archaeological endeavour. The challenges raised by Vygotsky are alive and well and the responses continue to evolve.

I now close this book in the confidence that the emergent cultural-historical imagination spawned by Vygotsky's writing will continue to generate new possibilities for research in the social sciences. We live in a world of multiple contradictions. We need a social science that articulates the complexities of the world that give rise to these contradictions and models human behaviour in the setting of its development. The boundaries that shape researchers' horizons often serve to severely constrain the imagination. As Sawyer notes:

> Socioculturalists have rarely drawn substantively on sociology, political science or history – disciplines that argue for the irreducibility of macro-level entities or structures such as social class, educational level, geographic region, race and ethnicity, social networks and institutional structures, and social power and its forms.
>
> (Sawyer, 2002, p. 301)

Avner Offer (2006) provides an intriguing discussion of the personal consequences of affluence. He attempts to move through an economic analysis infused with history and political theory to an account of personal aspiration and self-control in late capitalism. Whilst I do not agree with some of the psychological constructs he deploys (such as those derived from attachment theory), I applaud the move he makes to surface the economic features of the cultural-historical landscape and analyse the ways in which individual priorities are shaped. It is this kind of boundary-crossing that holds considerable potential for the future of research in the social sciences.

Vygotsky provides hope and inspiration and some of the conceptual tools that we need to fulfill the demands of a 'new' social science. Let us hope that the collective imaginations of the twenty-first century will generate the tools that enable the realisation of methodological goals established at the inception of the twentieth century.

Note

1 TLRP-ESRC study ESRC RES-139-25-0100 'Learning in and for Interagency Working' was co-directed by Harry Daniels and Anne Edwards. The research team included Paul Warmington, Deirdre Martin, Jane Leadbetter, David Middleton, Steve Brown, Anna Popova, Apostol Apostolov, Penny Smith, Ioanna Kinti, Mariann Martsin, and Sarah Parsons.

References

Abreu, G. and Elbers, E. (2005) 'The social mediation of learning in multiethnic schools: introduction', *European Journal of Psychology of Education* 20, 1: 3–11.

Ach, N. (1921) *Uber die begriffsbildung. Eine experimentelle Untersuchung*, Bamberg: C. Buchners Verlag.

Ageyev, V. (2003) 'Vygotsky in the mirror of cultural interpretations', in A. Kozulin, B. Gindis, V. Ageyev and S. Miller (eds) *Vygotsky's Educational Theory in Cultural Context*, 432–50, Cambridge: Cambridge University Press.

Agre, P.E. (1997) *Computation and Human Experience*, New York: Cambridge University Press.

Alexander, R. (2004) *Towards Dialogic Teaching: Rethinking Classroom Talk*, Cambridge: Dialogos.

Alexandrov, V.E. (2000) 'Biology, semiosis, and cultural difference in Lotman's semiosphere', *Comparative Literature* 52: 399–423.

Anderson, J.R., Reder, L.M. and Simon, H.A. (1996) 'Situated learning and education', *Educational Researcher* 25, 4: 5–11.

Anderson, J.R., Reder, L.M. and Simon, H.A. (1997) 'Situative versus cognitive perspectives: form versus substance', *Educational Researcher* 26, 1: 18–21.

Archer, M.S. (1988) *Culture and Agency: The Place of Culture in Social Theory*, New York: Cambridge University Press.

Archer, M.S. (1995) *Realist Social Theory: The Morphogenetic Approach*, New York: Cambridge University Press.

Baerentsen, K.B. and Trettvik, J. (2002) 'An activity theory approach to affordance', Oslo: NordiCHI, 19–23 October, 51–60.

Bakhtin, M.M. (1978) 'The problem of the text', *Soviet Studies in Literature* 14, 1: 3–33.

Bakhtin, M.M. (1981) *The Dialogic Imagination: Four Essays*, M. Holquist (ed.), M. Holquist and C. Emerson (trans.) *University of Texas Press Slavic Series 1*, Austin: University of Texas Press.

Bakhtin, M.M. (1984) *Problems of Dostoevsky's Poetics*, C. Emerson (ed. and trans.) *Theory and History of Literature 8*, Minneapolis: University of Minnesota Press.

Bakhtin, M.M. (1986) *Speech Genres and Other Late Essays*, C. Emerson and M. Holquist (eds), V.W. McGee (trans.) *University of Texas Press Slavic Series 8*, Austin: University of Texas Press.

Bakhurst, D. (1988) 'E.V. Ilyenkov and contemporary Soviet philosophy', unpublished PhD thesis, Exeter College, Oxford.

Bakhurst, D. (1991) *Consciousness and Revolution in Soviet Psychology: From the Bolsheviks to Evald Ilyenkov*, New York: Cambridge University Press.

Bakhurst, D. (1995) 'Lessons from Ilyenkov', *The Communication Review* 1, 2: 155–78.

Bakhurst, D. and Sypnowich, C. (1995) 'Introduction', in D. Bakhurst and C. Sypnowich (eds) *The Social Self: Inquiries in Social Construction*, 1–17, London: Sage.

Banks, A.P. and Millward, L.J. (2000) 'Running shared mental models as a distributed cognitive process', *British Journal of Psychology* 91: 513–31.

Barab, S.A. and Duffy, T. (2000) 'From practice fields to communities of practice', in D. Jonassen and S. Land (eds) *Theoretical Foundations of Learning Environments*, 25–56, New Jersey: Lawrence Erlbaum Associates, Inc.

Barnes, D. (1975) *From Communication to Curriculum*, London: Penguin.

Barton, D. (2001) 'Directions for literacy research: analysing language and social practices in a textually mediated world', *Language and Education* 15, 2–3: 92–104.

Bateson, G. (1972) *Steps to an Ecology of Mind*, Chicago: University of Chicago Press.

Beach, K. (1995) 'Activity as a mediator of sociocultural change and individual development: the case of school-work transition in Nepal', *Mind, Culture, and Activity* 2: 285–302.

Beach, K. (1999) 'Consequential transitions: a sociocultural expedition beyond transfer in education', *Review of Research in Education* 24: 101–39.

Bernstein, B. (1971) *Class, Codes and Control*, Vol. 1, *Theoretical Studies Towards a Sociology of Language*, London: Routledge & Kegan Paul.

Bernstein, B. (1977) *Class, Codes and Control*, Vol. 3, *Towards A Theory of Educational Transmissions*, 2nd revised edn, London: Routledge & Kegan Paul.

Bernstein, B. (1981) 'Codes, modalities and the process of cultural reproduction: a model', *Language in Society* 10: 327–63.

Bernstein, B. (1990) *The Structuring of Pedagogic Discourse*, Vol. 4, *Class, Codes and Control*, London: Routledge.

Bernstein, B. (1993) 'Foreword', in H. Daniels (ed.) *Charting the Agenda: Educational Activity after Vygotsky*, xiii–xxix, London: Routledge.

Bernstein, B. (1996) *Pedagogy, Symbolic Control and Identity: Theory, Research and Critique*, London: Taylor & Francis.

Bernstein, B. (1999) 'Vertical and horizontal discourse: an essay', *British Journal of Sociology of Education* 20, 2: 157–73.

Bernstein, B. (2000) *Pedagogy, Symbolic Control and Identity: Theory, Research, Critique*, revised edn, Lanham, MD: Rowman & Littlefield Publishers Inc.

Boaler, J. (1999) 'Participation, knowledge and beliefs: a community perspective on mathematics learning', *Educational Studies in Mathematics* 40: 259–81.

Bourdieu, P. (1977) *Outline of a Theory of Practice*, Cambridge: Cambridge University Press.

Bourdieu, P. (1988) *Homo Academicus*, Cambridge: Polity Press.

Bourdieu, P. (1998) *Practical Reason*, Cambridge: Polity Press.

Bourdieu, P. and Wacquant, L.J.D. (1992) *An Invitation to Reflexive Sociology*, Cambridge: Polity Press.

Bowers, J.S. (1996) 'Conducting developmental research in a technology-enhanced classroom', doctoral dissertation, Vanderbilt University, *Dissertation Abstracts International*, 57, 3433A.

Bowker, G.C. and Star, S.L. (1999) *Sorting Things Out*, Cambridge, MA: MIT Press.

Branco, A.U. and Valsiner, J. (1997) 'Changing methodologies: a co-constructivist study of goal orientations in social interactions', *Psychology and Developing Societies* 9, 1: 35–64.

Bredo, E. (1994) 'Reconstructing educational psychology: situated cognition and Deweyian pragmatism', *Educational Psychologist* 29, 1: 23–35.

Brighouse, T. (2002) 'The view of a participant during the second half – a perspective on LEAs since 1952', *Oxford Journal of Education* 28, 2–3: 188–96.
Brooks, R.A. (1991) 'Intelligence without representation', *Artificial Intelligence* 47: 139–59.
Brooks, R.A. (1999) *Cambrian Intelligence: The Early History of the New AI*, Cambridge, MA: MIT Press.
Brown, A.L. and Campione, J.C. (1990) 'Communities of learning and thinking, or a context by any other name', *Human Development* 21: 108–25.
Brown, A.L. and Campione, J.C. (1994) 'Guided discovery in a community of learners', in K. McGilly (ed.) *Classroom Lessons: Integrating Cognitive Theory and Classroom Practice*, 229–72, Cambridge, MA: MIT Press.
Brown, A.L. and Campione, J.C. (1996) 'Psychological theory and the design of innovative learning environments: on procedures, principles, and systems', in L. Schauble and R. Glaser (eds) *Innovations in Learning: New Environments for Education*, 289–325, Mahwah, NJ: Erlbaum.
Brown, J.S. and Duguid, P. (1991) 'Organizational learning and communities-of-practice: toward a unified view of working, learning and innovation', *Organization Science* 2: 40–57.
Brown, J.S. and Duguid, P. (2000) *The Social Life of Information*, Boston, MA: Harvard Business School Press.
Brown, J.S., Collins, A. and Duguid, P. (1989) 'Situated cognition and the culture of learning', *Educational Researcher* 18, 1: 32–42.
Bruner, J.S. (1986) *Actual Minds, Possible Worlds*, Cambridge, MA: Harvard University Press.
Bruner, J.S. (1990) *Acts of Meaning*, Cambridge, MA: Harvard University Press.
Bruner, J.S. (1996) *The Culture of Education*, Cambridge, MA: Harvard University Press.
Bruner, J. (1997) 'Celebrating divergence: Piaget and Vygotsky', *Human Development* 40: 63–73.
Bruner, J. (2005) 'Keynote presentation', First Congress of the International Society of Cultural and Activity Research (ISCAR), Seville, September.
Bruner, J.S., Goodnow, J.J. and Austin, G.A. (1956) *A Study of Thinking*, New York: Wiley.
Brushlinskii, A.V. (1994) 'Diskussii', *Psikhologicheskii zhurnal* 22, 4: 115–26.
Burke, K. (1969) *A Grammar of Motives*, Berkeley, CA: University of California Press. (Original work 1945.)
Burmenskaya, G. (1992) 'The development of Vygotsky's work', mimeograph of seminar at the Department of Developmental Psychology, Moscow Lomonosov State University, March 1992.
Calhoun, D., LiPuma, E. and Postone, M. (1993) *Bourdieu: Critical Perspectives*, Chicago: University of Chicago Press.
Candela, A. (1995) 'Consensus construction as a collective task in Mexican science classes', *Anthropology & Education Quarterly* 26, 4: 458–74.
Carraher, T.N., Carraher, D.W. and Schliemann, A.D. (1985) 'Mathematics in the streets and in schools', *British Journal of Developmental Psychology* 3: 21–9.
Center for Activity Theory and Developmental Work Research (2007) Available online: www.edu.helsinki.fi/activity/pages/chatanddwr/activitysystem/ (accessed 9 October 2007).
Chaiklin, S. (2003) '"The Zone of Proximal Development" in Vygotsky's analysis of learning and instruction', in A. Kozulin, B. Gindis, V. Ageyev and S. Miller (eds)

Vygotsky's Educational Theory in Cultural Context, 39–64, Cambridge: Cambridge University Press.

Chaiklin, S. and Lave, J. (eds) (1993) *Understanding Practice: Perspectives on Activity and Context*, Cambridge: Cambridge University Press.

Chatwin, B. (1987) *Songlines*, London: Penguin.

Clancey, W. (1993) 'The knowledge level reinterpreted: modelling socio-technical systems', *International Journal of Intelligent Systems* 8: 33–49.

Clancey, W.J. (1995a) 'Practice cannot be reduced to theory: knowledge, representations, and change in the workplace', in S. Bagnara, C. Zuccermaglio and S. Stuckey (eds) *Organizational learning and technological change*, 16–46, Berlin: Springer-Verlag.

Clancey, W.J. (1995b) 'A tutorial on situated learning', in J. Self (ed.) *Proceedings of the International Conference on Computers and Education (Taiwan)*, 49–70, Charlottesville, VA: AACE.

Clancey, W.J. (1997) *Situated Cognition: On Human Knowledge and Computer Representations*, Cambridge: Cambridge University Press.

Clancey, W.J. (2007) 'Scientific antecedents of situated cognition', in P. Robbins and M. Aydede (eds) *Cambridge Handbook of Situated Cognition*, 21–45, New York: Cambridge University Press.

Clark, A. (1997) *Being There: Putting Brain, Body, and World Together Again*, Cambridge, MA: MIT Press.

Clark, A. and Chalmers, D. (1998) 'The extended mind', *Analysis* 58, 1: 7–19.

Cobb, P. and Bowers, J. (1999) 'Cognitive and situated learning perspectives in theory and practice', *Educational Researcher* 28, 1: 4–15.

Cole, M. (1995) 'The supra-individual envelope of development: activity and practice, situation and context', in J.J. Goodnow, P.J. Miller and F. Kessel (eds) *Cultural Practices as Contexts for Development* 67: 105–18. San Francisco, CA: Jossey-Bass.

Cole, M. (1996) *Cultural Psychology: A Once and Future Discipline*, Cambridge, MA: Harvard University Press.

Cole, M. (2001) 'Kommentarii k kommentariam knigi "Kul'turno-istoricheskaia psikhologiia – nauka budushchego"', *Psikhologicheskii zhurnal* 22, 4 (July–August): 93–101 (quoted in Koshmanova, T.S. (2007) 'Vygotskian scholars: visions and implementation of cultural-historical theory', *Journal of Russian and East European Psychology* 45, 2: 61–95).

Cole, M. and Engeström, Y. (1993) 'A cultural-historical approach to distributed cognition', in G. Salomon (ed.) *Distributed Cognitions: Psychological and Educational Considerations*, 1–46, New York: Cambridge University Press.

Cole, M. and Gajdamaschko, N. (2007) 'Vygotsky and culture', in H. Daniels, M. Cole and J.V. Wertsch (eds) *The Cambridge Companion to Vygotsky*, 193–211, New York: Cambridge University Press.

Cole, M., Gay, J., Glick, J.A. and Sharp, D.W. (1971) *The Cultural Context of Learning and Thinking*, New York: Basic Books.

Coulson, S. (2001) *Semantic Leaps: Frame-shifting and Conceptual Blending in Meaning Construction*, Cambridge: Cambridge University Press.

Creese, A., Daniels, H. and Norwich, B. (2000) 'Evaluating teacher support teams in secondary schools: supporting teachers for SEN and other needs', *Research Papers in Education* 15, 3: 307–24.

Cussins, A. (1992) 'Content, embodiment and objectivity: the theory of cognitive trails', *Mind* 101: 651–88.

Daniels, H. (2001) *Vygotsky and Pedagogy*, London: Routledge.
Daniels, H. (2006) 'Analysing institutional effects in Activity Theory: first steps in the development of a language of description', *Outlines: Critical Social Studies* 2006, 2: 43–58.
Daniels, H. and Warmington, P. (2007) 'Analysing third generation activity systems: labour-power, subject position and personal transformation', *Journal of Workplace Learning* 19, 6: 377–91.
Daniels, H., Leadbetter, J., Soares, A. and McNab, N. (2007) 'Learning in and for cross-school working', *Oxford Review of Education* 33, 2: 125–42.
Daniels, H., Leadbetter, J. and Warmington, P., with Edwards, A., Brown, S., Middleton, D., Popova, A. and Apostolov, A. (2007) 'Learning in and for multi-agency working', *Oxford Review of Education* 33, 4: 521–38.
Das, J.P. (1995) 'Some thoughts on two aspects of Vygotsky's work', *Educational Psychologist* 30, 2: 93–7.
Davydov, V.V. (1977) *Arten der Verallgemeinerung im Unterricht* [Forms of generalization in education], Berlin: Volk und Wissen.
Davydov, V.V. (1982) 'Ausbildung der Lerntitigkeit' [Development of learning activity], in V.V. Davydov, J. Lompscher and A.K. Markova (eds) *Ausbildung der Le'rntatigkeit bei Schiilern*, 14–27, Berlin: Volk und Wissen.
Davydov, V.V. (1988) 'Problems of developmental teaching: the experience of theoretical and experimental psychological research', *Soviet Education* XX, 8: 3–87; 9: 3–56; 10: 2–42.
Davydov, V.V. (1989) *Udviklende undervisning pii virksomhedsteoriens grundlag* [Developmental teaching based on activity theory], Moscow: Sputnik.
Davydov, V.V. (1990) 'Types of generalization in instruction: logical and psychological problems in the structuring of school curricula', in J. Kilpatrick (ed.), J. Teller (trans.) *Soviet Studies in Mathematics Education*, Vol. 2, 56–83, Reston, VA: National Council of Teachers of Mathematics. (Original work published 1972.)
Davydov, V.V. (1993) 'The influence of L.S. Vygotsky on education, theory, research and practice', *Educational Researcher* 23: 12–21.
Davydov, V.V. (1995) 'The influence of L.S. Vygotsky on education theory, research and practice', *Educational Researcher* 24: 12–21.
Davydov, V.V. and Radzikhovskii, L.A. (1985) 'Vygotsky's theory and the activity oriented approach in psychology', in J.V. Wertsch (ed.) *Culture, Communication and Cognition: Vygotskian Perspectives*, 35–65, Cambridge: Cambridge University Press.
DeCorte, E., Greer, B. and Verschaffel, L. (1996) 'Mathematics learning and teaching', in D. Berliner and R. Calfee (eds) *Handbook of Educational Psychology*, 491–549, New York: Macmillan.
del Río, P. (1996) 'Building identities in a mass communication world: commentary on Steven Miles', *Culture & Psychology* 2, 2: 159–72.
del Río, P. (2002) 'The external brain: eco-cultural roots of distancing and mediation', *Culture & Psychology* 8, 2: 233–65.
del Río, P. and Álvarez, A. (1994) 'Tossing, praying and reasoning: the changing architectures of mind and agency', in J.V. Wertsch, P. del Río and A. Álvarez (eds) *Sociocultural Studies of Mind*, 215–47, Cambridge: Cambridge University Press.
del Río, P. and Álvarez, A. (1995) 'Directivity: the cultural and educational construction of morality and agency. Some questions arising from the legacy of Vygotsky', *Anthropology and Education Quarterly* 26, 4: 384–409.

del Río, P. and Álvarez, A. (2002) 'From activity to directivity. The question of involvement in education', in G. Wells and G. Claxton (eds) *Learning for Life in the 21st Century: Sociological Perspectives of the Future*, 145–178, London: Routledge.

del Río, P. and Álvarez, A. (2007) 'Inside and outside the Zone of Proximal Development: an eco-functional reading of Vygotsky', in H. Daniels, M. Cole and J.V. Wertsch (eds) *The Cambridge Companion to Vygotsky*, 276–306, New York: Cambridge University Press.

Dewey, J. (1981) 'The experimental theory of knowledge', in J.J. McDermott (ed.) *The Philosophy of John Dewey*, 136–177, Chicago: University of Chicago Press. (Original work published 1910.)

Diaz, M. (2001) 'The importance of Basil Bernstein', in S. Power, P. Aggleton, J. Brannen, A. Brown, L. Chisholm and J. Mace (eds) *A Tribute to Basil Bernstein 1924–2000*, 106–8, London: Institute of Education, University of London.

Diriwächter, R. and Valsiner, J. (2006) 'Qualitative developmental research methods in their historical and epistemological contexts', *Forum: Qualitative Social Research* 7, 1: Art. 8. Available online: www.qualitative-research.net/fqs-texte/1-06/06-1-8-e.htm.

Dyson, A. and Robson, E. (1999) *School, Family, Community: Mapping School Inclusion in the UK*, Leicester: Youth Work Press.

Elkonin, D.B. (1972) 'Toward the problem of stages in the mental development of the child', *Soviet Psychology* 4: 6–20.

Emerson, C. (1986) 'The outer word and inner speech: Bakhtin, Vygotsky and the internalization of language', in G.S. Morson (ed.) *Bakhtin: Essays and Dialogues on his Work*, 21–40, London: University of Chicago Press.

Engeström, Y. (1987) 'Learning by expanding: an activity-theoretical approach to developmental research', Helsinki: Orienta-Konsultit. Available online: lchc.ucsd.edu/MCA/Paper/Engestrom/expanding/toc.htm.

Engeström, Y. (1989) 'The cultural-historical theory of activity and the study of political repression', *International Journal of Mental Health* 17, 4: 29–41.

Engeström, Y. (1991) 'Activity theory and individual and social transformation', *Multidisciplinary Newsletter for Activity Theory* 7, 8: 14–15.

Engeström, Y. (1992) 'Interactive expertise: studies in distributed working intelligence', Helsinki: University of Helsinki, Department of Education, Research Bulletin 83.

Engeström, Y. (1993) 'Developmental studies on work as a test bench of activity theory', in S. Chaikin and J. Lave (eds) *Understanding Practice: Perspectives on Activity and Context*, 64–103, Cambridge: Cambridge University Press.

Engeström, Y. (1995) 'Objects, contradictions and collaboration in medical cognition: an activity-theoretical perspective', *Artificial Intelligence in Medicine* 7: 395–412.

Engeström, Y. (1996a) 'Development as breaking away and opening up: a challenge to Vygotsky and Piaget', *Swiss Journal of Psychology* 55: 126–32.

Engeström, Y. (1996b) 'Learning actions and knowledge creation in industrial work teams', paper presented at the international conference 'Work and learning in transition: toward a research agenda', sponsored by the Russell Sage Foundation, San Diego, CA, January 1996.

Engeström, Y. (1999a) 'Activity theory and individual and social transformation', in Y. Engeström, R. Miettinen and R.-L. Punamäki (eds) *Perspectives on Activity Theory*, 19–38, Cambridge: Cambridge University Press.

Engeström, Y. (1999b) 'Innovative learning in work teams: analyzing the cycles of knowledge creation in practice', in Y. Engeström, R. Miettinen and R.-L.

Punamäki (eds) *Perspectives on Activity Theory*, 377–404, Cambridge: Cambridge University Press.

Engeström, Y. (2000a) 'Making expansive decisions: an activity-theoretical study of practitioners building collaborative medical care for children', in K.M. Allwood and M. Selart (eds) *Creative Decision Making in the Social World*, 145–77, Amsterdam: Kluwer.

Engeström, Y. (2000b) 'Activity theory as a framework for analyzing and redesigning work', *Ergonomics* 43, 7: 960–74.

Engeström, Y. (2001a) 'Expansive learning at work: toward an activity theoretical reconceptualization', *Journal of Education and Work* 14, 1: 133–56.

Engeström, Y. (2001b) 'The horizontal dimension of expansive learning: weaving a texture of cognitive trails in the terrain of health care in Helsinki, Finland', paper presented at the international symposium 'New Challenges to Research on Learning', University of Helsinki, Finland, March 2001.

Engeström, Y. (2003) 'The horizontal dimension of expansive learning: weaving a texture of cognitive trails in the terrain of health care in Helsinki', in F. Achtenhagen and E.G. John (eds) *Meilensteine der beruflichen Bildung. Milestones of Vocational and Occupational Education and Training. Band 1, Volume 1: Die Lehr-Lern-Perspetive. The Teaching-learning Perspective*, 153–80, Bielefeld: W. Bertelsmann Verlag GmbH & Co.

Engeström, Y. (2004a) 'New forms of learning in co-configuration work', *Journal of Workplace Learning* 16, 1–2: 11–21.

Engeström, Y. (2004b) 'Object-oriented interagency: toward understanding collective intentionality in distributed activity fields', paper presented at the Sixth International Conference on Collective Intentionality, Siena, 10–13 October.

Engeström, Y. (2005a) 'Bumpy road to co-configuration: steps and obstacles in expansive organizational learning', paper presented at the Centre for Sociocultural and Activity Theory Research Inaugural Seminar, University of Bath, November.

Engeström, Y. (2005b) *Developmental Work Research: Expanding Activity Theory in Practice*, Berlin: Lehmanns Media.

Engeström, Y. (2006) 'Development, movement and agency: breaking away into mycorrhizae activities', in K. Yamazumi (ed.) *Building Activity Theory in Practice: Toward the Next Generation*, 1–43, Kansai: Kansai University Press.

Engeström, Y. (2007) 'Putting Vygotsky to work. The change laboratory as an application of double stimulation', in H. Daniels, M. Cole and J.V. Wertsch (eds) *The Cambridge Companion to Vygotsky*, 363–82, Cambridge: Cambridge University Press.

Engeström, Y. and Ahonen, H. (2001) 'On the materiality of social capital: an activity-theoretical exploration', in H. Hasan, E. Gould, P. Larkin and L. Vrazalic (eds) *Information Systems and Activity Theory, Vol. 2: Theory and Practice*, 56–87, Wollongong: University of Wollongong Press.

Engeström, Y. and Kerosuo, H. (2007) 'From workplace learning to inter-organizational learning and back: the contribution of activity theory', *Journal of Workplace Learning* 19, 6: 336–42.

Engeström, Y. and Miettinen, R. (1999) 'Introduction', in Y. Engeström, R. Miettinen and R.-L. Punamäki (eds) *Perspectives on Activity Theory*, 1–18, Cambridge: Cambridge University Press.

Engeström, Y., Brown, K., Christopher, L.C. and Gregory, J. (1997) 'Coordination, cooperation, and communication in the courts: expansive transitions in legal work', in M. Cole, Y. Engeström and O. Vasquez (eds) *Mind, Culture and Activity*, Cambridge: Cambridge University Press.

Engeström, Y., Engeström, R. and Kärkkäinen, M. (1995) 'Polycontextuality and boundary crossing in expert cognition: learning and problem solving in complex work activities', *Learning and Instruction* 5: 319–36.

Engeström, Y., Engeström, R. and Kerosuo, H. (2003) 'The discursive construction of collaborative care', *Applied Linguistics* 24, 286–315.

Engeström, Y., Engeström, R. and Vahaaho, T. (1999) 'When the center does not hold: the importance of knotworking', in S. Chaiklin, M. Hedegaard and U.J. Jensen (eds) *Activity Theory and Social Practice: Cultural-historical Approaches*, 345–74, Aarhus: Aarhus University Press.

Engeström, Y., Pasanen, A., Toiviainen, H. and Haavisto, V. (2005) 'Expansive learning as collaborative concept formation at work', in K. Yamazumi, Y. Engeström and H. Daniels (eds) *New Learning Challenges. Going Beyond the Industrial Age System of School and Work*, 47–77, Kansai: Kansai University press.

Engeström, Y., Puonti, A. and Seppänen, L. (2003) 'Spatial and temporal expansion of the object as a challenge for reorganizing work', in D. Nicolini, S. Gherardi and D. Yanow (eds) *Knowing in Organizations: A Practice-based Approach*, 133–59, Armonk: Sharpe.

Engeström, Y., Virkkunen, J., Helle, M., Pihlaja, J. and Poikela, R. (1996) 'Change laboratory as a tool for transforming work', *Lifelong Learning in Europe* 1, 2: 10–17.

Fairclough, N. (1992) *Discourse and Social Change*, Cambridge: Polity Press.

Fairclough, N. (2000) 'Discourse, social theory and social research: the discourse of welfare reform', *Journal of Sociolinguistics* 4: 163–95.

Fairclough, N. (2004) 'The dialectics of discourse'. Available online: www.geogr.ku.dk/courses/phd/glob-loc/papers/phdfairclough2.pdf (accessed 30 June 2004).

Farmer, F. (1995) 'Voice reprised: three etudes for a dialogic understanding', *Rhetoric Review* 13, 2: 304–20.

Fauconnier, G. and Turner, M. (2002) *The Way we Think: Conceptual Blending and Mind's Hidden Complexities*, New York: Basic Books.

Foucault, M. (1979) 'The life of infamous men', in M. Morris and P. Patton (eds) *Power, Truth, Strategy*, 76–91, Sydney: Feral.

Foucault, M. (1982) *The Archaeology of Knowledge and the Discourse on Language*, A.M. Sheridan-Smith (trans.), New York: Pantheon.

Foucault, M. (1992) 'What is an author?', in *Language, Counter-memory, Practice*, D.F. Bouchard and S. Simon (trans.), 124–7, New York: Cornell University Press.

Frawley, W. (1997) *Vygotsky and Cognitive Science: Language and the Unification of the Social and Computational Mind*, Cambridge, MA: Harvard University Press.

Gadamer, H.-G. (1979) *Truth and Method*, 2nd edn, London: Sheed & Ward.

Gee, J.P. (1996) *Social Linguistics and Literacies: Ideology in Discourses*, 2nd edn, London: Taylor & Francis.

Gee, J.P. (2000) 'Review: communities of practice in the new capitalism', *The Journal of the Learning Sciences* 9, 4: 515–23.

Gibson, J.J. (1986) *The Ecological Approach to Visual Perception*, Hillsdale, NJ: Lawrence Erlbaum.

Giddens, A. (1974) *Positivism and Sociology*, London: Heinemann.

Giddens, A. (1979) *Central Problems in Social Theory: Action, Structure, and Contradiction in Social Analysis*, Berkeley, CA: University of California Press.

Giddens, A. (1984) *The Constitution of Society: Outline of the Theory of Structuration*, Berkeley, CA: University of California Press.

Giddens, A. (1989) 'A reply to my critics', in D. Held and J.B. Thompson (eds) *Social Theory of Modern Societies: Anthony Giddens and his Critics*, 249–301, New York: Cambridge University Press.

Glassman, M. (1996) 'Understanding Vygotsky's motive and goal: an exploration of the work of A.N. Leontiev', *Human Development* 39: 309–27.

Gonzalez-Rey, F. (2002) 'L.S. Vygotsky and the question of personality in the cultural-historical approach', in D. Robbins and A. Stetsenko (eds) *Voices Within Vygotsky's Non-Classical Psychology: Past, Present, Future*, 77–98, New York: Nova Science.

Goodnow, J.J. (1976) 'The nature of intelligent behavior: questions raised by cross-cultural studies', in L.B. Resnick (ed.) *The Nature of Intelligence*, 129–42, Hillsdale, NJ: Erlbaum.

Goodwin, C. and Goodwin, M.H. (1996) 'Formulating planes: seeing as situated activity', in Y. Engeström and D. Middleton (eds) *Cognition and Communication at Work*, 61–95, New York: Cambridge University Press.

Goody, J. and Watt, I. (1968) 'The consequences of literacy', in J.R. Goody (ed.) *Literacy in Traditional Societies*, 23–46, Cambridge: Cambridge University Press.

Greenfield, P.M. (1993) 'Historical change and cognitive change: a two-decade follow-up study in Zinacantan, a Mayan community of southern Mexico', paper presented at the 60th Biennial Meeting of the Society for Research in Child Development, New Orleans, LA.

Greenfield, P.M. (1999) 'Cultural change and human development', in E. Turiel (ed.) *Culture and Development: New Directions in Child Psychology*, 37–59, San Francisco: Jossey-Bass.

Greenfield, P.M., Maynard, A. and Childs, C. (1997) 'History, culture, learning, and development', paper presented at the 62nd Biennial Meeting of the Society for Research in Child Development, Washington, DC.

Greeno, J.G. (1991) 'Number sense as situated knowing in a conceptual domain', *Journal for Research in Mathematics Education* 22: 170–218.

Greeno, J.G. (1997) 'On claims that answer the wrong questions', *Educational Researcher* 26, 1: 5–17.

Greeno, J.G. (1998) 'The situativity of knowing, learning, and research', *American Psychologist* 53: 5–17.

Greeno, J.G. (2006) 'Authoritative, accountable positioning and connected general knowing; progressive themes in understanding transfer', *The Journal of the Learning Sciences* 15, 4: 537–47.

Greeno, J.G. and the Middle School Mathematics Through Applications Projects Group (1998) 'The situativity of knowing, learning, and research', *American Psychologist* 53, 1: 5–26.

Greeno, J.G. and Moore, J.L. (1993) 'Situativity and symbols: response to Vera and Simon', *Cognitive Science* 17: 49–61.

Griffin, P. and Cole, M. (1984) 'Current activity for the future: the Zo-ped', in B. Rogoff and J.V. Wertsch (eds) *Children's Learning in the Zone of Proximal Development: New Directions for Child Development*, 45–63, San Francisco, CA: Jossey-Bass.

Gutiérrez, K., Baquedano-Lopez, P. and Tejada, C. (1999) 'Rethinking diversity: hybridity and hybrid language practices in the third space', *Mind, Culture, and Activity* 6, 4: 286–303.

Hakkarainen, K., Lonka, K. and Paavola, S. (2004) 'Networked intelligence: how can human intelligence be augmented through artifacts, communities, and networks?', paper presented at the Scandinavian Summer Cruise at the Baltic Sea (theme: *Motivation, Learning and Knowledge Building in the 21st Century*), 18–21 June (Organised by Karoliniska Institutet, EARLI SIG Higher Education and IKIT).

Hakkarainen, P. (2004) 'Editor's introduction: challenges of activity theory', *Journal of Russian and East European Psychology* 42, 2: 3–11.

Halliday, M.A.K. (1975) 'Talking one's way in', in A. Davies (ed.) *Problems of Language and Learning*, 8–26, London: Heinemann.

Hasan, R. (1992a) 'Speech genre, semiotic mediation and the development of higher mental functions', *Language Science* 14, 4: 489–528.

Hasan, R. (1992b) 'Meaning in sociolinguistic theory', in K. Bolton and H. Kwok (eds) *Sociolinguistics Today: International Perspectives*, 192–234, London: Routledge.

Hasan, R. (1995a) 'The conception of context in text', in P. Fries and M. Gregory (eds) *Discourse in Society: Systemic Functional Perspectives* (Meaning and Choice in Language: Studies for Michael Halliday) (ADPS50), 183–283, Norwood, NJ: Ablex.

Hasan, R. (1995b) 'On social conditions for semiotic mediation: the genesis of mind in society', in A.R. Sadovnik (ed.) *Knowledge and Pedagogy: The Sociology of Basil Bernstein*, 171–96, Norwood, NJ: Ablex.

Hasan, R. (1998) 'The disempowerment game: Bourdieu and language in literacy', *Linguistics and Education* 10: 25–87.

Hasan, R. (2001) 'Understanding talk: directions from Bernstein's sociology', *International Journal of Social Research Methodology* 4, 1: 5–9.

Hasan, R. (2002) 'Semiotic mediation and mental development in pluralistic societies: some implications for tomorrow's schooling', in G. Wells and G. Claxton (eds) *Learning for Life in the 21st Century: Socio-Cultural Perspectives on the Future of Education*, 89–123, Oxford: Blackwell.

Hasan, R. (2005) 'Semiotic mediation, language and society: three exotripic theories – Vygotsky, Halliday and Bernstein', in J.J. Webster (ed.) *Language, Society and Consciousness: Ruqaiya Hasan*, 46–67, London: Equinox.

Hasan, R. and Cloran, C. (1990) 'A sociolinguistic study of everyday talk between mothers and children', in M.A.K. Halliday, J. Gibbons and H. Nicholas (eds) *Learning Keeping and Using Language*, Vol. 1, 129–50, Amsterdam: John Benjamins.

Hatano, G. (1993) 'Time to merge Vygotskian and constructivist conceptions of knowledge acquisition', in E.A. Forman, N. Minick and C.A. Stone (eds) *Contexts & Learning: Sociocultural Dynamics in Children's Development*, 153–66, New York: Oxford University Press.

Hatano, G. and Wertsch, J.V. (2001) 'Sociocultural approaches to cognitive development: the constitutions of culture in mind', *Human Development* 44: 77–83.

Hedegaard, M. (1990) 'The zone of proximal development as basis for instruction', in L.C. Moll (ed.) *Vygotsky and Education: Instructional Implications and Applications of Sociohistorical Psychology*, 349–71, Cambridge: Cambridge University Press.

Hedegaard, M. (1995) 'Qualitative analyses of a child's development of theoretical knowledge and thinking in history teaching', in L. Martin, K. Nielsen and E. Tobach (eds) *Cultural Psychology and Activity Theory*, 293–325, Cambridge: Cambridge University Press.

Hedegaard, M. (1998) 'Situated learning and cognition: theoretical learning and cognition', *Mind, Culture, and Activity* 5, 2: 114–26.

Hedegaard, M. (2001) 'Learning through acting within societal traditions: learning in classrooms', in M. Hedegaard (ed.) *Learning in Classrooms: A Cultural Historical Approach*, Aarhus: Aarhus University Press.

Hedegaard, M. (2002) *Learning and Child Development: A Cultural-historical Study*, Aarhus: Aarhus University Press.

Hedegaard, M. (2007) 'The development of children's conceptual relation to the world, with focus on concept formation in pre-school children's activity', in H. Daniels, M. Cole and J.V. Wertsch (eds) *The Cambridge Companion to Vygotsky*, 246–75, New York: Cambridge University Press.

Hegel, G.W.F. (1977) *The Phenomenology of Spirit*, A.V. Miller (trans.), Oxford: Oxford University Press. (Original work published 1807.)

Heidegger, M. (1978a) *Being and Time*, Oxford: Blackwell.

Heidegger, M. (1978b) *Basic Writings*, London: Routledge.

Hicks, D. (1996) 'Discourse, learning, and teaching', *Review of Research in Education* 21: 49–95.

Hicks, D. (1999) 'Self and other in Bakhtin's early philosophical essays: prelude to a theory of prose consciousness', paper presented at the annual meeting of the AERA, Montreal, Canada.

Hill, W.C. and Hollan, J.D. (1994) 'History-enriched digital objects: prototypes and policy issues', *Information Society* 10: 139–45.

Hirst, W. and Manier, D. (1995) 'Opening vistas for cognitive psychology', in L.M.W. Martin, K. Nelson and E. Tobach (eds) *Sociocultural Psychology: Theory and Practice of Doing and Knowing*, 89–124, Cambridge: Cambridge University Press.

Hjörne, E. and Säljö, R. (2004) '"There is something about Julia": symptoms, categories, and the process of invoking ADHD in the Swedish school: a case study', *Journal of Language, Identity and Education* 3, 1: 1–24.

Hodkinson, P. (2004) 'Research as a form of work: expertise, community and methodological objectivity', *British Educational Research Journal* 30, 1: 9–26.

Hoffman, K.G. and Donaldson, J.F. (2004) 'Contextual tensions of the clinical environment and their influence on teaching and learning', *Medical Education* 38: 448–54.

Hollan, J., Hutchins, E. and Kirsh, D. (2000) 'Distributed cognition: toward a new foundation for human-computer interaction research', *Transactions on Computer-Human Interaction (TOCHI)* 7, 2 (Special issue on human–computer interaction in the new millennium, Part 2): 174–96.

Holland, D. and Cole, M. (1995) 'Between discourse and schema: reformulating a cultural-historical approach to culture and mind', *Anthropology and Education Quarterly* 26, 4: 475–90.

Holland, D., Lachicotte, L., Skinner, D. and Cain, C. (1998) *Identity and Agency in Cultural Worlds*, Cambridge, MA: Harvard University Press.

Holzman, L. (ed.) (1999) *Performing Psychology: A Post-modern Culture of the Mind*, London: Routledge.

Holzman, L. (2006) 'What kind of theory is activity theory?', *Theory & Psychology* 16, 1: 5–11.

Hughes, M. and Greenhough, P. (2006) 'Boxes, bags and videotape: enhancing home-school communication through knowledge exchange activities', *Educational Review* 58, 4: 471–87.

Hughes, M. and Pollard, A. (2006) 'Home-school knowledge exchange in context', *Educational Review* 58, 4: 385–95.

Hughes, M., Andrews, J., Feiler, A., Greenhough, P., Johnson, D., McNess, E., Osborn, M., Pollard, A., Salway, L., Scanlan, M., Stinchcombe, V., Winter, J. and Yee, W.C. (2003) 'Exchanging knowledge between home and school to enhance children's learning in literacy and numeracy', in S. Castelli, M. Mendel and B. Ravn (eds) *School, Family, and Community Partnership in a World of Differences and Changes*, 67–88, Gdansk: Ernape.

Hung, D.W.L. and Der-Thanq, C. (2001) 'Situated cognition, Vygotskian thought and learning from the communities of practice perspective: implications for the design of web-based e-learning', *Educational Media International* 38, 1: 3–12.

Hutchins, E. (1988) 'The technology of team navigation', in R.K.J. Galegher and C. Egido (eds) *Intellectual Teamwork: Social and Technical Bases of Cooperative Work*, 24–48, Hillsdale, NJ: Lawrence Erlbaum Associates.

Hutchins, E. (1995a) *Cognition in the Wild*, Cambridge, MA: MIT Press.

Hutchins, E. (1995b) 'How a cockpit remembers its speeds', *Cognitive Science* 19: 265–88.

Hutchins, E. and Klausen, T. (1992) 'Distributed cognition in an airline cockpit', in D. Middleton and Y. Engeström (eds) *Communication and Cognition at Work*, 15–34, Beverly Hills, CA: Sage Books.

Iaroshevskii, M.G. (ed.) (1991) *Repressirovannaia nauka*, Leningrad: Nauka (Vol. 1); St. Petersburg: Nauka (Vol. 2).

Ilyenkov, E.V. (1977) *Dialectical Logic. Essays on its History and Theory*, Moscow: Progress Publishers.

Ivic, I. (1989) 'Profiles of educators: Lev S. Vygotsky (1896–1934)', *Prospects* XIX, 3: 427–36.

Jayyusi, L. (1984) *Categorization and the Moral Order*, London: Routledge & Kegan Paul.

Johnson Laird, P.N. (1986) 'An artist constructs a science', *The Times Literary Supplement*, 15 August, 879–80.

John-Steiner, V. and Mahn, H. (1996) 'Sociocultural approaches to learning and development: a Vygotskian framework', *Educational Psychologist* 31: 191–206.

Karpov, Y.V. (2003) 'Vygotsky's doctrine of scientific concepts', in A. Kozulin, B. Gindis, V. Ageyev and S. Miller (eds) *Vygotsky's Educational Theory in Cultural Context*, 65–82, Cambridge: Cambridge University Press.

Knorr Cetina, K. (1999) *Epistemic Cultures: How Sciences Make Knowledge*, Cambridge, MA: Harvard University Press.

Knox, J.E. and Stevens, C. (1993) 'Vygotsky and Soviet Russian defectology: an introduction to Vygotsky', in R.W. Rieber and A.S. Carton (eds) *The Collected Works of L.S. Vygotsky, Vol. 2: Problems of Abnormal Psychology and Learning Disabilities*, 1–28, New York: Plenum Press.

Koshmanova, T.S. (2007) 'Vygotskian scholars: visions and implementation of cultural-historical theory', *Journal of Russian and East European Psychology* 45, 2: 61–95.

Kozulin, A. (1986) 'The concept of activity in Soviet psychology: Vygotsky, his disciples and critics', *American Psychologist* 41, 3: 264–74.

Kozulin, A. (1990) *Vygotsky's Psychology: A Biography of Ideas*, London: Harvester.

Kozulin, A. (1996) 'A literary model for psychology', in D. Hicks (ed.) *Discourse, Learning, and Schooling*, 145–64, New York: Cambridge University Press.

Kozulin, A. (1998) *Psychological Tools. A Sociocultural Approach to Education*, London: Harvard University Press.

Kozulin, A., Gindis, B., Ageyev, V. and Miller, S. (eds) (2003) *Vygotsky's Educational Theory in Cultural Context*, Cambridge: Cambridge University.

Langemeyer, I. (2005) 'Contradictions in expansive learning: towards a critical analysis of self-dependent forms of learning in relation to contemporary socio-technological change', *Forum Qualitative Sozialforschung/Forum: Qualitative Social Research* 7, 1: Art.

12. Available online: www.qualitative-research.net/1-06/06-1-12-e.htm (accessed 28 September 2007).

Lantolf, J. (2004) 'Sociocultural theory and second and foreign language learning: an overview of sociocultural theory', in K. van Esch and O. St. John (eds) *New Insights into Foreign Language Learning and Teaching*, 13–34, Frankfurt: Peter Lang Verlag.

Lave, J. (1977) 'Tailor-made experiments and evaluating the intellectual consequences of apprenticeship training', *The Quarterly Newsletter of the Institute for Comparative Human Development* 1: 1–3.

Lave, J. (1988) *Cognition in Practice: Mind, Mathematics and Culture in Everyday Life*, Cambridge: Cambridge University Press.

Lave, J. (1993) 'Situating learning in communities of practice', in L.B. Resnick, J.M. Levine and S.D. Teasley (eds) *Perspectives on Socially Shared Cognition*, 17–36, Washington, DC: American Psychological Association.

Lave, J. (1996) 'Teaching, as learning, in practice', *Mind, Culture, and Activity* 3: 149–64.

Lave, J. (1997) 'The culture of acquisition and the practice of understanding', in D. Kirshner and J.A. Whitson (eds) *Situated Cognition: Social, Semiotic, and Psychological Perspectives*, 63–82, Mahwah, NJ: Erlbaum.

Lave, J. and Wenger, E. (1991) *Situated Learning: Legitimate Peripheral Participation*, Cambridge: Cambridge University Press.

Lave, J. and Wenger, E. (1999) 'Legitimate peripheral participation', in P. Murphy (ed.) *Learners, Learning and Assessment*, 83–9, London: Paul Chapman.

Lave, J., Murtaugh, M. and de la Rocha, O. (1984) 'The dialectic of arithmetic in grocery shopping', in B. Rogoff and J. Lave (eds) *Everyday Cognition: Development in Social Context*, 67–94, Cambridge, MA: Harvard University Press.

Lea, M. and Nicoll, K. (eds) (2002) *Distributed Learning*, London: RoutledgeFalmer.

Leach, J. and Scott, P. (1995) 'The demands of learning science concepts: issues of theory and practice', *School Science Review* 76: 47–51.

Leadbetter, J., Daniels, H., Brown, S., Edwards, A., Middleton, D., Popova, A., Apostolov, A. and Warmington, P. (2007) 'Professional learning within multi-agency children's services: researching into practice', *Educational Research* 49, 1: 83–98.

Leander, K. (2002) 'Locating Latanya: the situated production of identity artifacts in classroom interaction', *Research in the Teaching of English* 37: 198–250.

Lee, C.D. (2007) *Culture, Literacy, and Learning: Blooming in the Midst of the Whirlwind*, New York: Teachers College Press.

Lemke, J. (1988) 'Genres, semantics and classroom education', *Linguistics and Education* 1: 81–99.

Lemke, J. (1990) *Talking Science: Language, Learning and Values*, Norwood, NJ: Ablex.

Lemke, J. (1995) *Textual Politics: Discourse and Social Dynamics*, London: Taylor & Francis.

Lemke, J. (1997) 'Cognition, context, and learning: a social semiotic perspective', in D. Kirshner (ed.) *Situated Cognition Theory: Social, Neurological, and Semiotic Perspectives*, 37–55, New York: Erlbaum.

Leontiev, A.N. (1978) *Activity, Consciousness and Personality*, Englewood Cliffs, NJ: Prentice Hall.

Leontiev, A.N. (1981a) 'The concept of activity in psychology', in J.V. Wertsch (ed.) *The Concept of Activity in Soviet Psychology*, 23–46, Armonk, NY: M.E. Sharpe.

Leontiev, A.N. (1981b) *Problems of the Development of the Mind*, Moscow: Progress Publishers.

Leontiev, A.N. (1997) 'On Vygotsky's creative development', in R.W. Rieber and J.

Wollock (eds) *The Collected Works of L.S. Vygotsky, Vol. 3: Problems of the Theory and History of Psychology,* 9–34, New York: Plenum Press. (Original work 1927.)

Leontiev, A.N. (1998) 'Uchenie o srede v pedologicheskih rabotakh Vygotskogo', *Voprosy psikhologii* 1: 108–24.

Leontiev, A.N. (2005) 'Study of the environment in the pedological works of L.S. Vygotsky: a critical study', *Journal of Russian and East European Psychology* 43, 4: 8–28.

Lidz, C.S. and Elliot, J.G. (eds) (2000) *Dynamic Assessment: Prevailing Models and Applications,* London: JAI.

Lindkvist, L. (2005) 'Knowledge communities and knowledge collectivities: a typology of knowledge work in groups', *Journal of Management Studies* 42, 6: 1189–210.

Linehan, C. and McCarthy, J. (2001) 'Reviewing the "Community of Practice" metaphor: an analysis of control relations in a primary school classroom', *Mind, Culture, and Activity* 8, 2: 129–47.

Lompscher, J. (1984) 'Problems and results of experimental research on the formation of theoretical thinking through instruction', in M. Hedegaard, P. Hakkarainen and Y. Engeström (eds) *Learning and Teaching on a Scientific Basis,* 293–358, Risskov: University of Aarhus, Institute of Psychology.

Lompscher, J. (ed.) (1985) *Persünlichkeitsentwicklung in der Lerntatigkeit* [Personality development through learning activity], Berlin: Volk und Wissen.

Lorenz, E. (2001) 'Models of cognition, the contextualisation of knowledge and organisational theory', *Journal of Management and Governance* 5: 307–30.

Lotman, Y.M. (1990) *Universe of the Mind. A Semiotic Theory of Culture,* A. Shukman (trans.), Bloomington, IN: Indiana University Press.

Lotman, Y. (1994) 'Text within a text', *Publications of the Modern Language Association* 109: 377–84.

Ludvigsen, S. (in press) 'What counts as knowledge: learning to use categories in computer environments', in R. Säljö (ed.) *ICT and Transformation of Learning Practices,* Amsterdam: Pergamon, Elsevier Science Ltd.

Luria, A.R. (1976) *Cognitive Development: Its Cultural and Social Foundations,* Cambridge, MA: Harvard University Press.

Luria, A. and Vygotsky, L.S. (1930) *Studies in the History of Behaviour,* Moscow: Progress Publishers.

Macdonald, C.A. (2006) 'The properties of mediated action in three different literacy contexts in South Africa', *Theory & Psychology* 16, 1: 51–80.

Makitalo, A. and Säljö, R. (2002) 'Talk in institutional context and institutional context in talk: categories as situated practices', *Text* 22, 1: 57–82.

Märtsin, M. (2007) 'From triangles to runaway-objects and mycorrhizae activities: an overview of the Engeströmian version of activity theory', mimeograph, Bath: Centre for Sociocultural and Activity Theory, University of Bath.

Marx, K. (1972) 'Theses on Feuerbach', in R. Tucker (ed.) *The Marx-Engels Reader,* 143–5, New York: W.W. Norton.

Marx, K. (1973) *Grundrisse,* London: Penguin. (Original work 1858.)

Marx, K. (1976) *Capital: A Critique of Political Economy Volume 1,* London: Penguin. (Original work 1883.)

Matusov, E. (1998) 'When solo activity is not privileged: participation and internalization models of development', *Human Development* 41: 326–49.

Matusov, E. (2007) 'Applying Bakhtin scholarship on discourse in education: a critical review essay', *Educational Theory* 57, 2: 215–37.

Maybin, J. (1999) 'Framing and evaluation in 10–12 year old school children's use of appropriated speech, in relation to their induction into educational procedures and practices', *Text* 19, 4: 459–84.

Mehan, H. (1979) *Learning Lessons: Social Organization in the Classroom*, Cambridge, MA: Harvard University Press.

Mercer, N. (1995) *The Guided Construction of Knowledge: Talk Amongst Teachers and Learners*, Clevedon: Multilingual Matters.

Mercer, N. (2000) *Words and Minds: How we Use Language to Think Together*, London: Routledge.

Mercer, N. and Littleton, K. (2007) *Dialogue and the Development of Children's Thinking*, London: Routledge.

Mercer, N., Dawes, L., Wegerif, R. and Sams, C. (2004) 'Reasoning as a scientist: ways of helping children to use language to learn science', *British Educational Research Journal* 30: 359–77.

Mercer, N., Wegerif, R. and Dawes, L. (1999) 'Children's talk and the development of reasoning in the classroom', *British Educational Research Journal* 25, 1: 95–111.

Meshcheryakov, B. (2007) 'Terminology in L. S. Vygotsky's writing', in H. Daniels, M. Cole and J.V. Wertsch (eds) *The Cambridge Companion to Vygotsky*, 155–77, New York: Cambridge University Press.

Middleton, D. (2007) 'Making the difference in interagency working: professional learning in communicating what matters', mimeograph.

Middleton, D. and Brown, S.D. (2005) *The Social Psychology of Experience: Studies in Remembering and Forgetting*, London: Sage Publications.

Miettinen, R. and Peisa, S. (2002) 'Integrating school-based learning with the study of change in working life: the alternative enterprise method', *Journal of Education and Work* 15, 3: 303–19.

Mills, W.C. (1959) *The Sociological Imagination*, Oxford: Oxford University Press.

Minick, N.J. (1985) 'L.S. Vygotsky and Soviet activity theory: new perspectives on the relationship between mind and society', unpublished PhD thesis, Northwestern University, IL.

Minick, N. (1987) 'The development of Vygotsky's thought: an introduction', in R.W. Rieber and A.S. Carton (eds) *The Collected Works of L.S. Vygotsky*, Vol. 1, 17–38, New York: Plenum Press.

Mintrop, H. (2004) 'Fostering constructivist communities of learners in the amalgamated multi-discipline of social studies', *Journal of Curriculum Studies* 36, 2: 141–58.

Moll, L.C. (1990) 'Introduction', in L.C. Moll (ed.) *Vygotsky and Education. Instructional Implications and Applications of Sociohistorical Psychology*, 1–30, Cambridge: Cambridge University Press.

Moll, L. (1997) 'The creation of mediating settings', *Mind, Culture, and Activity* 4: 191–9.

Moll, L. and Greenberg, J. (1990) 'Creating zones of possibilities: combining social contexts for instruction', in L. Moll (ed.) *Vygotsky and Education*, 319–48, Cambridge: Cambridge University Press.

Moll, L.C. and Whitmore, K.F. (1993) 'Vygotsky in classroom practice: moving from individual transmission to social transaction', in E.A. Forman, N. Minnick and C. Addison Stone (eds) *Contexts for Learning*, 19–42, New York: Oxford University Press.

Moll, L., Amanti, C., Neff, D. and Gonzalez, N. (1992) 'Funds of knowledge for teaching: using a qualitative approach to connect homes and classrooms', *Theory Into Practice* 31, 2: 132–41.

Moll, L., Tapia, J. and Whitmore, K. (1993) 'Living knowledge: the social distribution of cultural resources for thinking', in G. Salomon (ed.) *Distributed Cognitions*, 139–63, Cambridge: Cambridge University Press.

Moran, S. and John-Steiner, V. (2003) 'Creativity in the making: Vygotsky's contemporary contribution to the dialectic of development and creativity', in K.R. Sawyer, V. John-Steiner, S. Moran, R.J. Sternberg, D.H. Feldman, H. Gardner, J. Nakamura and M. Csikszentmihalyi (eds) *Creativity and Development*, 61–90, Oxford and New York: Oxford University Press.

Morgan, D. (1998) 'Sociological imaginings and imagining sociology: bodies, auto/biographies and other mysteries', *Sociology* 32, 4: 647–63.

Nelson, K. (1995) 'From spontaneous to scientific concepts: continuities and discontinuities from childhood to adulthood', in L.M.W. Martin, K. Nelson and E. Tobach (eds) *Sociocultural Psychology: Theory and Practice of Doing and Knowing*, 229–49, Cambridge: Cambridge University Press.

Newman, D., Griffin, P. and Cole, M. (1989) *The Construction Zone: Working for Cognitive Change in School*, Cambridge: Cambridge University Press.

Newman, F. and Holzman, L. (1993) *Lev Vygotsky: Revolutionary Scientist*, London: Routledge.

Nilholm, C. and Säljö, R. (1996) 'Co-action, situation definitions and sociocultural experience: an empirical study of problem-solving in mother-child interaction', *Learning and Instruction* 6, 4: 325–44.

Norman, D.A. (1993) 'Cognition in the head and in the world: an introduction to the special issue on situated action', *Cognitive Science* 17, 1: 1–6.

Nunes, T., Schliemann, A.D. and Carraher, D.W. (1993) *Street Mathematics and School Mathematics*, Cambridge: Cambridge University Press.

Offer, A. (2006) *The Challenge of Affluence*, Oxford: Oxford University Press.

Olson, D.R. (1976) 'Towards a theory of instructional means', *Educational Psychologist* 12: 14–35.

Petrovsky, A. (1990) *Psychology in the Soviet Union: A Historical Outline*, Moscow: Progress Publishers.

Piaget, J. (1924) *Le jugement et le raisonnement chez l'enfant*, Neuchatel: Delachaux et Niestle.

Piaget, J. (1972) 'Intellectual evolution from adolescence to adulthood', *Human Development* 15: 1–12.

Piaget, J. (1995) *Sociological Studies*, L. Smith (ed.), London: Routledge.

Prawat, R.S. (1999) 'Cognitive theory at the crossroads: head fitting, head splitting, or somewhere in between?', *Human Development* 42, 2: 59–77.

Puzyrei, A.A. (2007) 'Contemporary psychology and Vygotsky's cultural-historical theory', *Journal of Russian and East European Psychology* 45, 1: 8–93.

Ratner, C. (1997) *Cultural Psychology and Qualitative Methodology. Theoretical and Empirical Considerations*, v–xv, London: Plenum Press.

Ratner, C. (1998) 'Prologue', in R.W. Rieber (ed.) *The Collected Works of L.S. Vygotsky: Vol. 5, Child Psychology*, New York: Plenum Press.

Ratner, C. (2002) *Cultural Psychology: Theory and Method*, New York: Kluwer Academic/Plenum.

Riegel, K.F. (1976) 'The dialectics of human development', *American Psychologist* October, 689–700.

Rikowski, G. (1999) 'Education, capital and the transhuman', in D. Hill, P. McLaren, M.

Cole and G. Rikowski (eds) *Postmodernism in Educational Theory: Education and the Politics of Human Resistance*, 50–4, London: Tufnell Press.

Rikowski, G. (2002a) 'Fuel for the living fire: labour-power!', in A. Dinerstein and M. Neary (eds) *The Labour Debate: an Investigation into the Theory and Reality of Capitalist Work*, 179–202, Aldershot: Ashgate.

Rikowski, G. (2002b) 'Methods for researching the social production of labour-power in capitalism', research seminar, University College Northampton, 7 March.

Rockwell, E. (1999) 'Recovering history in the study of schooling: from the *Longue Durée* to everyday co-construction', *Human Development* 42: 113–28.

Rogoff, B. (1982) 'Integrating context and cognitive development', in M.E. Lamb and A.L. Brown (eds) *Advances in Developmental Psychology*, Vol. 2, 125–70, Hillsdale, NJ: Erlbaum.

Rogoff, B. (1990) *Apprenticeship in Thinking: Cognitive Development in Social Context*, New York: Oxford University Press.

Rogoff, B. (1992) 'Three ways to relate person and culture: thoughts sparked by Valsiner's review of *Apprenticeship in Thinking*', *Human Development* 35: 316–20.

Rogoff, B. (1995) 'Observing sociocultural activity on three planes: participatory appropriation, guided participation, and apprenticeship', in J.J. Wertsch, P. del Río and A. Álvarez (eds) *Sociocultural Studies of Mind*, 139–64, Cambridge: Cambridge University Press.

Rogoff, B. (1997) 'Evaluating development in the process of participation: theory, methods, and practice building on each other', in E. Amsel and A. Renninger (eds) *Change and Development*, 265–85, Hillsdale, NJ: Erlbaum.

Rogoff, B. (1998) 'Cognition as a collaborative process', in D. Kuhn and R.S. Siegler (eds) *Handbook of Child Psychology: Vol. 2, Cognition, Perception, and Language*, 5th edn, 679–744, New York: Wiley.

Rogoff, B. (2003) *The Cultural Nature of Human Development*, New York: Oxford University Press.

Rogoff, B. and Chavajay, P. (1995) 'What's become of research on the cultural basis of cognitive development?', *American Psychologist* 50, 10: 859–77.

Rogoff, B. and Lave, J. (1984) *Everyday Cognition: Its Development in Social Context*, Cambridge, MA: Harvard University Press.

Rogoff, B., Matusov, E. and White, C. (1996) 'Models of teaching and learning: participation in a community of learners', in D. Olson and N. Torrance (eds) *The Handbook of Education and Human Development: New Models of Learning, Teaching, and Schooling*, 388–415, Oxford: Blackwell.

Rojas-Drummond, S. and Alatorre, J. (1994) 'The development of independent problem solving in pre-school children', in N. Mercer and C. Coll (eds) *Explorations in Sociocultural Studies, Vol. 3: Teaching, Learning and Interaction*, 161–75, Madrid: Infancia y Aprendizaje.

Rojas-Drummond, S. and Mercer, N. (2004) 'Scaffolding the development of effective collaboration and learning', *International Journal of Educational Research* 39, 1–2: 99–110 (special issue on group work, edited by P. Blatchford and P. Kutnick).

Rojas-Drummond, S., Mercer, N. and Dabrowski, E. (2001) 'Collaboration, scaffolding and the promotion of problem solving strategies in Mexican pre-schoolers', *European Journal of Psychology of Education* XVI, 2: 179–96.

Roth, W.M. (2007a) 'Heeding the unit of analysis', *Mind, Culture, and Activity* 14, 3: 143–9.

Roth, W.M. (2007b) 'The ethico-moral nature of identity: prolegomena to the development of third-generation cultural-historical activity theory', *International Journal of Educational Research* 46: 83–93.

Roth, W.M. and Lee, Y.J. (2007) '"Vygotsky's Neglected Legacy": cultural-historical activity theory', *Review of Educational Research* 77, 2: 186–232.

Roth, W.M., Hwang, S.W., Goulart, M. and Lee, Y.J. (2005) *Participation, Learning and Identity*, Berlin: International Cultural-Historical Human Sciences.

Rowlands, S. (2000) 'Turning Vygotsky on his head: Vygotsky's "scientifically based method" and the socioculturalist's "social other"', *Science and Education* 9: 537–75.

Sacks, H. (1992) *Lectures on Conversation*, Oxford: Blackwell.

Sakharov, L. (1994) 'Methods for investigating concepts', M. Vale (trans. 1990), in R. van der Veer and J. Valsiner (eds) *Vygotsky Reader*, 73–99, Oxford: Blackwell.

Säljö, R. (1994) 'Minding action: conceiving the world versus participating in cultural practices', *Nordisk Pedagogik* 2: 71–80.

Säljö, R. (2002) 'My brain's running slow today – the preference for "things ontologies" in research and everyday discourse on human thinking', *Studies in Philosophy and Education* 21: 389–405.

Salomon, G. (1993a) 'Editor's introduction', in G. Salomon (ed.) *Distributed Cognitions: Psychological and Educational Considerations*, xi–xxi, Cambridge: Cambridge University Press.

Salomon, G. (1993b) 'No distribution without individuals' cognition: a dynamic interactional view', in G. Salomon (ed.) *Distributed Cognitions: Psychological and Educational Considerations*, 111–38, Cambridge: Cambridge University Press.

Sameroff, A.J. (1980) 'Development and the dialectic: the need for a systems approach', in W.A. Collins (ed.) *The Concept of Development – Minnesota Symposia on Child Psychology* 15: 83–103.

Sarangi, S. and Roberts, C. (1999) 'Introduction: discursive hybridity in medical work', in S. Sarangi and C. Roberts (eds) *Talk, Work and Institutional Order: Discourse in Medical, Mediation and Management Settings*, 473–503, Berlin: Mouton de Gruyter.

Sawyer, K. (2002) 'Unresolved tensions in sociocultural theory: analogies with contemporary sociological debates', *Culture & Psychology* 8, 3: 283–305.

Saxe, G.B. (1988) 'Candy selling and math learning', *Educational Researcher* 17, 6: 14–21.

Saxe, G.B. (1991) *Culture and Cognitive Development: Studies in Mathematical Understanding*, Hillsdale, NJ: Erlbaum.

Saxe, G. (2004) 'Practices of quantification from a socio-cultural perspective', in A. Demetriou and A. Raftopoulos (eds) *Developmental Change: Theories, Models, and Measurement*, 241–64, New York: Cambridge University Press.

Saxe, G.B. and Esmonde, I. (2005) 'Studying cognition in flux: a historical treatment of *Fu* in the shifting structure of Oksapmin mathematics', *Mind, Culture, and Activity* 12, 3–4: 171–225.

Scaife, M. and Rogers, Y. (1996) 'External cognition: how do graphical representations work?', *International Journal of Human-Computer Studies* 45: 185–213.

Schedrovitsky, G.P. (1982) 'The Mozart of psychology: an imaginary exchange of views', in K. Levitin (ed.) *One is Not Born a Personality*, 59–63, Moscow: Progress Publishers.

Schoultz, J., Säljö, R. and Wyndhamn, J. (2001) 'Conceptual knowledge in talk and text: what does it take to understand a science question?', *Instructional Science* 29: 213–36.

Scribner, S. (1984) 'Studying working intelligence', in B. Rogoff and J. Lave (eds) *Everyday Cognition: Its Development in Social Context*, 9–40, Cambridge, MA: Harvard University Press.

Scribner, S. (1985) 'Vygotsky's uses of history', in J.V. Wertsch (ed.) *Culture, Communication, and Cognition: Vygotskian Perspectives*, 119–45, Cambridge: Cambridge University Press.

Scribner, S. and Cole, M. (1981) *The Psychology of Literacy*, Cambridge, MA: Harvard University Press.

Seifert, K. (2002) 'Sociable thinking: cognitive development in early childhood education', in O. Saracho and B. Spodek (eds) *Contemporary Perspectives on Early Childhood Curriculum*, 15–40, Greenwich, CT: Information Age Publishing.

Seltzer, K. and Bentley, T. (2001) *The Creative Age: Knowledge and Skills for the New Economy*, London: DEMOS.

Sfard, A. (1998) 'On two metaphors for learning and the dangers of choosing just one', *Educational Researcher* 27, 2: 4–13.

Sherin, M.G., Mendez, E.P. And Louis, D.A. (2004) 'A discipline apart: the challenge of "Fostering a Community of Learners" in a mathematics classroom', *Journal of Curriculum Studies* 36, 2: 207–32.

Shore, B. (1996) *Culture in Mind*, New York: Oxford University Press.

Shulman, L.S. and Sherin, M.G. (2004) 'Fostering communities of teachers as learners: disciplinary perspectives', *Journal of Curriculum Studies* 36, 2: 135–40.

Shweder, R.A. (1990) 'Cultural psychology – what is it?', in J.W. Stigler, R.A. Shweder and G. Herdt (eds) *Cultural Psychology: Essays on Comparative Human Development*, 1–43, New York: Cambridge University Press.

Sidorkin, A.M. (1999) *Beyond Discourse: Education, the Self and Dialogue*, New York: State University of New York Press.

Silverman, D. and Torode, B. (1980) *The Material Word: Some Theories of Language and its Limit*, London: Routledge.

Smolka, A. (2005) 'The authoring of institutional practices: discourse and modes of participation of subjects', *Culture & Psychology* 11, 3: 359–76.

Spurrett, D. and Cowley, S. (2004) 'How to do things without words: infants, utterance-activity and distributed cognition', *Language Sciences* 26, 5: 443–66.

Stetsenko, A. (2007) 'Agency and society: lessons from the study of social change', *International Journal of Psychology* 42, 2: 110–12.

Suchman, L.A. (1987) *Plans and Situated Actions: The Problem of Human-Machine Communication*, New York: Cambridge University Press.

Suchman, L. (1993) 'Response to Vera and Simon's situated action: a symbolic interpretation', *Cognitive Science* 17, 1: 71–5.

Tharp, R.G. and Gallimore, R. (1988) *Rousing Minds to Life: Teaching, Learning, and Schooling in Social Context*, Cambridge: Cambridge University Press.

Thomas, A. (2005) 'Children online: learning in a virtual community of practice', *E-Learning* 2, 1: 27–38.

Thompson, M. (2005) 'Structural and epistemic parameters in communities of practice', *Organization Science* 16, 2: 151–64.

Thorne, S.L. (2005) 'Epistemology, politics, and ethics in sociocultural theory', *The Modern Language Journal* 89: 393–408.

Toomela, A. (ed.) (2003a) *Cultural Guidance in the Development of Human Mind*, Westport, CT: Ablex.

Toomela, A. (2003b) 'How should culture be studied?', *Culture & Psychology* 9, 1: 35–45.

Tuomi-Grohn, T., Engeström, Y. and Young, M. (2003) 'From transfer to boundary-crossing between school and work as a tool for developing vocational education: an introduction', in T. Tuomi-Grohn and Y. Engeström (eds) *Between School and Work: New Perspectives on Transfer and Boundary-crossing*, 1–15, Amsterdam: Pergamon.

Vadeboncoeur, J. (2003) 'Cultural tools and cognition: a co-revolutionary relation', *Discourse: Studies in the Cultural Politics of Education* 24, 3: 385–92.

Valsiner, J. (1988) *Developmental Psychology in the Soviet Union*, Brighton: Harvester.

Valsiner, J. (1990) *Culture and Human Development*, Lexington, MA: Lexington Books.

Valsiner, J. (1991) 'Building theoretical bridges over a lagoon of everyday events', *Human Development* 34: 307–15.

Valsiner, J. (1997) *Culture and the Development of Children's Action: A Theory of Human Development*, 2nd edn, New York: John Wiley and Sons.

Valsiner, J. (1998a) 'Dualisms displaced: from crusades to analytic distinctions', *Human Development* 41: 350–4.

Valsiner, J. (1998b) *The Guided Mind: A Sociogenetic Approach to Personality*, Cambridge, MA: Harvard University Press.

Valsiner, J. (2004) 'Three years later: culture in psychology – between social positioning and producing new knowledge', *Culture & Psychology* 10, 1: 5–27.

Valsiner, J. and Van der Veer, R. (1993) 'The encoding of distance: the zone of proximal development and its interpretations', in R.R. Cocking and K. Ann Renninger (eds) *The Development and Meaning of Psychological Distance*, 35–62, Hillsfield, NJ: Erlbaum Associates.

Valsiner, J. and Van der Veer, R. (2000) *The Social Mind: Construction of the Idea*, Cambridge: Cambridge University Press.

Van der Veer, R. (1994) 'The concept of development and the development of concepts of education and development', in Vygotsky's *Thinking, European Journal of Psychology of Education* 9, 4: 293–300.

Van der Veer, R. (1997) 'Some major themes in Vygotsky's theoretical work – an introduction', in R.W. Rieber and J. Wollock (eds) *The Collected Works of L.S. Vygotsky, Vol. 3: Problems of the Theory and History of Psychology*, 1–7, New York: Plenum Press. (Original work 1927.)

Van der Veer, R. (2001) 'The idea of units of analysis: Vygotsky's contribution', in S. Chaiklin (ed.) *The Theory and Practice of Cultural-historical Psychology*, 93–106, Aarhus: Aarhus University Press.

Van der Veer, R. and Valsiner, J. (1991) *Understanding Vygotsky: A Quest for Synthesis*, Oxford: Blackwell.

Van der Veer, R. and Van Ijzendoorn, M. (1985) 'Vygotsky theory of the higher psychological processes – some criticisms', *Human Development* 28, 1: 1–9.

Vann, K. and Bowker, G.C. (2001) 'Instrumentalizing the truth of practice', *Social Epistemology* 15, 3: 247–62.

Vasilyuk, F. (1991) *The Psychology of Experiencing: The Resolution of Life's Critical Situations*, Hemel Hempstead: Harvester.

Vera, A.H. and Simon, H.A. (1993a) 'Situated action: a symbolic interpretation', *Cognitive Science* 17, 1993: 7–48.

Vera, A.H. and Simon, H.A (1993b) 'Situated action: reply to William Clancey', *Cognitive Science* 17, 1993: 117–33.

Veresov, N.N. (1992) 'Kul'tura i tvorchestvo kak psikhologicheskie idei', *Voprosy psikhologii* 1–2: 124–8.

Veresov, N. (1999) *Undiscovered Vygotsky*, Berlin: Peter Lang.

Veresov, N. and Hakkarainen, P. (2001) 'Editors' introduction: psychology at the limit, or the limits of psychology (Part I)', *Journal of Russian and East European Psychology* 39, 1: 3–6.

Victor, B. and Boynton, A. (1998) *Invented Here: Maximizing your Organization's Internal Growth and Profitability*, Boston, MA: Harvard Business School Press.

Virkkunen, J., Engeström, Y., Helle, M., Pihlaja, J. and Poikela, R. (1997) 'The change laboratory – a tool for transforming work', in T. Alasoini, M. Kyllönen and A. Kasvio (eds) *Workplace Innovations – A Way of Promoting Competitiveness, Welfare and Employment*, 45–67, Helsinki: Ministry of Labour.

Vygotsky, L.S. (1929) 'The problem of the cultural development of the child II', *Journal of Genetic Psychology* 36: 415–34.

Vygotsky, L.S. (1978) *Mind in Society: The Development of Higher Psychological Processes*, M. Cole, V. John-Steiner, S. Scribner and E. Souberman (eds and trans.), Cambridge, MA: Harvard University Press.

Vygotsky, L.S. (1981a) 'The development of higher forms of attention', in J.V. Wertsch (ed.) *The Concept of Activity in Soviet Psychology*, 189–240, New York: Sharpe.

Vygotsky, L.S. (1981b) 'The genesis of higher mental functions', in J.V. Wertsch (ed.) *The Concept of Activity in Soviet Psychology*, 144–88, Armonk, NY: M.E. Sharpe.

Vygotsky, L.S. (1981c) 'The instrumental method in psychology', in J.V. Wertsch (ed.) *The Concept of Activity in Soviet Psychology*, 134–43, Armonk, NY: M.E. Sharpe. (Original work 1960.)

Vygotsky, L.S. (1983) 'From the notebooks of L.S. Vygotsky', *Soviet Psychology* XXI, 3: 3–17.

Vygotsky, L.S. (1986) *Thought and Language*, Cambridge, MA: MIT Press. (Original work 1934.)

Vygotsky, L.S. (1987a) *The Collected Works of L.S. Vygotsky, Vol. 1: Problems of General Psychology*, R.W. Rieber and A.S. Carton (eds), New York: Plenum Press. (Original work 1933–4.)

Vygotsky, L.S. (1987b) 'Lectures on psychology', in R.W. Rieber and A.S. Carton (eds) *The Collected Works of L.S. Vygotsky, Vol. 1: Problems of General Psychology*, New York: Plenum Press. (Original work 1933–4.)

Vygotsky, L.S. (1987c) 'Thinking and speech', in R.W. Rieber and and A.S. Carton (eds) *The Collected Works of L.S. Vygotsky, Vol. 1: Problems of General Psychology*, 39–285, New York: Plenum. (Original work 1934.)

Vygotsky, L.S. (1989) 'Concrete human psychology', *Soviet Psychology* 27, 2: 53–77.

Vygotsky, L.S. (1993) *The Collected Works of L.S. Vygotsky, Vol. 2: Problems of Abnormal Psychology and Learning Disabilities*, R.W. Rieber and A.S. Carton (eds), New York: Plenum Press.

Vygotsky, L.S. (1994) 'The socialist alteration of man', in *The Vygotsky Reader*, 175–84, Oxford: Basil Blackwell. (Original work 1930.)

Vygotsky, L.S. (1997a) *The Collected Works of L.S. Vygotsky, Vol. 3: Problems of the Theory and History of Psychology*, R.W. Rieber and J. Wollock (eds), New York: Plenum Press. (Original work 1927.)

Vygotsky, L.S. (1997b) *Educational Psychology*, Boca Raton, FL: Saint Lucie Press. (Original work 1921–3.)

Vygotsky, L.S. (1997c) *The Collected Works of L.S. Vygotsky, Vol. 4: The History of the Development of Higher Mental Functions*, R.W. Rieber (ed.), New York: Plenum Press. (Original work 1924–34.)

Vygotsky, L.S. (1998a) *The Collected Works of L.S. Vygotsky, Vol. 5: Child Psychology*, R.W. Rieber (ed.), New York: Plenum Press. (Original work 1928–31.)

Vygotsky, L.S. (1998b) 'Consciousness as a problem in the psychology of behavior', in N. Veresov (ed.) *Vygotsky before Vygotsky*, 185–202, Oulu: Oulu University Press. (Original work 1925.)

Vygotsky, L.S. (1999) 'Tool and sign in the development of the child', in R.W. Rieber (ed.) *The Collected Works of L.S. Vygotsky, Vol. 6: Scientific Legacy*, New York: Plenum.

Vygotsky, L.S. (2004) 'Imagination and creativity in childhood', *Journal of Russian and East European Psychology* 42, 1: 7–97.

Wardekker, W.L. (1998) 'Scientific concepts and reflection', *Mind, Culture, and Activity* 5, 2: 143–54.

Warmington, P. (2005) 'From activity to labour: commodification, labour-power and contradiction in activity theory', *Contradictions in Activity Symposium*, First International Congress of the International Society for Cultural and Activity Research (ISCAR), Seville, 20–24 September.

Wartofsky, M. (1973) *Models*, Dordecht: D. Reide.

Wegerif, R. (2007) 'From dialectic to dialogic: a response to Wertsch and Kazak', in T. Koschmann (ed.) *Theorizing Learning Practice*, 29–54, Mahwah, NJ: Erlbaum.

Wegerif, R. and Mercer, N. (1997) 'Using computer-based text analysis to integrate quantitative and qualitative methods in the investigation of collaborative learning', *Language and Education* 11, 4: 271–87.

Wegerif, N., Mercer, N. and Dawes, L. (1999) 'From social interaction to individual reasoning; an empirical investigation of a possible socio-cultural model of cognitive development', *Learning and Instruction* 9: 493–516.

Wells, G. (1999) *Dialogic Inquiry: Toward a Sociocultural Practice and Theory of Education*, Cambridge: Cambridge University Press.

Wenger, E. (1998) *Communities of Practice: Learning, Meaning and Identity*, Cambridge: Cambridge University Press.

Wenger, E., McDermott, R. and Snyder, W. (2002) *Cultivating Communities of Practice*, Boston, MA: Harvard Business School Press.

Wertsch, J.V. (1979) 'From social interaction to higher psychological processes: a clarification and application of Vygotsky's theory', *Human Development* 22: 1–22.

Wertsch, J.V. (1985a) *Vygotsky and the Social Formation of Mind*, Cambridge, MA: Harvard University Press.

Wertsch, J.V. (ed.) (1985b) *Culture, Communication, and Cognition: Vygotskian Perspectives*, New York: Cambridge University Press.

Wertsch, J.V. (1985c) 'The semiotic mediation of mental life: L S Vygotsky and M M Bakhtin', in E. Mertz and R.A. Parmentier (eds) *Semiotic Mediation: Sociocultural and Psychological Perspectives*, 223–56, New York: Academic Press.

Wertsch, J.V. (1991) *Voices of the Mind: A Sociocultural Approach to Mediated Action*, Cambridge, MA: Harvard University Press.

Wertsch, J.V. (1993) 'Commentary', *Human Development* 36: 168–71.

Wertsch, J.V. (1994) 'The primacy of mediated action in sociocultural studies', *Mind, Culture, and Activity* 1, 4: 202–8.

Wertsch, J.V. (1995) 'The need for action in sociocultural research', in J.V. Wertsch, P. del Río and A. Álvarez (eds) *Sociocultural Studies of Mind*, 56–74, New York: Cambridge University Press.

Wertsch, J.V. (1998) *Mind as Action*, New York: Oxford University Press.

Wertsch, J.V. (2000) 'Vygotsky's two minds on the nature of meaning', in C.D. Lee and P. Smagorinsky (eds) *Vygotskian Perspectives on Literacy Research: Constructing Meaning through Collaborative Inquiry*, 19–30, New York: Cambridge University Press.

Wertsch, J.V. (2002) *Voices of Collective Remembering*, New York: Cambridge University Press.

Wertsch, J.V. (2005) 'Essay review of "Making human beings human: Bioecological perspectives on human development" by U. Bronfenbrenner', *British Journal of Developmental Psychology* 23: 143–51.

Wertsch, J.V. (2007) 'Mediation', in H. Daniels, M. Cole and J.V. Wertsch (eds) *The Cambridge Companion to Vygotsky*, 178–92, New York: Cambridge University Press.

Wertsch, J.V. and Kazak, S. (2007) 'Saying more than you know in instructional settings', in T. Koschmann (ed.) *Theorizing Learning Practice*, 134–67, Mahwah, NJ: Erlbaum.

Wertsch, J. and O'Connor, K. (1994) 'Multivoicedness in historical representation: American college students' accounts of the origins of the United States', in J.V. Wertsch (ed.) *Journal of Narrative and Life History* 4 (Special Issue on Historical Representation): 295–330.

Wertsch, J.V. and Rupert, L.J. (1993) 'The authority of cultural tools in a sociocultural approach to mediated agency', *Cognition and Instruction* 11, 3–4: 227–39.

Wertsch, J.V. and Stone, C.A. (1985) 'The concept of internalization in Vygotsky's account of the genesis of higher mental functions', in J.V. Wertsch (ed.) *Culture, Communication and Cognition: Vygotskian Perspectives*, 162–79, New York: Cambridge University Press.

Wertsch, J.V. and Toma, C. (1995) 'Discourse and learning in the classroom: a sociocultural approach', in L.P. Steffle and J. Gale (eds) *Constructivism in Education*, 159–75, Hillsdale, NJ: Erlbaum.

Wertsch, J.V. and Tulviste, P. (1992) 'L. S. Vygotsky and contemporary developmental psychology', *Developmental Psychology* 28, 4: 548–57.

Wertsch, J.V. and Tulviste, P. (1996) 'L.S. Vygotsky and contemporary developmental psychology', in H. Daniels (ed.) *An Introduction to Vygotsky*, 53–74, London: Routledge.

Wertsch, J.V., del Río, P. and Álvarez, A. (1995) 'Sociocultural studies: history, action and mediation', in J.V. Wertsch, P. del Rio and A. Alvarez (eds) *Sociocultural Studies of Mind*, 1–34, New York: Cambridge University Press.

Wertsch, J.V., McNamee, G.D., McLane, J.B. and Budwig, N.A. (1980) 'The adult-child dyad as a problem solving system', *Child Development* 51: 1215–21.

Wertsch, J.V., Minick, N. and Arns, F.J. (1984) 'The creation of context in joint problemsolving', in B. Rogoff and J. Lave (eds) *Everyday Cognition: Its Development in Social Context*, 151–71, Cambridge, MA: Harvard University Press.

Wertsch, J.V., Tulviste, P. and Hagstrom, F. (1993) 'A sociocultural approach to agency', in E.A. Forman, N. Minick and C.A. Stone (eds) *Contexts for Learning: Sociocultural Dynamics in Children's Development*, 225–56, Oxford: Oxford University Press.

Whitcomb, J. (2004) 'Dilemmas of design and predicaments of practice: adapting the "Fostering a Community of Learners" model in secondary school English language arts classrooms', *Journal of Curriculum Studies* 36, 2: 183–206.

Wortham, S. (2001) 'Interactionally situated cognition: a classroom example', *Cognitive Science: A Multidisciplinary Journal* 25, 1: 37–66.

Wortham, S. (2006) *Learning Identity: The Joint Emergence of Social Identification and Academic Learning*, Cambridge: Cambridge University Press.

Wozniak, R.H. (1975) 'A dialectic paradigm for psychological research: implications drawn from the history of psychology in the Soviet Union', *Human Development* 18: 18–34.

Yaroshevsky, M. (1989) *Lev Vygotsky*, Moscow: Progress Publishers.

Yaroshevsky, M. (1990) *A History of Psychology*, Moscow: Progress Publishers.

Zinchenko, V.P. (1996) 'Ot klassicheskoi k organicheskoi psikhologii', *Voprosy psikhologii* 5: 7–20.

Index

Abreu and Elbers 149, 168
Ach, N. 48
activity theory: activity system 122, 166–7; boundary-crossing 128–9; change 164; cognitive trails 129–30, 144; cultural history 123–6; development 121–3; developmental work research 131–43; dialogicality 127; expansive learning 126–7; hierarchical structure 119; inter-school work 143–7; interventionist research 115–47; labour power 130–1; learning 143–7; mediation 121–2; objective/affective motives 120; Russian school 115–21
Ageyev, V. 17
Agre, P.E. 87
Alexander, R. 65
Alexandrov, V.E. 63
Alvarez, Amelia 69–71
Anderson, J.R. 84–5
anti-reductionism: development 70; methodology 34–45; unity 34–6, 43
Archer, M.S. 52, 53, 54
artefacts: mediation 7–11, 76; production 148–50

Baerentsen and Trettvik 42
Bakhtin, M.M. 6, 58, 62, 63, 65, 71, 113, 114, 127, 154, 161
Bakhurst, D. 9, 13, 30
Banks and Millward 79
Barab and Duffy 98–100
Barnes, Douglas 72
Bateson, Gregory 80–1, 126
Beach, K. 92
Bernstein, B. 6, 7, 18, 19, 45, 105, 149–57, 159, 160, 162, 163, 164, 166, 168, 170
Bernstein, Nicholas 22, 112

Blonsky 45
Boaler, J. 93, 106
boundary-crossing 128–9
Bourdieu, P. 97, 105, 161
Bowers, J.S. 92
Bowker and Star 151
Bozhovich 43
Bredo, E. 91
Brighouse, T. 135
Brooks, R.A. 87
Brown and Campione 108
Brown, Seely D. 63, 67, 68, 95, 96, 98, 99
Bruner, J.S 10, 57, 58, 67, 105
Brushlinskii, A.V. 2
Burke, K. 58–60
Burmenskaya, G. 107

Calhoun, D. 151
Candela, A. 71, 72, 75
Carraher, T.N. 93
Chaiklin, S. 20, 22, 25, 107
Chatwin, Bruce 129
city metaphor 1–2, 177
Clancey, W.J. 86–7, 88, 91
Clark, Andy 80
Cobb and Bowers 102
cognition: cognitive revolution 3; cultural bias 93–4; distributed *see* distributed cognition; learning 104; situated cognition 84–6
cognitive ethnography 79–83
cognitive trails 129–30, 144
Cole, Michael 10, 12, 32, 50, 51, 77, 79, 81, 84, 86, 93, 94, 116, 117, 118, 166, 167
communication: conduit model 62, 63; tool development 141–3; voice 62–5

communities of practice: applications 106–9; characteristics of communities 99; community defined 96; developments 100–3; knowledge 98–100; power/conflict/history 97–8; situated action 91–113; situated cognition 84–6; theory 94–7
concepts: scientific/everyday 14–19, 40–1
constructivist pedagogy 108
creativity: development 66–7; Zone of Proximal Development (ZPD) 22–3, 112
cultural development: generic law 12
cultural history: activity theory 123–6; contradictions 125; Cultural Historical Activity Theory (CHAT) 117, 155–61, 164, 168; cultural-historical theory 44–5; discourse 152–5; expansive transformations 125–6; five principles 123–6; historicity 124; history of ideas 124
culture: bias and cognition 93–4; sociocultural *see* sociocultural tradition; transformation of cultures of learning 140
Cussins, A. 129, 130, 145
cybernetic epistemology 80–1

Daniels, Harry 2, 29, 121, 130, 132, 135, 157, 158
Das, J.P. 30
Davydov, V.V. 18, 26, 27, 29, 34, 104, 111, 116, 118
DeCorte, E. 84–5
del Río, Pablo 69–71
development: anti-reductionism 70; creativity 66–7; cultural development 12; learning 41; social situation 42; wider situation 71–5; ZPD *see* Zone of Proximal Development
developmental method: background 13–14, 24; perspective 33–4
developmental work research (DWR): activity theory 131–43; application 132–43; communication 141–3; expansion of the object 136–41; forming the consortium 138; managing conflict 143; multiple objects 137–8; professional fear 143; professional identity 139–40; projects 139; tool development 141–3; transformation of cultures of learning 140

Dewey, J. 98
dialectical perspective: background 12–13, 32; dialogical models 65–6; psychology 12; research 31–4, 36, 41, 43, 44
dialogical models 65–6, 127
Diaz, M. 160
Diriwächter, R. 114
discourse: cultural history 152–5; discursive psychology 107–8; Zone of Proximal Development (ZPD) 24
distributed cognition: cognitive ethnography 79–83; external representations 88–90; historical change dynamics 83–4; origins 77–8; research 76–90; shared/distributed models 78–9; situated development of theory 86–7
Down 126
dual stimulation: method 45–50
Dyson and Robson 110

egocentric speech 37–8
Elkonin, D.B. 164–5, 167
Emerson, C. 37–8
emotional experience 43–4
Engeström, Y. 4, 11, 24, 25, 77, 79, 81, 115–34, 141, 145, 146, 147, 152, 155, 160, 161, 164, 165, 169, 170
Esmonde, Indigo 83–4
ethnography: cognitive ethnography 79–83
expansive learning 126–7

Farmer, F. 64, 65
Forbidden Colours Task 47–8
fossilized behavior 33, 36
Frawley, W. 116

Gadamer, H.-G. 103
Gal'perin 107
Gee, James Paul 108–9, 112
genetic method 13–14, 24
Gestalt theory 2, 35, 36
Gibson, J.J. 10, 42, 44
Giddens, Anthony 52, 53, 93
Glassman, M. 120
Gonzalez-Rey, F. 43
Goodnow, J.J. 62, 93
Goodwin and Goodwin 82
Goody and Watt 93
Greenfield, P.M. 84
Greeno, J.G. 84, 88–9, 92, 95, 107
Griffin and Cole 22, 69, 112, 166, 167
Gutiérrez, Kris 112

habitus 105
Hakkarainen, P. 117, 119, 120, 146
Hasan, R. 5–6, 7, 154, 160, 162, 163
Hatano, G. 55, 102
Hedegaard, M. 18, 104, 105, 111, 150
Hegel, Georg Wilhelm Friedrich 2, 120, 152
Heidegger, M. 65, 93
Hicks, D. 65, 108
hierarchical knowledge: structure 18–19
higher mental functioning: lower/higher elementary functioning 25–7; social origins 12–13
Hill, W.C. 82
Hirst and Manier 3
historical change dynamics 83–4
historically based psychology 14, 45
historicism 36
history: cultural *see* cultural history
Hjörne and Säljö 150, 151
Hodkinson, P. 97, 98, 103
Hoffman and Donaldson 108
Hollan, J. 77–83
Holland, D. 10, 96, 161, 162, 164
Holzman, L. 24–5, 30, 116
Hughes, Martin 109
Hutchins, Edwin 56, 77–9, 83

Iaroshevskii, M.G. 2
Ilyenkov, E.V. 9, 10, 13, 125
institutions: activities 150–1; historical products 168–78; level of analysis 148–50; post-Vygotskian research 148–78; regulation 150–1; structure 151–2
instructional approach 18
Ivic, I. 41, 168

Janet, Pierre 2, 54
Jayyusi, L. 167
John-Steiner, V. 32, 76
Johnson Laird, P.N. 49

Karpov, Y.V. 18, 19, 112
Kerosuo, H. 129
Knorr Cetina, K. 130
knotworking 128
knowledge: communities of practice 98–100; empirical 105; funds of knowledge and third spaces 109–14; hierarchical knowledge 18–19; narrative 105; theoretical/dialectical 105
Knox and Stevens 8

Koshmanova, T.S. 2
Kozulin, A. 2, 8, 11, 30, 65, 107, 115, 117–18

Langemeyer, I. 119
Lantolf, J. 52
Lave, J. 28, 51, 56, 76, 86–7, 91–9, 102–7, 109, 114
Leander, K. 10
learning: activity theory 143–7; cognition 104; development 41; expansive learning 126–7; identity formation 96; inter-school work 143–7; minimal model 173–4; situated *see* situated learning; transformation of cultures of learning 140; Zone of Proximal Development (ZPD) 76
Lee, Carol 112, 123, 124, 125, 177
Lemke, Jay 97–8, 103, 149, 154, 165, 167
Leontiev, A.N. 2, 22, 36, 112, 115–17, 119–21, 130, 162, 165, 167
Lewin 33, 45
Lidz and Elliot 21
Lindkvist, L. 101
Lineham and McCarthy 107–8
Lompscher, J. 104
Lotman, Y.M. 63, 71
Ludvigsen, S. 151
Luria, A.R. 14, 49, 84

Macdonald, C.A. 59
Makitalo and Säljö 148, 150, 151, 167, 168
Märtsin, M. 119, 130
Marx, Karl Heinrich 2, 3, 33–5, 107, 110, 111, 116, 121, 123, 130, 152, 168
Matusov, E. 113, 114
Maybin, J. 65
mediation: activity theory 121–2; cultural context 57–62; explicit/implicit 5–7; mediated action 57–62; pentad 58–60; properties 60–1; semiotics 4–8, 27, 59, 64; social theory 4–7; tools/signs/artefacts 7–11, 76; triangular representation 4–5
Mehan, H. 94
Mercer, N. 65, 72, 74, 75
Meshcheryakov, B. 29
Middleton, D. 24, 63, 67, 68, 173, 174
Miettinen and Peisa 119
Miller, George 49
Minick, N.J. 27, 30, 31, 34, 37, 38, 41, 43, 49, 148

Mintrop, H. 108
Moll, Luis 109, 110, 111, 112
Moran, S. 32
Morgan, D. 1

Nelson, K. 27
Newman, F. 30
Norman, D.A. 85, 86
Nunes, T. 51, 83

Offer, Avner 178
Olson, D.R. 93

perezhivanie 43–4
Petrovsky, A. 107
Piaget, Jean 21, 37–8, 51, 79, 93
Prawat, R.S. 8
process ontology 55–7
Propp, Vladimir 68
psychology: cognitive revolution 3; cultural artefacts 7, 11; developmental psychology 22, 25, 26; dialectical perspective 12; discursive psychology 107–8; ecological/social influence approach 53, 86; higher/lower processes 26; historically based 14, 45; methodological individualism 53, 86; psychological tools 7–9, 11, 27; stimuli 4, 8
Puzyrei, A.A. 1–2, 177

Ratner, C. 25, 44, 116, 149, 150
reciprocal teaching 63
reflexes 5, 25, 27, 34
reflexology 36, 46, 117
remembering 67–9
research: overview 29–49
Rockwell, E. 72
Rogoff, B. 51–3, 55, 86, 93, 94, 95, 101, 102, 107, 109, 113, 114
Rojas-Drummond, S. 71
Roth, W.M. 115, 117, 119, 120, 123, 124, 125, 131, 162, 168, 177
Rowlands, S. 110, 111
Russian Revolution: education 3
Russian school: activity theory 115–21; cultural history 2; reflexology 36, 46, 117

Sacks, H. 167
Sakharov, Leonid 37, 48–9
Säljö, R. 59, 72, 148, 150, 151, 167, 168
Salomon, M. 77

Sander, Friedrich 46
Sarangi and Roberts 176
Sawyer, K. 12, 52–7, 81, 85–7, 93, 94, 102, 114, 115, 178
Saxe, Geoffrey B. 53, 54, 83–4, 102
scaffolding metaphor 22, 24, 69
Scaife and Rogers 88
Schedrovitsky, Georgy 30
Scribner, Sylvia 51, 83, 84, 93, 94
Seifert, K. 95
semiotics: artefacts 10; invisible 6, 7; linguistics 4, 5, 6; mediation 4–8, 27, 59, 64
sense meaning 27–8
separability 52–5
Sfard, A. 89–90, 95
Sherin, M.G. 108
Shif, Zhozefina Il'inichna 14, 39, 40
Shore, B. 79
Shulman, L.S. 108
Silverman and Torode 162
situated action: beyond within the head models 92–3; communities of practice 91–113; methods for situated accounts 93–4; transfer from situation to situation 91–2, 95
situated cognition 84–6
situated learning: implications 103–6; interpretation 91, 93, 99–100; theory 86
Smolka, Ana 71
social positioning 160–4
social theory: mediation 4–7
sociocultural tradition: appropriation and mastery 66–7; mediated action 57–62; methodological individualism 53, 86; process ontology 55–7; separability 52–5; studies 51–75; transformation of theories 69–71; voice 62–5
Spurrett and Cowley 80
Suchman, L. 82, 86, 92, 93, 95, 104

Tharp and Gallimore 22
Thinking Together 73–5
Thomas, A. 108
Thompson, M. 108
Thorne, S.L. 115, 116
Toomela, A. 54
transfer: situation to situation 91–2, 95
Tuomi-Grohn, T. 92

Valsiner, Jaan 12, 20, 21, 22, 29, 31, 32, 40, 46, 47, 49, 53, 54, 114, 116

Van der Veer, R. 2, 12, 16, 20, 21, 26, 29–32, 35, 36, 40, 43, 46, 49, 53, 54, 116
Van Ijzendoorn, M. 26
Vann and Bowker 106, 107
Vasilyuk, F. 44, 147
Vera and Simon 86
Veresov, N.N. 2, 26–7, 30, 75
Virkkunen, J. 134
voice: multi-voicedness 127; sociocultural tradition 62–5
Vygotskian theory: overview 1–28
Vygotsky blocks 48–9

Wardekker, W.L. 16
Warmington, P. 121, 130, 132
Wartofsky, M. 10, 11
Wegerif, R. 65, 66
Wells, G. 65

Wenger, E. 28, 56, 86, 93, 95, 96, 97, 98, 99, 100, 103, 105, 106
Werner, Heinz 46
Wertsch, James V. 2, 4–7, 10, 14, 23–4, 26, 29, 45, 47–8, 51–2, 54–71, 75, 78, 86, 113, 149, 150, 154, 168
Whitcomb, J. 108
Wortham, S. 87
Wright Mills, Charles 1

Yaroshevsky, M. 2, 3, 107

Zinchenko, V.P. 2
Zone of Proximal Development (ZPD): assessment/instruction 20–2; creativity 22–3, 112; forms of discourse 24; learning 76; scaffolding metaphor 22, 24, 69; theoretical background 19–25, 107, 111, 112

eBooks – at www.eBookstore.tandf.co.uk

A library at your fingertips!

eBooks are electronic versions of printed books. You can store them on your PC/laptop or browse them online.

They have advantages for anyone needing rapid access to a wide variety of published, copyright information.

eBooks can help your research by enabling you to bookmark chapters, annotate text and use instant searches to find specific words or phrases. Several eBook files would fit on even a small laptop or PDA.

NEW: Save money by eSubscribing: cheap, online access to any eBook for as long as you need it.

Annual subscription packages

We now offer special low-cost bulk subscriptions to packages of eBooks in certain subject areas. These are available to libraries or to individuals.

For more information please contact webmaster.ebooks@tandf.co.uk

We're continually developing the eBook concept, so keep up to date by visiting the website.

www.eBookstore.tandf.co.uk